A World among These Islands

A World among These Islands

Essays on Literature, Race, and National Identity in Antillean America

Roberto Márquez

University of Massachusetts Press

AMHERST AND BOSTON

Copyright © 2010 by Roberto Márquez
Printed in the United States of America

LC 20100030870
ISBN 978-1-55849-851-8 (paper); 850-1 (library cloth)

Designed by Dennis Anderson
Set in Sabon by House of Equations, Inc.
Printed and bound by Thomson-Shore, Inc.

Library of Congress Cataloging-in-Publication Data

Márquez, Robert.
    A world among these islands : essays on literature, race, and national identity in Antillean
America / Roberto Márquez.
        p. cm.
    Includes bibliographical references and index.
    ISBN 978-1-55849-850-1 (library cloth : alk. paper) —
    ISBN 978-1-55849-851-8 (pbk. : alk. paper)
    1. Caribbean literature—History and criticism.   2. National characteristics, Caribbean,
in literature.   3. Race in literature.   4. Caribbean Area—In literature.   I. Title.
    PN849.C3M345 2010
    809'.89729—dc22   2010030870

British Library Cataloguing in Publication data are available.

For
Elena Rose Márquez,
Alina, Avián, Valerie
and their new generation of outriders
and legatees

Contents

Acknowledgments

ORIGINALLY PRESENTED as part of a (1975) conference "effort to rescue literary studies of the Caribbean from its long-standing invisibility and oblivion," "Beyond a Critical Insularity" was first published in a special (Summer 1983) issue of *Ideologies and Literature,* edited by Ileana Rodríguez and Marc Zimmerman. The *Latino(a) Research Review* published "Raza, racismo, e historia: 'Are All My Bones from There?'" in its vol. 4, no. 3 (Winter 2000) issue. In slightly different form, it originated as the keynote address before the Symposium on Afro-Latinos and the Issue of Race in the New Millennium held at Brooklyn College, on October 21, 2000. A Spanish version was also presented before the Colloquium on *Americanidade compartilhada* held at the Universidade Federal Fluminense, Niterói, Rio de Janeiro, Brazil, on November 9–10, 2000. "Nationalism, Nation, and Ideology: Trends in the Emergence of a Caribbean Literature" first appeared as the concluding chapter in Franklin W. Knight and Colin A. Palmer's *The Modern Caribbean* (Chapel Hill: University of North Carolina Press, 1989); "Seeing Fragments/Whole" in *Review: Latin American Literature and Arts* 60 (Spring 2000).

"Sojourners, Settlers, Castaways, and Creators: Of Puerto Rico Past and Puerto Ricans Present" was originally presented before the Japanese Association for American Studies annual meeting held at Hitotsubashi University, Kunatachi, Japan, on April 5, 1992, and subsequently published in *The Massachusetts Review* 36, no. 1 (Spring 1995). "One Boricua's Baldwin" first appeared in *American Quarterly* 42, no. 3 (September 1990), and "Boricuas, Jíbaras, and Jibaristas: Of Memory, Memoir, and Mimicry" in the *Latino Review of Books* 2, no. 1 (Spring 1996).

"Soul of a Continent" originally appeared in *American Quarterly* 41, no. 4 (December 1989); "A Poet's Century" as my "Prefatory Remarks" to the centennial edition of translations of Nicolás Guillén's poetry, *My*

Last Name, published in London by Mango Publishers (2002). "The Stoic and the Sisyphean: John Hearne and the Angel of History," presented originally to the Seminar of the Program in Atlantic History, Culture, and Society at The Johns Hopkins University, April 1981, was first published in *Anales del Caribe* 3 (1983). "Grenada: History, Neo-colonialism, and Culture in the Contemporary Caribbean," delivered as the keynote address at a symposium, *After Grenada: Caribbean Writing in the Face of Intervention,* held at Northeastern University, May 14, 1984, appeared in *Contributions in Black Studies*, no. 6 (1984). Under the title "An Anatomy of Racism," "El Señor Presidente" was previously published in *NACLA Report on the Américas* 25, no. 4 (February 1992), and "The Pirate Ambush of Remorse" in *Review: Latin American Literature and Arts* 44 (January–June, 1991).

I wish here to express my thanks and appreciation to all these different publications, venues, and institutions, their editors, organizers, and directors, for the initial opportunity and warm welcome they gave to this work.

A World among These Islands

Introduction

FOUNDATIONAL SITE and crucible of the European colonial (and later United States neocolonial) enterprise in the Americas, the Caribbean is also the world pioneering locale of that complex process of transnational globalization and "modernity" that was there first set in motion. It was in this archipelago of isles (rimlands, enclaves, and territories)[1] coupled and swung between our hemisphere's two continents that the worldwide reach and integration of the planet's once mutually isolated spheres had its most decisive early modern birthing. The unaccustomed intimacy, assorted content, and commingling of different geographies, peoples, economies, cultures, intrasocietal conflicts and the brusque convergence of their respective histories which came of that original encounter evolved eventually to become an enduring aspect of the ordinary experience of all humanity. The alchemy of that fateful beginning also, in due course, saw in the Caribbean the emergence of a world all its own, wholly distinct, of many worlds constructed, ebullient, integral, and new. That process of commingling, predictably enough, became a patent constant and unique attribute of the archipelago's own distinctive historical development, individual character, and cultural personality.

A region of continuous human commerce and exchange, of fusions fraught or fruitful, of a ceaseless and ubiquitous *Creolization,* the Caribbean is thus also a more than ordinarily privileged and compelling location for sustained engagement with and rewarding study of that initial encounter's subsequent and broadly American New World unfolding. Its legacies are, certainly, still evident in our own contemporary train of multinational clash, transnational encounter, domestic structural displacements, periodic social reconfigurations, and variable convergences, with all that train's no less dramatic freight of demographic shifts, unprecedented population transfers out of ancestral homelands, and burgeoning (multi-)metropolitan Caribbean (im)migrant enclaves and Antillean postcolonial diasporas. The reciprocal cultural force and

I

energy of these diasporas' emergent New Creoles who, in Aimé Césaire's (Martinique, 1913–2008) apt and canny phrase, so evidently "belong to no nationality ever contemplated by the chancelleries" inescapably bring fresh dimension, novel conceptions, alternative definitions, and uncommon challenge to more traditionally accented discussions and debates about the precincts, confines, encompassing reach as well as inclusive scope of "the nation," its apposite citizenry, authoritatively communal "identity," culturally emblematic icons, "national" concerns and priorities.

In tandem with all the many other historic changes which likewise marked the Caribbean's passage through the last several centuries, these transitive New Creole communities' very existence and increasingly self-assertive vigor "abroad" and "at home" resist as, partially or entirely, inadequate all but unavoidably neologistic identifiers—AmeríRican and Dominican-York are just two examples—of their bi-directional reality and so doubly maverick condition. They thus vitally and provocatively stimulate reassessment, new *(re)historizations,* and critical revisions of previously customary and commandingly select, too patrician ex-clusive notions of the proper—territorial, linguistic, ethnic, racial, or cultural—frontiers of "the national" and its proper sphere(s).

An area and subject so richly protean and vibrantly effervescent would seem a point of singular attraction and keen interest to an Ameri-can academy so frequently drawn, in triumphal content or apprehensive disquiet, to "melting pots" and "the clash of civilizations," lately enticed by the topical appeal of a sometimes hazily grounded, fitfully or ir-regularly accentuated "Atlantic Space" and increasingly absorbed by the chic theoretical seductions of the postmodern turn. The Caribbean, for all that, is still most often positioned on the tangential outer banks and subsidiary margin of its endeavor's accustomed focal core, scholarly provinces, and sustained concentration—save as it periodically erupts in disconcerting portent, unsettling revolution, or natural catastrophe, abruptly to thrust itself unbidden to stage center of a then suddenly rapt attention. More often than not generally approached in isolated single country or sectoral fragment fashion, the archipelago's more fully di-mensioned complexity, heterogeneous coherence, overarching integrity and cohesion are just as frequently likely to be all but virtually ignored, to remain largely veiled, effectively disregarded. The more obvious vir-tues of this time-honored single country or individual provincial sub-division stress and concentration notwithstanding, the comparatively restrictive ambit of its otherwise appropriate particularizations can thus similarly diminish vital recognition of the parallel significance, the shaping weight and importance, of a more amply comprehensive, equally definitive *Caribbean* context and landscape; and even, to some extent, a sufficient appreciation of its own selected terrain's unique idiosyncrasy and personality as at once inextricably constituent element and discrete expression of that wider Caribbean's larger composite integrity, disparate yet convergent singularity.

Perhaps nowhere has this customary practice's more reductive point of view, its tacit or explicit disaggregations and practical parceling, been so regularly in evidence as in our habitual segregations and fragmentation of the area's literary heritage and history.

Neither easily contained, entirely grasped, nor sufficiently encompassed within the boundaries of any single language or likewise predictably familiar and too circumscribed classificatory prototype or categorical mold, the Caribbean's literature has been, and for the most part is still, nearly invariably assayed along strictly delimited, reciprocally cut-off fractional lines. Thus because it is selectively appropriated, habitually placed, and only partially incorporated (as a usually subsidiary subdivision) within the purview of other regions, domains, subjects, or intellectual agendas, its own organic totality, independent specificity, and autonomous reality, in consequence and effect, disappear from immediate awareness or sustained consideration. Recognition of *that* reality essentially evaporates in the neglected interstices between more narrowly stipulated realms, into that virtual no-man's land lying between and beyond the standard divisions, cliquish jurisdictions, and exclusionary conclaves into which the academy is most typically ordered and by which it is most commonly oriented. Aspiring to a prospect and outlook at once more analytically consistent with and comprehensive enough comfortably to embrace the Caribbean's thus variously unruly and accordingly "undisciplined" densities of necessity obliges a measure of venturesome and unsanctioned cross-territorial travel, not wholly unlike that of the undocumented émigré's fugitive border-crossings.

It was ultimately in response to the recurring dissatisfactions, dubious constrictions, synthetic fissures, complacent subordinations, often telling silences and partialities which that unwarranted disappearance of the more abundantly ample, if eccentric, wholeness of the Caribbean's literature and literary history seemed so frequently to create or encourage, the questions it thus left unanswered or provoked, that, a

Spanish-Harlem-born-and-raised Puerto Rican "New Creole" student, scholar, and critic, I early on and decisively committed to that pan-Caribbean vision and perspective whose more fully integrative premises underpin the informing attitude, perception, and structural order of *A World among These Islands*.

When initially I ventured into the groves of academe as a full-fledged and eager undergraduate, in the fall of 1962, it was with a gnawing impatience and curiosity, an unsated hunger and yearning for that knowledge that might serve rationally to explain and make useful communal sense and instrumentality of my and my species' place and role on the planet. It was, after all, the urgent and growing force of that hunger which turned my energies to the chancy gamble of two years of preparatory night schooling, away from the aviation mechanic's career I had been trained for and earlier envisioned, and increasingly to that vibrant intersection of literature, social, and cultural history to which I have since been devoted.

Entering as an English and American Literature major, I was soon enough and progressively drawn beyond that discipline's conventionally assumed or approved national, ethnic, and linguistic precincts. I tended more naturally to incline away, as well, from its then typically too sharp divorce between the "strictly literary," "history," and other forms of critical appraisal and experience. Although I was otherwise stirred by and admiring of the impressive array of texts, authors, themes, settings, and all that "wit. . . to advantage dressed" which "the field" so authoritatively claimed as its own, the increasingly felt absences and lacunae in its selected tradition, preferred affiliations, and tacit hierarchies at the same time gradually loomed ever and more unfulfillingly larger. To combine my abiding enthusiasm and commitment to the writing and writers of the English-speaking world, and not least within it that of African-Americans, Antilleans, and other writers emerging from "the developing world," with an equally strong and gathering interest in the history and literature(s) of Spain, Latin America, and *the(ir)* Caribbean, I turned successively to concentrations in Spanish and in Comparative Literature, only to find there, for all the equally compelling literary vitality and power of their respective canons, comparable conceits, and an analogue inattention to those varied natives of my person no less palpable or condescending, if in different language, idiom, or inflection.

Ever more emphatically devoted, more intimately and unequivocally involved, during my postgraduate and subsequent years, in the daily uncoiling drama and radically changing realities of Latin—and Latino—American life (much as with the contemporary poetry and prose with which as teacher, translator, editor, and critic I was similarly occupied), I decisively set my compass, with an avid personal zest and resolve, to critical scrutiny of the comparatively neglected literary production, intellectual and social evolution of the Caribbean to which my own background, experience, and sympathies beckoned. In contrast to the Hispano-centric bias and practice still wide-spread among many of my Latin American(ist) colleagues, and so rather heretically, my own definition of the region was waywardly and insistently inclusive of its English-, French-, and other-language-speaking areas, as well as of the enclaves of Antilleans abroad, particularly in the United States. The Caribbean's faceted individuality, no less than the insufficiently acknowledged regional and world historical centrality of, for example, the Haitian Revolution, thereby emerged all the more forcefully. If I was first most obviously drawn to the poetry and creative work of, among others, Nicolás Guillén, it was not least because, beyond the uniquely Cuban context and texture of the larger drama of race, nationality, nation-building, and national self-affirmation it directly engages and embodies, its poignant candor and the incisive boldness and originality of its artful interrogations—"Does all my skin come from that Spanish marble? . . . Is there nothing more than this which you have written . . . ?"—revealed too a wider and directly accessible *Caribbean* amplitude of perception and implication resonant with and very much akin to my own view of the scope and complexity of such matters. Its notable historical sensibility and major thematic inflections likewise underscored the Antilles' idiosyncratically eclectic New World density, cultural inventiveness, and dynamic development. It was—and remains—an elected as much as a discovered affinity.

Along with the equally pertinent emphasis of its signature themes and foci, the pivot of that affinity lay in that holistic perception of the Caribbean as an organic totality, historically inclusive in my view of its "Mainland Passage" extensions and external frontier, which more and more unmistakably became the vital center of gravity and piloting definition of "my subject": a definition at once more apt, encompassing, and essentially germane, if possibly more analytically ambitious, than those more compartmentally circumscribed ones I had earlier met with and which were more regularly on offer. An archipelagic outlook, with a particular inclination to the critical enterprise of a genuinely

pan-Caribbean literary criticism concomitant with it, has, in consequence and of necessity, consistently been the steering and permanently
fixed star in the universe of my intellectual venture, vocation, and trajectory. It is ultimately to the different coordinates, shifting milieu, changing atmospheric conditions, variable accents and inflections of that outlook and that enterprise to which the essays gathered here variously
testify and bear a material witness: it is to these they speak, and around
these that they were composed and are primarily ordered.

The book is divided into three interlinked yet discrete topical sections. The essays in the first of these are, as its title indicates, so many
efforts at (and arguments for) "Seeing the Caribbean Whole." With the
Antilles writ large as their primary point of departure, they critically examine and emphasize the evolving stages, enduring legacies, structural
features, and effects of a long historical progression commonly shared,
with circumstantial adaptations and variation, across the archipelago.
It is that historical development and literary evolution which crucially
shaped, informed and *oriented* the area's concrete human experience
and its social, political, and intellectual vernaculars which, as its literary tradition's context and subsoil, ultimately nourished the content,
substance, and coordinates of a discernible Caribbean cosmos and esthetic of various idiom, dialect, and tonality that they strive at once to
illustrate and reveal.

From the pre-Columbian roots of the original colonial pact and the
lasting inheritance—of imperial, racial, caste, and class presumption, division, and confrontation—which it universally bequeathed, and which
have analogous manifestations of more recent vintage, to the emancipa-
tory epochal divide of shaping contour and social topography introduced by the Haitian Revolution, to the still later impact and cultural
influence of the Cuban and Grenadian revolutions, it is to the inexo-
rability, evolving dialectic, and gathering power of the past's material
immediacy in the present (and to the alert critic of Antillean verse and
prose) that these essays equally draw the reader's attention. Each is an
expression of the central premise which, to a greater or lesser degree,
lies at the heart of this entire collection: that for all of their protean,
polychromatic diversity, and however apparently fragmented, these
"islands" all comprise a world: a distinctive and cohesive congregation
of territories (and their diasporas) with—in the words of the Dominican
poet Pedro Mir—a "common scent, a very household / air . . . / the same

sweat, the same postures," "a single heart for [all its plural] national hardships."

Framed by the urgency to move "Beyond a Critical Insularity" and that call for "nothing less than a comprehensive literary history of perhaps encyclopedic scope" with which this section begins, in the early seventies, and by the appearance and review, more than two decades later, of *A History of Literature in the Caribbean* in three volumes in which that call appears to find sympathetic echo, with which in "Seeing Fragments/Whole" it concludes, the section also indirectly charts, as in that final essay's surveying trace, the perceptible extremities of a certain arc of emergence.

No less vitally pan-Caribbean in underlying assumption, the essays in "Notes of a 'Nother Rican," the second part, predominantly focus on Puerto Rico, Puerto Rican literary and sociohistorical experience, and their "New Creole" incarnations and expressions in the lives and writing of Boricuas in the United States. The work of a second-generation historical product and legatee of the earliest, most enduring and continuous of the great pre– and post–World War II national waves of migration to the United States from the Caribbean, these essays hence similarly accentuate that particular angle of vision and comparative positioning of perception which, as root and pivot, are inextricable from that larger informing perspective.

Suggestive of that quality of "explanatory or critical comment appended to a passage or text," the element and attitude of circumstantial or provisional hachure which ultimately defines all our essayings, the wider elasticity of resonance of the section's title is, at the same time, deliberate, willfully ambiguous, and poly-connotative. Signifying a more than single dimension or unidirectional authorial *not otherness,* it is also meant colloquially to evoke anomalous variance, that *neither, nor,* as well as *here and there*—in Spanish, *ten con ten*—dialectic is intrinsic to the contemporary insular experience of Diaspora. Phonically, it, in addition, correctly intimates that the essays included in this section are the work of but one more, merely *another,* among the assorted multitude of Ricans who, born, raised, and resident in the United States or on the ancestral isle, are all equally heir to the history and epochal undulations of an entire archipelago. It further and simultaneously insinuates an unmistakable *difference* in kind, character, experience, or texture from that typically anticipated of an emergent type or class that lacks still its properly apposite descriptive nomenclature and genuinely proper name, a name beyond mere addendum or too frequently insufficient tag-on appeals to that which such folk *are not, are not quite, not exactly,* or *anymore.* A neologism of vernacularly precise inflection and particularity but still elusive specificity seemed an especially fitting way of pointing to that unprecedented human tangibility of our Diaspora's New Creoles, which so often remains beyond the power of our inherited—conventionally nationalist or fashionably academic—vocabularies either aptly to convey, suitably to reflect, or fully to accommodate without a palpable hedging, patronizing disquiet, or discomfiture. It is with the complex interconnectedness of all these various dimensions, and the historic roots, process of articulation, contemporary dramas of social change, and creative expression of this *'Nother* Boricua subject, sensibility, and notion of nation—to which the author's own odyssey bears some testimony—that the essays in this part are primarily concerned.

The final segment, "Occasions, Views, and Reviews," turns to Caribbean writers, political and cultural figures, or signal events from the region's other Spanish-speaking, as well as Anglophone and Francophone territories and the ways in which their work or influence relates to and engages the collection's more general themes of literature, race, nation, and national identity. Thus complementing and integral to the Caribbean totality it forms with the previous two sections, it shares the nature of their confrontation with the area's durable historical legacies, period clashes, and history unreconciled, the collective or individual achievement, current insolvency, or unforeseen disenchantments that their activity, impact or individual partisanship reveal as emblematic, singly and together, of a major moment of transition not yet entirely over—this is the guiding thread, the common theme that runs through it. These are, as well, among the nuclei around which all three sections variously, in Antillean fashion, converge as a single totality.

Notes

1. Most obviously perhaps in the case of Guyana, Surinam, Guiana, and Belize but only relatively less so in the predominantly Spanish- (or Portuguese-) speaking areas of several Latin American countries' Atlantic coasts, these Caribbean rimlands and territories have, among other things and more often than not, been historically generally oriented outward toward the sea and otherwise are—regionally, linguistically, culturally, in all or some combined measure of

these—comparative isolates in their adjacent continental environment, habitat, or surroundings. They are thus more than just arguably or merely metaphorically so many continentally "insular" enclaves and equally part of a wider, variously integrated broader Caribbean orbit, experience, and cultural sphere: part, that is, of that world of "islands" from which this collection takes its title.

SEEING THE
CARIBBEAN WHOLE

I know from here that I and distant others
Alien only by twang and dialect have unity / . . . /
I praise those who see a world among these islands

DEREK WALCOTT

Beyond a Critical Insularity

We in the Caribbean are already integrated.
It is only the Governments who don't know it.

GEORGE BECKFORD

SPEAKING BEFORE a group of translators, literary critics, and teachers of literature gathered at a meeting of the Comparative Literature Association, some while ago now, and to all appearances the only Caribbeanist among this distinguished assembly, I took occasion to address what strikes me still as the obligation more fully to engage the Antillean archipelago as a single cohesive totality, our need of a conceptual outlook and critical vision which, doing no violence to any of its sub-regional units or individual insular particularities, will nonetheless allow us analytically to approach the Caribbean, its literature and culture, as the locus and world-historical setting of the organically linked and inter-related societies that it is.

It is, I began, a truism bordering on the trite to say that the Caribbean is a region of great linguistic, ethnic, and cultural variation and diversity. We are daily reminded by the media, billboards, travel agents, and tourists of the extraordinary and above all "exotic" variety which, we are regularly informed, is the essential touchstone of the place. Beneath this miscellaneously vibrant and polychromatic multiplicity there is, nonetheless, an equally emblematic, if not as often recognized or acknowledged similitude of historical, social, and cultural experience that, all assertions to the contrary notwithstanding, give this singular region its distinctive character and holistic integrity.

Though the region was forged in the crucible of conflict, of great power rivalries, of slave revolt and revolution, of caste, class, and intraregional confrontation, its more obvious heterogeneities can all too often conceal, as the waters surrounding its islands and mainlands veil from our view its subterranean geographic interlinkings, the striking and vital connections that lie below the area's shimmering surface. It was, after all, the decisive historical encounter—economically, politically, socially, culturally, and biologically—of the indigenous, African, Asian, and different European settler populations in this place which ubiquitously led to the distinctive transformation of its variously contentious individual components and the creation of a new cultural synthesis whose most irrefutably characteristic feature, throughout the archipelago, is that dialectical transcendence and unprecedented originality typical of every syncreticism. Indeed, one would be perfectly justified in arguing, with the Cuban ethnologist Rogelio Martinez Furé, the existence of nothing less than an Antillean Civilization. Insisting on the overarching similarities and consequences of the region's folk traditions, this writer goes on to emphasize:

> This incessant clash of civilizations, of reciprocal influences among the cultures of Western Europe and Africa, fusing upon the Indian humus—including the contributions of some Asian civilizations—and conditioned by the relations of production of slavery, the sugar economy, the slave trade, and the colonial regime, has historically created cultural links that find expression in our traditions of music and dance, the popular arts, oral literature, eating habits, religious concepts and common superstitions, to the point that we can speak of an Antillean Civilization, a civilization that has local variants—determined by the presence of the dominant (Spanish, French, English, etc.) culture, which does not preclude its existence at the level of the popular (folk) culture, despite the variety of languages or forms of the official cultures. These languages have themselves suffered the impact of the Indo-Antillean and African languages, thus producing a Creole speech in every one of our islands.[1]

The written literatures produced in the non-Creole and Creole dialects alike, in whatever language, no less forcefully argue the existence of this Antillean Civilization. Enriched by its linguistic range and multiplicity, if thereby more dependent on translation for its inter-island, nonexclusive distribution and impact, that literature, like the folk lore it so often draws inspiration from, is at once various, multivalent, and one. Whatever its ostensible language—and I say ostensible because, though to all appearances it is written in some of the major, more conventionally orthodox languages of Europe, the forging and enunciation of a properly Antillean literary idiom and inflection is in fact one of its principal achievements—that literature, no less the product of that clash and collusion of civilizations, is likewise the creatively inventive epitome of its remarkably coherent diversity, cultural richness, and originality. Whatever the island of origin, and allowing for local variation—determined, again, by the character and identity of the experience with the traditionally dominant metropolitan hub and the temperament (not to mention political outlook) of the individual writer—one invariably everywhere encounters homologous premises, equivalent dilemmas, analogous concerns—an identifiably correlated sense of the collective historical experience: a palpable, idiosyncratically *Caribbean* ambiance. Alejo Carpentier's focus on Guadaloupe and Haiti as the setting and subject of, respectively, *El siglo de las luces* (*Explosion in a Cathedral*) and *El reino de este mundo* (*The Kingdom of This World*), telling and significant in itself, far from diminishing, gives richer depth and meaning to his undeniable and distinctive *cubanía*. A writer of exceptional talent, acuity, and historical sensitivity, he is hardly alone in this: I can think of no Antillean writer about which, to some extent or other, this could not be said. That the realities of colonialism and neocolonialism have so often prevented this literature from moving easily across the archipelago's linguistic borders, or that we ourselves have been only too complicitiously respectful of them or the proprietary, orbital claims of Europe, the United States, or our own local elites, does not alter the facts. One can still hear in the Barbadian Edward Kamau Brathwaite's

> I
> must be given words to refashion futures
> like a healer's hand
> I
> must be given words so that the bees
> in my blood's buzzing brain of memory
> will make flowers, will make flocks of birds,
> will make sky, will make heaven,
> the heaven open to the thunderstone and the volcano
> and the unfolding land

a younger brother of the Martiniquen author of *Cahier d'un retour aux pays natal* with his "j'aurais des mots assez vastes pour vous contenir" and his "français antillais." The family resemblance extends forward and back, to the work of Eugenio María de Hostos, José Martí, J. J. Thomas, and Frantz Fanon; Jacques Roumain, Pedro Mir, Nicolás Guillén, C. L. R. James, Martin Carter, Derek Walcott, and Anthony McNeil; José Luis González, Juan Bosch, the Marcelin brothers, Edgar

Mittelholzer, and H. G. de Lisser; Jan Carew, Luis Rafael Sánchez, George Lamming, Andrew Salkey, Samuel Selvon, Simone Schwarz-Bart, Merle Hodge, Marion Patrick Jones, Karl Toulanmanche, Etnairis Rivera, Pedro Pietri, and Roger Mais; V. S. Reid, Michael Anthony, Edmundo Desnoes, Sonny Ladoo, César Leante, Orlando Patterson, René Marqués, John Hearne, Léon Damas, Jean Dieudonné Garçon, Anthony Phelps—whose most recent book is significantly entitled *Et moi, je suis une île*—and all the rest. These writers are all as ineluctably linked to each other as they are separated from Europe (using the apt metaphor of yet another member of this widely extended family, Jean Rhys) by a *Wide Sargasso Sea*. The Haitian poet and novelist René Depestre did no more than recognize that kinship when he wrote: "I believe that in the Antilles we have the right to speak of a literature of identity which expresses itself in French, in English . . . in Spanish[, and in Dutch, their various dialects and Creoles]. I believe that the impassioned search for identity is the first element of unity that appears when you compare the lines of force of our diverse literatures."[2]

It is not, of course, the only one. The encounter with history, to become its subject rather than its object, the repossession of the physical and spiritual landscape therein implied, and the *realisme merveilleux* of our particular New World synthesis, all interrelated, are equally compelling. Édouard Glissant, author of *Le Quatrième Siècle* and several other works might well have echoed Depestre by seeing in these "lines of force" evidence of the growing acknowledgment of a decisive *Antillanité*. I doubt that, seen in this context, either of them would find much cause to argue with Césaire's succinct and thoroughly Antillean observation that, as one of the colonized and a Black man not unfamiliar with the modern Caribbean's contemporary experience of Diaspora, "Je ne suis d'aucune nationalité prévue par les chancelleries."[3]

But the objectively demonstrable presence of that *Caribbeanness* is one thing. It is quite another to act consistent with the recognition of its existence above and beyond language. Our conventional cultural-political establishments persist still in constricting the compass of their (and our) vision to the "orbit" of, respectively, the "British" West Indies, the "French" Antilles, the "Spanish" or "Dutch" Caribbean and, hence, to the constructed borders which are no more than the enduring legacy of colonialism and now out-of-date imperial inheritance. V. S. Naipaul's "Mimic Men" continue everywhere in evidence. A Dominican or a Puerto Rican is, consequently, prevented—except as he or she is able to read it in the original—from seeing a part of themselves reflected in the work of a Guadeloupean or Jamaican—and vice versa. The author of the poem quoted above not long ago informed me that he was entirely unaware of the work of Aimé Césaire until well after the publication of his own *Rights of Passage:* His apprenticeship, he pointed out, was passed in the company of the more immediately accessible Eliot, Pound, and various English poets. It is the characteristic Caribbean experience. In this sense, we might be said to be truly insular. Even the very extra-official Caribbean Artists' Movement, which has already done a great deal to foment and encourage the development of a more genuinely Antillean consciousness, remains primarily and almost exclusively a phenomenon of the Anglophone Antilles.

Cuba, so far as I can determine, is the only Caribbean nation with a consciously Antillean cultural policy, the only one since the sixties regularly to translate and promote the work of Caribbean writers working in languages other than its own Spanish. The Instituto del Libro and Casa de Las Américas are both sponsors of special editions devoted to the literatures of the Anglophone islands. If similar anthologies exist in the "French Antilles" I have yet to see them. Cuba's is still the only edition of Jean Price-Mars's classic work, *Ainsi parle l'uncle,* in an area language other than French. It shares with the Dominican Republic the honor of having translated the landmark contemporary novel of Price-Mars's fellow Haitian Jacques Stéphen Alexis, *Compère General Soleil,* in an edition which became quickly exhausted and is now out of print. There is a Mexican edition of Alexis's *L'espace d'un cillement,* but I am not aware that it has circulated to any great extent within the archipelago. None of these works are, in any case, available to English-speaking readers.[4] Translations of the work of Glissant, Mir, and Wilson Harris in regional languages other than their own are equally wanting. And the list goes on . . .

That was back in 1974. At the time, I was directing myself to "The Politics of Translation"[5] as it impinges on and directly affects the Caribbean and its literature. I was trying to demonstrate, with specific example, how the common lack of any authentically Antillean policy on the matter is intimately related to a structural totality and outlook demanding analysis in the context of the Caribbean's colonial history and, of course, the economically subordinate position and still culturally insecure horizons of national elites caught, with the urban and rural masses they are anxious to contain or to disgorge, in the press of an increasingly globalized economy. I was attempting to articulate how the failure to come to terms with Caribbean Literature, writ large, on even so apparently pedestrian a level as the mere identification and immediate accessibility of its texts significantly contributes to the perpetuation of a too narrowly constricted vision of it, of ourselves and of our collective history; to the region's continued balkanization and to a confirmation of the relationships of dominant authority and power which have historically produced it.

The development of a less insular, more comprehensive and properly Caribbean literary criticism is, obviously, still in its infancy. That, it seems to me, is not entirely unrelated to a still widespread ignorance of the texts outside—and, indeed, even within—the particular sub-regions which produced them. That, in part, is my reason for reiterating remarks originally intended specifically to address the problem of translation. I continue to believe that the need to make that crucial element and rich body of our primary source material more generally accessible is a priority of no little urgency. It unavoidably impinges on the efficacy and broader impact of any holistic criticism of Caribbean Literature which seeks, as it must, to extend its influence beyond the sphere of a small professional coterie of the cognoscenti. The anachronistic categories of definition and persistent neglect of the area, except within the parameters of "orbital" assumptions, are, after all, already embodied in a pedagogical tradition, in curricula models, and in the present departmental structures of colleges and universities within and outside of the Caribbean. A challenge to the universal validity of those categories presupposes, at the very least, some questioning of the organizational assumptions and conceptual limits within which those structures currently operate. For their programmatic description and categories, the values taken for granted by that pedagogical tradition, are a tacit postulation of the texts and issues that they take as their proper domain and concern. They are, to borrow a term from Raymond Williams, part of a "Selective Tradition." It is no coincidence, for example, that the literature courses typical of conventional Latin American Studies programs almost invariably reflect a strictly Hispanophone—and, more often than not, patrician—bias. John LaRose goes to the heart of more than one problem when, in a recent personal letter, he writes: "I eschew the word Latin America as a global ethnocultural term for a whole geography of Central-South America and the Caribbean. I regard it as a term of cultural aggression against Afro- and Indo- and other ethnic Americans within that geography." I am of the opinion that our too-wide ignorance of the texts significantly contributes to the continuing enshrinement of that misrepresentation of reality.

But there is another reason for beginning as I have. What I said three years ago in the context of translation seems to me just as, if not more, applicable to Caribbean Literary Criticism. Our most important critics are, with almost no exceptions, still not, strictly speaking, *Caribbean* critics. They are rather critics of the literature of some (usually linguistic) fragment of the area. Some, like Guyana's Gordon Rohlehr, are thorough, deep, and sensitive commentators with a keen perception of the sociohistorical factors helping to shape the full range of cultural production within their regional sector. His essays on everything from the novel, the telling anxieties of V. S. Naipaul, the poems of Walcott and Brathwaite, and the origins and meaning of the calypso to the relationship between literature and the folk, the angst of the younger "urban" poets of the English-speaking territories and the emerging work of the newer writers of fiction like Garth St. Omer are among the most substantive and original I have read on those subjects. José Luis González, as literary critic and cultural historian, and—insofar as they are both similarly concerned with the oral tradition and its impact on emerging cultural patterns—Martinez Furé are, to some extent, among Rohlehr's immediate counterparts outside the Anglophone areas. Some, like Lilyan Kesteloot, Naomi Garret, Michael Dash, and Wilbert Roget prefer to examine almost exclusively the salients of a particular literary movement, author, or country; or, like Janheinz Jahn, begin with some suggestive comparative construct, such as "Neo-Africanism," in which, for all its apparent pertinence, the Caribbean is in the final analysis, invariably ancillary to a more overarching thematic obsession with some transhistorical soul. There are those, like G. R. Coulthard, whose work intimates, and so is a first step toward, a criticism of genuinely Caribbean scope but who lack the theoretical and social vision which would have given that work still greater depth and solidity, even more compelling pioneering stature. Others, (one thinks of Michael Gilkes, Kenneth Ramchand, and A. J. Seymour) conscientiously eschew social history, save by broad reference, as not strictly essential to their primary task as critics, in favor of a kind of psychological emphasis "where the integrity of the personality is almost always the subject"[6] or, as in the case of the latter two, a colonial variant of the New Criticism or modified version of Eliot's *Christianity and Culture*. Others still are frankly imperial in their premises and approach the region of the Caribbean which seduces their interest as an overseas extension of some province of European culture. Auguste Viatte's *Histoire littéraire de l'Amérique française des origins à 1950* is one of the more striking examples of this critical presumption. Gerald Moore's *The Chosen Tongue: English Writing in the Tropical World*, for all its subtlety, and not a few Hispanophone exegetes, for all their influence, seem to me also to belong to that tradition.

Whatever their particular achievements or shortcomings, however, these critics all have one thing in common: their failure to come to terms with the literature and culture of the Caribbean as a whole. The occasional recent essays of René Depestre, José Antonio Portuondo, Sylvia Wynter, Roberto Fernández Retamar, Edward Brathwaite, and Jan Carew are still exceptional, so many tentative, exploratory forays into what for the majority largely remains still a *terra incognita*. But there are, for all that, increasing signs of a growing pressure for a vital readjustment of our critical lenses. *Caliban* and *Contradictory Omens* are no more than the advance guard of a gathering Pan-Caribbean consciousness struggling to make the necessary connections between our singularly several selves, and to identify the particular ways in which class, caste, race, ideology, and the colonial context have, in each and in every one of our subunits, creatively interacted to produce a "slow, uncertain but organic progress (from imitation/initiation to invention), evolving into ac/act/accent, style and possibility,"[7] that *Creolization* which is the linchpin of our history.

I expect it is clear that, in my opinion, the critic of Caribbean Literature has to be more than "mere" literary critic. He or she has, too, to be as fully conversant as possible with the historiography and social history of the entire area, sensitive to ideological currents and, most particularly, to the submerged tradition—Edward Brathwaite's "little Tradition"—of the folk and the ways in which it finds expression in all forms of literary and cultural production. It should also be clear that what I would like ideally to see, in consequence, —and believe we desperately need—is nothing less than a comprehensive literary history of perhaps encyclopedic scope; a work that, taking the entire archipelago as its legitimate province, will combine the all-embracing theoretical ambition of Darcy Ribeiro's *The Americas and Civilization*, the dialectical rigor and dynamic appreciation of complex economic and social forces of Moreno Fraginals's *The Sugarmill*, with an equally keen regard for the peculiar integrity and materiality of esthetic conceptions and cultural production which, with Marx himself, fully recognizes that "Works of art are not just passively consumed; they develop (and, in a way, create) the faculties by which they can be enjoyed."[8]

It seems to me possible critically to delineate some of the principal characteristics of an already extent Caribbean esthetic, an esthetic that even as it pays due and indispensable heed to local particularity, demonstrably extends and coheres beyond linguistic boundaries. I am especially struck by how the current preoccupation with identity and the historical among our novelists and poets is intimately related to, among other things, decisive changes in the region's ethno-class and economic configurations during the last century and our own: to the area-wide destruction or displacement of the traditional plantocracies and *hacendado* elites, the emergence of an urban and rural proletariat, itself increasingly displaced to become part of a multinational migrant army of surplus labor. Equally central has been the rise to prominence of a class of *mestizo* and (in its broadest sense) "colored" professionals of variously populist, social-democratic or socialist and, in any case, generally nationalist outlook striving to establish its own hegemony and to give ideological substance to its claims of national representation and for control of the state in the face of these various changes, which include the demise of the old colonial regimes and the aggressive, imperial expansion of the United States, its corporations, cultural influence, and tourists. The Caribbean's writers and poets are directly involved and implicated, as eyewitnesses and participants, in this process. These factors, consequently, bear directly on the formulation of esthetic notions and our need as critics to distinguish, within the recognition of their common *Caribbeanness,* between the plantocratic nationalism of a Herbert de Lisser, in Jamaica, the *hacendado* Creole nostalgia and historical pessimism of a René Marqués, in Puerto Rico, and, say, the "proletarian" irreverence and "Creole" piqong of Trinidad's Samuel Selvon and the extraordinary historical optimism beneath the elegiac tones of a Pedro Mir or a Nicolás Guillén.

It seems increasingly clear, too, that key elements of this Caribbean esthetic were, however inchoately, already imminent and emerging earlier than the nineteenth and early twentieth centuries in which we usually locate them. Corroborating the practical, pragmatic, instrumental character of the "Creative Literature of the British West Indies during the Period of Slavery," Edward Kamau Brathwaite thus goes on to tell us:

The people who wrote about the West Indies during the period of slavery were Englishmen or English-oriented creoles who accepted slavery as something "given," even though some of them might have disapproved of it as a "system." The work they produced was therefore "tropical English." Their models were the metropolitan masters, Dryden, Pope, Prior, James Thomson, Cowper, Thomas Gray, the early Byron in poetry; or worse, minor imitations of these. The prose fiction, on the other hand, reveals less obvious imitation because most of the novels on the West Indies during the period are picaresque and autobiographical in nature. Their limitations stem from the fact that few of them were able to record a truly convincing experience.[9]

With the proper contextual qualifications, changes of emphasis, and specific source materials in question the transposition would require, this could also stand as a fairly accurate description of the early colonial literature of Spanish America prior to independence and, in the Antilles, of the Francophone islands through the better part of the nineteenth century. It is only relatively—and mostly chronologically—less true of the Hispanophone islands, where the Enterprise of the Indies was initially begun. Only to the extent that the preoccupations—cultural, social, and political—felt on the continent after 1826 had a palpable repercussion and gave some stimulus to the growing uneasiness with a strictly peninsular sense of its cultural and "national" identity may it be said to be inapplicable. One is, for all that, reminded of the abolitionist circle of writers gathered around the Cuban Domingo del Monte. Certainly among them, too, one encounters what Brathwaite aptly refers to as "the tyranny of the model" as well as various "migrations of association,"[10] the same derivative clichés of the romantic landscape, a not quite authentic voice mingled in with one that is absolutely genuine. And, as Brathwaite goes on to emphasize, "the voice is crucial. It can transform the scene, even though its elements are local, into something quite 'other'."[11]

This last is a critical observation, one central to any notion of a Caribbean esthetic, to the vital characterization of any literature which, like that of the Antillean archipelago, has (im)migration, colonial dependence, uprooting, exile, and Diaspora as decisively central facts of its cultural life, ordinary living experience, and historical ambience; and some of whose most emblematic works have, indeed, sometimes actually been produced and, until fairly recently, also frequently first published outside the area. The degree to which these "migrations of association" operate, what their relative strength and intensity may be in any given place, varies, of course. But I think that the dynamic tension between them and a specifically Caribbean consciousness in the period of slavery and afterwards is both widespread and well worth exploring. If we do not all and everywhere pass through the region's evolutionary stages at the same time or rate of speed, there is nonetheless compelling evidence to assert that, these disphasures notwithstanding, we do everywhere all go through homologous and comparable evolutionary stages.

The same issue can be equally taken up with respect to the work of the earliest chroniclers of the region. Elsa Goveia, in *A Study on the Historiography of the British West Indies to the End of the Nineteenth Century,* has already done a magnificent job of paving the way for this kind of investigation. Her work will be indispensable to those who follow, searching out the relevance of the work of the chroniclers to presumed or imminent esthetic categories. Despite its title, I might add, her work does not limit itself to the Anglophone islands.

Very little work has, thus far, been done on the former Dutch colonies, exclusive of Guyana. The Dutch Antilles, in consequence, offers a particularly fertile area for study, one that must not be omitted from our consideration, which will give fuller, indispensable dimension to a criticism of authentically Pan-Caribbean scope.

As an original and recurring structural feature of Caribbean life and experience, the subject and theme of immigration too, it seems to me, have also yet to be sufficiently or thoroughly enough dealt with. The enduring Caribbean linkages, loyalties, "double vision," and challenges posed to still powerfully influential, but no longer apt or analytically viable,— exclusively territorial, and strictly bounded, linguistically purist—notions of nation and national identity by the sociohistorical claims, familial, literary, and esthetic connections evident in that growing branch of Caribbean writing that has emerged and is now being produced by Caribbean or Caribbean-descendent folk living in London, New York, Paris, Madrid, Amsterdam,Toronto, and Montreal, among other overseas metropolitan cities, similarly demand to be critically examined as a Diaspora branch of the Caribbean's many-limbed tree. And not merely the work typical of those transients and occasional sojourners who throughout the region's history have, for one reason or another, stationed themselves temporarily abroad, but also that by those such as Pedro Pietri, Paule Marshall, Dionne Brand, and others who—transplanted, born, or brought up there—more or less permanently reside in those metropoles' Caribbean enclaves. Any sustained examination of their work will, of course, raise some serious material and theoretical questions about our subject, questions which, thorny as they are, increasingly demand to be addressed. Bringing new vision and novel perspective to old dramas and problems, their work similarly brings new and unprecedented dimensions and complexities to the usually stipulated terms of our ongoing discussion of them.

To remind us all that, in any event, the idea of one integral Caribbean is not so novel a notion as the conventional resistance to it may lead one to believe, I would like to conclude these remarks with three observations, written from varying vantage and at different points in the archipelago's still unfolding history and which, it seems to me, speak directly to the question.

Writing in the 1690s and early 1700s, the French Dominican missionary and so-called Pirate's Priest, Père Jean-Baptiste Labat (1663–1738), confessed himself forcefully struck by what he unambiguously observes to be the cultural integrity and singular identity of the Antilles. "I have traveled everywhere in your sea of the Caribbean," he notes in one of his seminal journal's entries, with arresting insight and a remarkably modern inflection,

> . . . from Haiti to Barbados, to Martinique and Guadaloupe, and I know what I am speaking about. . . . You are all together, in the same boat, sailing on the same uncertain sea . . . citizenship and race unimportant, feeble little labels compared to the message that my spirit brings to me: that of the position and predicament which History has imposed upon you . . . I saw it first with the dance . . . [:] the merengue in Haiti, the beguine in Martinique and today I hear, *de mon oreille morte*, the echo of calypsos from Trinidad, Jamaica, St. Lucia, Antigua, Dominica and the legendary Guiana. . . . It is no accident that the sea which separates your lands makes no difference to the rhythm of your body.[12]

During the Second War for Cuban Independence (1895–1898) and amid his sustained effort to ensure that in what he called "Our America" the colony would not ultimately live on to undermine his vision of a republic of all and for the good of all, and all too keenly aware of the very real obstacle to that end which the region's territories' mutual isolation represented, José Martí likewise repeatedly cautioned his fellow Antilleans. "Nations that don't know one another," he averred just seven years before the "Splendid Little War" of 1898 which signaled the

United States' debut as an imperial power in the area, "should quickly become acquainted, as people who are soon to face a common foe."[13]

From one of our own contemporaries, the Barbadian novelist George Lamming, comes this equally admonitory counsel: "We, West Indians, shall travel the road of self-mutilation, if we do not quickly reconvene, and assume our tasks as men and women of one country."[14]

Alerts all which literary critics, no less than any other ordinary citizen, could do worse than to heed.

Notes

1. Rogelio Martinez Furé, "Diálogo imaginario sobre folklore," *La Gaceta de Cuba* 121 (marzo 1974): 16.

2. René Depestre, "Problemas de la identidad del hombre negro en las literaturas antillanas," *Casa de las Américas* (diciembre 1968), 19.

3. Aimé Césaire, *Cahier d'un retour au pays natal* (Paris: Présence Africaine, 1956), 63.

4. It would be nearly a decade and more after this was written that, with the publication of *So Spoke the Uncle*, Magdaline W. Shannon's translation of Price-Mars's text, and of *In the Flicker of an Eyelid*, Carrol F. Coates and Edwidge Danticat's translation of Alexis's *L'espace d'un cillement*, both in 1983, some of their work would begin, slowly, to be available in English. Coates's translation of *Compère Général Soleil, General Sun, My Brother*, would not appear until 1999. *Monsieur Toussaint*, a play by Glissant, eventually appeared in an English translation by Juris Silenieks in 1981. Betsy Wing's translations of Glissant's poems published in his collections *Le sel noir, Le sang rive*, and *Boises, Black Salt*, did not finally appear until 1998; her edition of *The Collected Poems of Édouard Glissant* and translation of the novel *Le Quatrième Siècle* (*The Fourth Century*) were published in 1994 and 2001, respectively. A book of Pedro Mir's verse would not be available until Jonathan Cohen and Donald D. Walsh published their translations of it in the anthological compilation *Countersong to Walt Whitman and Other Poems*, in 1993.

5. See "The Politics of Translation and the Literature of the Caribbean," *Revista Chicano-riqueña*, año IV (verano 1976): 48–56.

6. Michael Gilkes, *Racial Identity and Individual Consciousness in the Caribbean Novel*, The Edgar Mittelholzer Memorial Lectures, Fifth Series, 1974 (Georgetown, Guyana: Ministry of Information and Culture National History and Arts Council, 1975), p. 43. See also *Wilson Harris and the Caribbean Novel* (London: Longman Group Limited, 1975), p. xxv.

7. E. K. Brathwaite, *Contradictory Omens: Cultural Diversity and Integration in the Caribbean* (Mona, Jamaica: Savacou Publications, 1974), 21.

8. S. S. Prawer, *Karl Marx and World Literature* (Oxford: Clarendon Press, 1976), 290.

9. E. K. Brathwaite, "Creative Literature of the British West Indies during the Period of Slavery," *Savacou* 1, no. 1 (June 1970): 48.

10. Ibid., 55 and 58.

11. Ibid., 54.

12. Gordon K. Lewis, *The Growth of the Modern West Indies* (New York: Monthly Review Press, 1968), p. 46.

13. José Martí, *Nuestra América,* ed. Roberto Fernández Retamar (Havana: Casa de Las Américas, 1974), p. 21.

14. George Lamming, "The West Indian People," *New World Quarterly* 2, no.2 (1966) 63–64.

Raza, racismo, e historia

"Are All My Bones from There?"

For Hortense J. Spillers and Ana Pizarro

Does all my skin (I should have said),
Does all my skin come from that Spanish marble?
My frightening voice, too, the harsh cry in my throat?
Are all my bones from there? . . .
Is there nothing more than that which you have written. . . . ?
Nicolás Guillén, "My Last Name: A Family Elegy"

It must now surely be apparent to all at the start of a new millennium that the strategies of artful dodging and denial which all too often tend still to meet provocative questions about race, racism, and history such as that lyrically posed by Nicolás Guillén in the early 1950s are now even more inadequate and untenable than they have always been. Certainly the accelerating surge of consciousness among Afro-Latino Americans themselves—not to mention, among several other factors, the quantum growth of scholarly attention to and increasing general interest in these matters since the sixties—makes such evasions more and more difficult comfortably to conjure up or convincingly to sustain. This, of course, does not prevent them from being conjured up. The need to speak candidly about such matters in our Americas continues, then, to be a pressing and knotty task of some moment.

Against a still powerful millennial tradition predisposed to ignore, diminish, marginalize, or otherwise to dismiss the central place and impact of the descendants of the African in this hemisphere, we, alas, must still contend with and regularly confront the legacies, historic weight, and continuing provocation of a history decisively marked by genocidal violence, the trade in and exploitation of Africa's humanity, the slave-like indenture of Asia's millions, the pigmentocratic pretension and still omnipresent patrician disdain for the working majority of our region's contemporary inheritors of the Conquistador's mantle on both sides of the Río Grande.

To articulate the historical coordinates and survey the decisive compass points by which we all, and Latin Americans of African descent most particularly, have been crucially shaped and "oriented" as peoples in and of the New World remains, for precisely that reason, an imperative and essential operation, one preliminary to any effective devising of more genuinely appropriate strategies of both communal dialogue and the working out of the forms and frameworks best suited to promote authentically democratic conceptions of our polities, the overall integrity, general health, and material welfare of our communities. It is precisely that kind of critically preliminary inventory of our common inheritance of "race, racism, and history" and its fallout to which this essay aims to contribute.

I. Root and Matrix: The Crusades

The roots and structural matrix of New World notions of race, and of Iberian racialist thought in particular, were already well in place before the Columbian landfall. A promontory of Asia, long subject to Asian depredations, and comparatively undeveloped tributary of that more sumptuous and self-sufficient scimitar of territory extending south beyond the Strait of Gibraltar and eastward through Alexandria, Arabia, Persia, India, and China, Europe first created a cohesive consciousness of itself as a defensive, aggressively oppositional negation of the more advanced and sophisticated civilizations on whose periphery it lay. At the center of its historic project of unity under the banner of Christendom, initially embodied in the Crusades, was the wish eventually to effect a displacement of the multilateral potency and omnipresence of Africa and Asia.

Medieval Europe's first, though abortive, experience in long-distance colonization, the Crusades represented a general mobilization behind the congregational idea of an ideal—or imagined—community of a Europe united against the "infidel" and the "barbarian." Nodal points in the vocabulary of a militant Christianity, each of these concepts ethnocentric premises and comparative hierarchy was to remain relatively constant, unvarying, and stable. As a result,

From the end of the twelfth century until the beginning of the sixteenth, the term *barbarus* [which, beyond its etymological origins in Greek, we have reason to believe may have originally indicated a specific community of African people], or whatever vernacular form it might take, had come to acquire two closely related meanings. As a term of classification it applied broadly to all non-Christian peoples, and more loosely might be used to describe any race, whatever its religious beliefs, which behaved in savage or "uncivil" ways. In both cases, the word implied that any creature so described was somehow an imperfect human being. . . . By and large, for any serious purpose, "barbarian" was a word reserved for those who neither subscribed to European religious views, nor lived their lives according to European social norms.[1]

By so inclusive and adaptively elastic a definition, of course, practically the whole of the then known world outside of Christian Europe was, in varying degrees, "Barbarian."

The Crusades similarly transformed the natives of the Holy Lands: From a presence traditionally hardly even noticed, if at all, by a host of religious European pilgrims, they passed to the category of inopportune local obstacle, recalcitrant nemesis or awesome military impediment.[2] The Crusades, in consequence, "created a huge market for a comprehensive, integral, entertaining, and satisfying image of the enemy's [religious] ideology . . ." The general public, Maxime Rodinson goes on to explain, "demanded an image be presented that would show the abhorrent side of Islam by depicting it in the crudest fashion possible so as to satisfy the . . . taste for the marvelous so noticeable in all the work of the period."[3] Europe's symptomatic heraldic turn to Greece, rather than to its Egyptian colonizers or to its later Arab interpreters, and to Rome did little to dampen this rather tendentious proclivity. A generic, peremptory distinction between fellow denizen and outsider, between naturally freeborn "citizen" and alien, inferior "barbarian" was, in fact, the prime meridian of Aristotelian sociology and politics. The force of this discrimination implied a convergence and tacit fusion of geo-political, ethnological, and cultural categories by which communal origin, putative "race," and communal public standing became so many mutually confirming aspects of a single contingency: the nature of one's specific ancestral affiliation and pedigree. Transition to the analogous convergence, in the Spain of the Catholic Kings and post-Columbian America, between strictly religious, cultural or ethnic, and "racial" categories would, in consequence, involve no particularly difficult conceptual leap. That passage had, in effect, already been anticipated and authorized by Herodotus's depictions of "Indians of the South [who] were black and were related to the Ethiopians, an identification that was to remain firmly embedded in European popular thought until the sixteenth century."[4] After several centuries of Islam's continuing expansion and, on the Iberian Peninsula especially, its undeniable and enduring general influence, moreover, the tangible material benefits, the seductive intellectual and cultural authority of Muslim civilization on the European domestic scene itself began increasingly to prove a problematic presence.

As the historic prolongation of the Crusades, it only remained for the Iberian *Reconquista* and Spain's introduction of the "sifting out" idea of a *pureza de sangre* finally to bring the notion of a congregational Christian orthodoxy into more intimate alignment with categories of culture and "nationality" that, though ostensively religious, affinitive, and behavioral, could in practice only be certified by recourse to genealogical appeals and, so, inescapably to biological categories of essential inheritance and "race." Ethno-religious, social-behavioral, and racial-biological categories were in this way conflated. Civil claim to political and economic rights, the recognition of one's citizenship status, social and cultural prestige would henceforth all be a correlative of the automatic hierarchy, the superior civic and public standing forever conferred by that genealogical certification. Its absence became the predetermined and equally permanent token of a secular marginality, of fundamental insufficiency, and an obligatory subordination: the material emblem of shameful taint or discrediting contamination. The general resonance and force of this novel inflection would quickly convert proper nouns like *Moro*, *Negro*, and *Etiopé*, as well as neologisms like *Converso* and *Marrano*, their various cognates and derivatives, into socially charged adjectives: so many epithets and proximate synonyms in comparative alienness and a stipulated deficiency or inferiority.

This is the subsoil from which contemporary Latin Americans' racially inflected use of words like *morejón*, *morocho*, *morochón*, and *morlaco* all emerge; and which made of *Moreno*—also originally derived from *Moro*—the connotatively protean vernacular synonym of *Negro* that it still remains. It is also the context that gave us the metaphorical description for that most traditional of Antillean rice dishes: *Moros y cristianos*. Seen as the ultimate culmination and institutional consolidation of the European Crusades' final success, the absolutist modern state inaugurated by Spain's monarchs had, by 1492, thus already effectively committed itself to an equally absolute "racialist" ethnocentrism. In that sense too, alas, Spain was the first authentically modern state.

The exploratory expeditions of the Iberians in the western Mediterranean and the African Atlantic that were the immediate precursors of the Enterprise of the Indies, also identifiably marked by the stamp of the Crusades, were among this emerging ethnic absolutism's early proving grounds. It was the occupation of the Balearic isles, the discovery and settlement of the Azores, and the brutal colonization of the Canary Islands that provided the colonial models and immediate precedents for the structural terms, racial attitudes, and governing assumptions that informed conquest and settlement in the American colonies. Certainly, there was virtually nothing that would later be done or said as regards the New World's indigenous peoples or the African slaves imported there to replace them which had not already been foreshadowed and rehearsed on the sugar plantations of Madeira or in the rhetoric and debates about, for example, the "primitive" temperament and "pagan" character of the Canary Islanders.[5]

The Portuguese voyages, slave raids, and commercial *factorias* down the long coast of Africa that, between the 1440s and the 1490s, made sub-Saharan Blacks a significant and regular presence (as bondsmen, domestic servants, and showy symbols of hidalgo wealth and social station) in major cities like Lisbon, Oporto, Madrid, Valencia, Barcelona, Cadiz, and Seville were also the template and original source of supply of the labor that would shortly be bound for the New World. Forerunners of the later Triangular Trade, they also preceded it in the purveying of pejorative and self-serving images of Blacks as the accursed children of Ham who, as the chronicler Gomes Eannes de Zurara put it in the 1460s, "should be subject to all the other races of the world."[6]

In brief, by the time Columbus arrives on the scene, even if the dream of a united Christendom had already begun visibly to fracture along sectarian and national lines, something of an ideological consensus and the terms of Europe's "racial" engagement with the Americas had, in fact, already been achieved. Arab, Jew, African, and out-island Indigene, as so many expressions of the "barbarous," "pagan," and "primitive," had emerged as cognate versions of the aberrant, divinely condemned, and "racially" differentiated Other. The lethal conceit of the Christian West to which that noxious equation gave rise, moldy with the accretions of more modern times, is still very much alive and kicking.

II. Columbian Landfall to the Haitian Revolution

It was no coincidence that the hubris of this conceit should be so clearly reflected in the very first acts of Columbus—and of the entire procession of European successors that followed in his wake. There was his almost immediate declaration that the darker-skinned inhabitants of the unfamiliar world he came upon "ought to make good and skilled servants" for the paleface parvenu, that "with fifty men we could subjugate them all and make them do what we want."[7] His—and his sovereigns'— missionary zeal and utopian vision of a polity which, accepting only fully certified "Old Christians" among those immigrating ultimately to rule and hold dominion in the new territories, aimed to secure and to guarantee, from the get-go, a *pureza de sangre* even more immaculate and unsullied than the metropolis itself could ever reliably demonstrate. The imposition of the system of *encomienda* which Columbus was the first to force upon Native American societies, bringing them unrelenting holocaust and devastation, was calculated to complement that vision. Turning to the trade in Africans to fill the vacuum left by the decimation of the labor pool in his initial plan seemed logical enough to a Genoese sailor who had already taken direct part in and was intimately familiar with the Guinea trade. The final upshot was, in any event, a pejorative identification of race and the laboring classes which became as enduringly commonplace as it was ineluctable.

The mere possession of a white skin, indicating your European provenance and rights of eminent domain, was now by itself the conclusive badge and sign of a presumptively superior humanity and comparatively privileged social condition. Categories of class, social place, economic function, and ethnic identity effectively fused into each other, becoming virtually indistinguishable and mutually self-confirming. Refashioned and newly configured onto the society of feudal ranks, orders, and estates that was the Conquistador's European inheritance there was now grafted a *Society of Race* and racial castes.

If the facts of miscegenation (which made a blended population of *mestizos,* mulattos, *zambos, zambuagos, pardos, grifos, cuaterones,* and such a presence of growing demographic heft) threatened to destabilize that axial hinge of the colonial pact, then a *pigmentocracy* of complexions could be invoked to second the aristocracies of economic and social class. This would keep everyone in their comparatively proper place. To a greater or lesser extent and except for the adaptive variations and relative modifications specific local or regional conditions sometimes allowed or required, this *Society of Race* and racial castes is the one by which the Americas have all been historically shaped and socially articulated. It is the society out of which the distinctive particularity of the Afro-Latino experience ultimately comes. Those who, from the Amerindian Caribs to the runaway *cimarrón* and insurrectionary slave, resisted or otherwise rejected this society's equations, defined out of the polity and out of the categories of a shared humanity, had necessarily to be strategically isolated from its center, as the *palenques* and alternative communities of the Maroons all were; or had to be unceremoniously subdued, extirpated, annihilated, and erased from memory. It was this society that made the trade in slaves, the sugar plantation, and manor house latifundia its defining signature forms. Its defense of them (which from the 1640s onward accelerated to include—and predominately— Spain's French, English, Dutch, and Danish rivals in the Americas) led to that second great demographic transformation which, bringing multiple millions of Africans across the Middle Passage, so dramatically changed the region's overall *complexion*. More often than not, if ironically not exactly intended, it also effected that widening *Africanization* of popular local life, culture, and experience its architects came most deeply to fear. This is the society that, from Columbus to the irruptive triumph of the Haitian Revolution, had virtually no structural competitors and whose racial protocols reigned generally supreme across the American landscape.

It was the Haitian Revolution, rather than the earlier American Revolution or the later Wars of Latin American Independence that first most unambiguously challenged this society's incumbency and shook it to its deepest foundations. Thomas Jefferson, who shared the American Founding Fathers' belief that Blacks, "whether originally a distinct race, or made distinct by time and circumstances, are inferior to the whites in the endowments both of body and mind,"[8] deliberately restricted the racial reach of his otherwise magnificent document of colonial liberation by ultimately consenting with them to the United States Constitution's acceptance of slavery that has haunted this nation ever since. The white Creole elites of South America, then as now wary of the democratizing aspirations to a new and more equitable social dispensation on the part of the Amerindian, blacks, mulattos, pardos, and the varied *castas* of "colored folk," also strove to limit the scope of revolution to their own racial sector. They, as well, wanted to guarantee that the new republics they were bringing into existence would effectively allow them to exercise, in Bolívar's strikingly telling phrase, "an active domestic tyranny."[9] In the aftermath of victory, the Liberator made his views of its racial and caste boundaries even more plain. In a letter of 1826, soliciting General José Antonio Páez's help in warding off the dangers he saw emerging, he lashed out against those with less autocratic outlooks, concluding apprehensively with:

> We shall not [even] speak of the democrats and fanatics, or say anything about the persons of color, for to enter the bottomless abyss of these problems is to bury reason therein as in the house of death. What can we expect of so violent, so frenzied a clash of passions, rights, demands, and principles? Chaos is less fearful than this terrible scene, and, though we turn our eyes from it, it will neither disappear nor cease to haunt us in all its terror. Believe me, my dear General, a great volcano lies at our feet, and its rumblings are not rhetorical; they are physical and very real. . . . Who [, he demands to know,] shall restrain the oppressed classes? Slavery will break its yoke, each shade of complexion will seek mastery, and . . . [t]he latent feelings of hatred among the various sections will break out anew.[10]

This was simultaneously the achievement, the hovering permanent threat, and worst nightmare of the *Society of Race*. If the white Creole Venezuelan's contextual predicament was not always precisely the same as the white Virginia planter's, the response of their class to it proved, in practice, that their dreads and preoccupations were tantamount to identical. Bolívar, it may merit mention, was not unmindful of what had already transpired in San Domingue.

The only successful slave revolt in history, the Haitian Revolution's "transformation of slaves, trembling in hundreds before a single white man, into a people able to organise themselves and defeat the most powerful European nations of the day"[11] exploded the arrogance and overweening presumption of *The Society of Race*. Occurring at the height of the system of slavery and in what was then one of the most impressively profitable of this hemisphere's colonies, its victory struck that society an unexpectedly stunning blow, a blow whose profound impact and reverberations would long resonate and were vividly and palpably felt across the region. Every state and every colony in which the standardized Authority of the White remained the cardinal coordinate of social relations,—that is to say, all of them—shaken from cozy complacency, were dramatically and henceforth put on notice: *Haiti could happen here.* The only American state founded and brought into being specifically and deliberately to reject, root and branch, the racial status quo and its customary implications, the Black Republic by its very existence stood in sensational defiance of the presumed universalism of White Authority. A potential safe haven, it also offered comfort, tangible encouragement, and a powerful example to blacks and all those still unfree. But for the fact of Haiti, the process of abolition and emancipation would everywhere have certainly been more attenuated and delayed than it was. Historic culmination and *bête noire* of the *Society of Race,* Haiti became that society's image of threatening total ruin and catastrophe.

III. After the Haitian Revolution

The structural features of the years after the Haitian Revolution can, for our purposes, be synthesized and reduced to essentially two major stages and three different, though mutually overlapping trends. In the first stage, which runs unevenly and was experienced differentially from the initial to the final decades of the nineteenth century, there is the political (re)consolidation and strategic regrouping of the area's directing white Creole elites. There is also, in the face of the racial composition of their own populations, their explicit postulation of polities and notions of "nationality" and "national culture" which assume the theologies and raciological hierarchies of white supremacy. This almost uniformly leads them openly to ventilate their growing anxieties and uneasiness with the future portent and potentialities of the non-European elements of their societies' demographic makeup and general inheritance. That *Anxiety of Race,* whose effect lingers to this day, is, in fact, one of the prominent characteristics of the nation-building process, from the headwaters of the Mississippi to Tierra del Fuego. From Jefferson and Bolívar to Antonio Saco and Domingo Faustino Sarmiento, from Manuel Alonso's Puerto Rico to Francisco García Calderón's Perú, it is the central trope and recurring motif of this initial stage.

Taking for granted that whatever form of state had already or might eventually emerge would—and rightly should—be ruled by local whites, this was the atmospheric climate from which even the era's most radically progressive liberals—one thinks of the Manuel González Prada of *Horas de Lucha* or the José Martí of "Mi raza" and "The Charlestown

Earthquake"—were not themselves immune. The particular forms of this *Anxiety of Race* might vary, but its defining lines of force were always clear enough.

On the South American continent there was, on the one hand, the emancipated white Creoles' chiding and troubled lament that, alas, mother Spain was not—economically or otherwise—authentically European. As one of those Frenchman they were fond of reading so succinctly put it: it is "Africa begins at the Pyrenees." [12] It was, therefore, its presumptively "backward" legacies that as post-colonials they had inherited and were now unfortunately burdened with.

There was, on the other hand, the almost universal brooding about the racial inferiority and congenital incapacity for progress and modernity of their local non-white populations and the noxious effects which, it was alleged, miscegenation had had—and, if not checked, would continue to have—on the developmental prospects of Latin America. Race, that is, lay at the very heart of Latin American society's difficulties and underdevelopment. "The race question," the Peruvian García Calderón was neither the first nor the last to insist,

> is a very serious problem in American history: it explains the progress of some nations, the decadence of others; it is the key to the incurable malady which is lacerating America. Finally, many other secondary phenomena depend upon it: general wealth, industrial organization, the stability of governments, and the steadfastness of patriotism. It is necessary, therefore, [he concludes] that the continent have an unswerving policy, based on the study of the problems posed by race, just as there is an agrarian policy in Russia, a protectionist policy in Germany and a policy of free-trade in England. [13]

The empirical implementation of such a policy could—and did—include a range of options, from the comparatively "benign" (educational uplift, a more broadly generalized program of assimilation to "white" social and cultural norms, vocational typecasting) to the deadly fatal.

In the Caribbean, where the Spanish Empire had decided to reinvent itself in the aftermath of the Battle of Ayacucho and the shattering failure of European military intervention in Haiti, there was first the sustained and deliberate campaign to isolate, destabilize, generally discredit, and economically punish the Black Republic. This, it was hoped, would discourage a repetition of its historic audacity and contain the reach of its seditious example. The unrelenting crusade of propaganda that Robert Lawless has suitably dubbed *Haiti's Bad Press* [14] was a key part of this effort, and our regular neglect of Haiti's formative impact and continuing influence on the history of our islands and continents remains a testament to its enduring efficacy.

There was, at the same time, an immediate sharpening of racist white fears of the *Africanization* of the Caribbean. In the Spanish-speaking islands, in particular, this took the form of defending and insisting upon the racially "white" identity of the properly "national" citizenry, and of *this* citizenry's obsession with the security implications of demographic encirclement and the putative menace of racial war. Both provoked a radical reassertion of the authoritative polity's "whiteness" and, its numbers now augmented by the influx of loyalist *peninsulares* and conservative Creole whites fleeing Haiti and the revolutions on the continent, a heightening of its racial identification with the European metropolis. That, after 1834–48, when the rest of the region had either already ended or was embarked upon the process of ending slavery, Spain's remaining New World colonies were actually providing it with a new lease on life was something which certainly did not bode well for— and indeed would significantly retard—Afro-Antillean friendly attitudes and policies. It was, in fact, the wish to secure the power and extend the reach of an elsewhere declining system which, until the 1860s, made intimate allies of Antillean and Southern North American plantocrats and nourished their common dream of a plantation empire stretching from the Carolinas to Central America and beyond.

The Dominican Republic's proximity made its ruling classes especially nervous and sensitive to Haiti's looming presence. The Revolution's commitment to end slavery in Hispaniola and its wish to secure its exposed eastern flank had in fact brought Spanish Santo Domingo under Haitian sovereignty from the 1820s to 1844. The independence with which it inaugurated its subsequent national life was, thus, actually predicated on a radical rejection of the Haitian revolutionary alternative. This was one of the factors which, in significant part, contributed to its being the only Latin American territory willingly to submit, albeit briefly, to a restoration of Spanish colonial authority. Its later promotion of the image of a Christianized, Spanish-educated cacique, Enriquillo, as national symbol of its distinctly Latin American genesis, at once deliberately associated the origins of the republic with a native aboriginal past and circumvented the formative gravity of the black and mulatto presence. That the Amerindian was now conveniently extinct made him all the more attractive as a symbol. Dominicans, in any case, were thereby tacitly defined as being, in some sense, *Indian*. Local blacks, by contrast, could be cast—as former President Joaquin Balaguer was still casting them in 1989[15]—as "foreigners" and "Haitians": they effectively ceased to exist as constitutive elements of the *real* nation.

The Cuban patriciate, too, unambiguously asserted, with Antonio Saco, that "Cuban nationality is formed by the white race."[16] Their successful bid to replace San Domingue as sugar supplier to the world, in addition, did not only precipitate a new rise of the plantation, a reinvigoration of the slave trade, and the explosive growth of a second slavery. The need for protection from their own slaves would bring them into a conservative colonial alliance with Spain as its "Ever Faithful Isle." As in Puerto Rico, it would also lead this patriciate to explicitly marginalize its people of African origin and closely to monitor the racial and social line it strove to maintain between whites, black slaves, and the free population of color. While they invariably concurred with their continental brethren that the purer your stock of "whiteness" the better, *Antillanos* were barely more sanguine that if miscegenation was a problem it could, properly managed, just as well provide something like a solution. By controlling the inflow of slaves brought in by the trade, and over time diluting the relative blackness of the local population of colored folk, a *mejoramiento de la raza*, they reasoned, might be possible. *De la raza negra, se entiende.*[17]

The result, in the islands and on the continent, was the white elite's institution of social and immigration policies calculated to reduce or mitigate the general heft and influence of local non-whites, to realign and reconfigure the demographic balance between the races so as to insure the continued social and economic dominance of Creole whites. To govern, as Juan Bautista Alberti would insist, is to populate. But preferably with white Europeans. The promotion of their migration became everywhere the rage. There could even be a certain ecumenical catholicity in it. "I want families and single colonists," Antonio Saco averred. "I want artisans, merchants, writers and scholars: in a word, I want all kinds of people as long as they have white faces. . . ."[18] It was a sentiment which—echoed from one end of the hemisphere to the other—was, in fact, to bring in new waves of just such immigrants.

The trend toward theoretically more congregational, racially inclusive notions of the national polity which, from the late 1860s through the 1890s, also typified this stage retained a heavy dose and clearly detectable patina of the previous decades' inflections. Its comparatively more integrative declensions were not incompatible with racist premises, formulations, or bias. Part of the strategic accommodation and adaptation to the accumulating pressures of local ethno-social realities and shifting demographics, it nonetheless presumably allowed for fractionally more democratic and racially more encompassing definitions of the national community. The role of the state and the genuine statesman was now increasingly and ideally—as best they could—pragmatically to conform, to administer, and to reconcile the interests and diverse claims of the various branches of the national household.

The clearest, most radically sincere and integrative racial formulation of this relatively more ecumenical modality was, perhaps, José Martí's fresh definition of the nation as "more than white, more than black, more than mulatto."[19] It undoubtedly gave strategic point, mediating leverage, social heft, political efficacy, and revolutionary authority to the white Creole's congregationalism and, in Cuba specifically, to Martí's uncommon assault on the sophistry and pseudo-science of contemporary raciologists.

However prescient and enlightened, the man who defiantly affirmed "This is not the century of the struggle among races, but rather the century of the affirmation of rights,"[20] "say human and you declare the entitlement to all rights,"[21] could still regularly conceive the emancipation of the slave as the philanthropic gesture of benevolent whites to whom the Black was, as a result, beholden and his gratitude obliged. Nor was the white Creole radical of the era who in himself most splendidly resumed "the soul of a continent" entirely beyond effectively succumbing to the seductions of that conventional stereotyping derived from a tacitly and unilaterally decreed racial hierarchy of cultures. Though he disapproved of the word *race* and quarreled with those whose worldview depended on it, he nonetheless frequently employed it, as normally accepted, in ways which could come dangerously close to their irrationalism and mystic imprecisions. The insinuative ambiguities of his celebrated sentence "La raza es una patria major"[22] in the context of a society and social climate whose racialist predisposition Martí knew only too well is but one, among many, examples of this.

The dominant school of thought and a central tenet in this later trend, in any case, was still the assumption, implicit or expressed, that the white man was the natural superior of the black. Whereas in the United States a single drop of Negro blood condemned one to status as the three-fifths part of a human being, in the countries to the south

Domingo Del Monte's earlier expressed desire to bring about, if not necessarily by violent means, "the diminishment, the extinction if it were
possible, of the Negro race"[23] in his country still retained a more than
passing hold on the prevailing climate of opinion. It was a consummation which might be said actually to have reached something of a fulfill-
ment in the virtual disappearance of the Afro-Argentinean community
so few of us now remember.[24] In practice, in any case, Blacks were still
invariably relegated to the menial tasks and hidden backs rooms of the
national house, and very little had substantially changed in that household's overarching domestic hierarchies and prevailing social consensus,
or in the condescending character typical of communal attitudes and
ordinary race relations.

In the second stage, which stretches from the last decade of the nineteenth century into the charged air of our own day, a maverick and
intensifying if equivocal reevaluation of emphasis, terms, images, and
operative definitions begins gradually to emerge. Against the backdrop
of the Creole white (and *mestizo*) elites' own abrupt diminishment to
the comparatively unaccustomed condition and status of dismissible
"natives" and "colored folk," there is, first, the almost immediate in-
jured and angry reaffirmation of their historically certificated social
and cultural aristocracy. One result is a conservative resurgence of an
identification of Latin America with its European cultural roots and
inheritance. Along with a new surge in the region's anticolonial mood,
this also brought a Hispanophile rehabilitation of Spain as epic motherland and the rise of a radical Latinism in which a clash of regional
Civilizations—the Anglo-Saxon and the Iberian—is the central motif.

Faced with the menacing strength, imperial vigor, and economic and
cultural threat of North American power, extolling the virtues of Iberian idealism over Yankee pragmatism becomes almost *de rigueur.* This
Latinism's emphasis on the innate, numinous moral and spiritual superiority of descendants of the Iberian also clearly gave a racialist tinge
to that heightened populist nationalism whose roots lie in it. Reinstated
as spiritual fount and cultural motherland, Spain became, only too conspicuously, the token of a racial badge. "We are all Spaniards," Luis
Lloréns Torres declared, insisting too on the alabaster hue of "our soul,
our Spanish racial spirit."[25] It was one of the tics of the time that lingers
with us yet. One of this tic's corollary ideas was the persistent refusal
to accord, in the face of all evidence to the contrary, any but ancillary
cultural value to the presence of the Black. Tomás Blanco's declaration

of 1942 to the effect that "our colored population is completely Hispan-ized and the African contributions to our environment are very slight, except in our musical folklore"[26] was a view generally shared by more than just the majority of Cuban and Puerto Rican Creoles to whom it was first addressed. "Our general culture," he no less quaintly went on, echoing sentiments then common throughout Latin America "is white, Western, with few and very slight non-Spanish influences . . . our people is not black . . ." More "scientifically" fastidious than most, he even went so far to as emphasize that, under the circumstances, "the amount of black blood [involved] matters very little."[27]

Calculated to demonstrate the comparatively benign, presumptively compassionate nature of Latin American servitude relative to its North American variant, a "we was a good massa" revision of the domestic histories of slavery in Spanish times and colonies, which deliberately minimized and muted all its harshness and brutal realities, generally went hand in hand with its self-serving pastorals. The oft-repeated nug-get that, to all intents and purposes, racism effectively did not exist there was another favorite trope of this mythmaking. The implications of the fact that Spain, in addition to having been the first to bring it to the New World, was also the last of the European colonial powers to outlaw and end slavery was, of course, invariably ignored, overlooked, or conveniently forgotten.

The conferral (or denial) of symbolic passports of national authen-ticity, in accordance with the presumed unique and special status of Spanish among the world's languages, and the patrician demand of something more than the usual socio-culturally appropriate linguistic registers and etiquette—the hysterical and ahistorical call for a hope-lessly illusory *pureza de lengua*—from the regional diasporas which this elite has itself created, is one of the more covert forms this Hispanophile outlook has more recently assumed.

From the early '20s onward, this general process of revision and re-evaluation would also entail a reappraisal and rearticulating of the role of miscegenation as a factor acting upon the body politic. What an ear-lier time postulated as its regressive genetic and social impact comes now to be regarded as the catalytic mechanism which, having already achieved the nation's *mulatez* or *mestizaje,* would ultimately produce the vast and universal hybridization of a cosmic race. What previous generations had roundly condemned as an enervating, deteriorative agent was now increasingly celebrated as democratically synthesizing force and as signal source of our national and regional racial and cultural particularities.

As a more progressive and liberal alternative to the traditionally dominant Hispanophile discourse, this ideology of Creole *mestizaje* openly acknowledged the ubiquitous presence and cultural influence of the black ancestor. Drawing inspiration from a plethora of long untapped popular experience and tradition, its adherents' occasionally "scandalous" promotion of *negrismo* offered an obvious challenge to more conventional dogma and orthodoxy. To the extent it did so, it represented an important insurgent break. From the Argentine to *Los nuyores* and beyond, "the Negro danced while boulevards applaud[ed]."[28]

The new modality, though, too often proved to be, in fact, *más negrista que negra, más moda que mulata.* Its emphasis on the historical facts of *mestizaje* was not always incompatible with continuing confirmation of some of the most objectionable clichés of a racialist stereotyping, in which, as Luis Palés Matos put it, "the negress . . . sings / her . . . domestic animal's life / . . . smell[ing] of earth, of savagery, of sex," while "Africa grunts: Ñam. Ñam."[29] With relatively few exceptions, its identification with the concrete person and specific material condition of the black seemed all too often to be merely a literary and exotic domestic theme: *pura literatura,* tending to the abstract, socially detached, and oftentimes internally inconsistent and contradictory.

Even as the new emphasis on *mestizajes* announced a certain shift in the cultural politics of the region, then, it revealed important lines of continuity with some of the racialist thinking of the past. If some still assumed the course of syncretism would best *always* run in the direction of a comparative *whiteness* and *away from* the extremities of blackness, others tacitly conveyed the idea of a national and cultural hierarchy in which blacks would, at best, be domestic junior partners and Africa, save as the process of *mestizaje* tended to whiten her descendants, a still accessory addendum to a fundamentally inviolate core which remained, in its essence, Creole Spanish and, above all,—*white*.

Emerging to become our region's predominant cultural discourse and official national cultural doctrine since the 1950s, the ideology of *mestizaje,* so conceived, is not unproblematic and compels a certain critical caution and wariness. The critique of its more dubious elements and unexamined racial assumptions is, in fact, one of the central features of the current moment that gathers intensity with every passing year. That the sharpest and most pointed edge of that critique comes increasingly from Afro-Latin Americans themselves does not seem to me either casual or coincidental. The general rise of the black presence and its power in the world (which followed upon African Independence, the American Civil Rights Movement, the crisis of négritude in the French Antilles and the rise of new forms of Black Nationalism in the English Caribbean) further promoted the radical thoroughness of this critique. It also informed its gathering urgency and the sometimes positively dismissive pitch of its tone. "The repugnant alienation suffered by the [Latin American] black," it was now more frequently and openly heard, to the obvious discomfort of some, "has been crushing, constant, and systematic."[30] "The most omnipresent and original datum about [anti-Black Latin American racism]," many now even more boldly proclaimed, "is the absurd and obstinate negation of its existence."[31]

The Afro-Latino population in the United States played an especially salient and crucial role in the development and emergence of this critique. The greater comparative consciousness of the layered intricacies of race its North American experience gave it contributed mightily to the unmasking of the more covert and courtly class and racial protocols of Latin American convention. It also placed it in the strategic pivot between the two realities and at the transnational center of any debate on the issue. It continues to occupy that unique and historically critical position. How it will ultimately discharge and effectively realize all the potentialities of that singular positioning will continue to be among the key issues we will have regularly to deal with in the new millennium. The centrality of its role will almost certainly grow in the years ahead. Uniquely located, and whether as encouraging advocates, collegial collaborators, or candid critics, it is also increasingly well poised to assume the burdens and responsibilities of this strategic position. Seeing to the removal of the offensive representations of Afro-Latinos still daily purveyed on the soaps and outlets of Telemundo and Univisión here and in every corner of Spanish America (which the history I've outlined here makes still generally and uncritically admissible at a time when they would not pass muster on even the most conservative of American networks, for all *their* shortcomings), for example, is one among the several areas where the U.S. Latino community's strategic locus and experience give it an especially privileged place, opportunity, and power, the conscientious exercise of which would have an undoubtedly very salutary general effect. What is clear, in any event, is that that community has already had, and will continue to have a role of major consequence to play in the years and decades that lie ahead.

More dialectically rhizoid then accustomed versions of the ideology of *mestizaje,* the discourse of *creolization* which, since the 1970s, has entered the debate appears to be more amply inclusive and extensively embracing. Certainly it offers a more broadly comprehensive and inter-active idea of hybridity and a wider horizon of promising possibilities. Restive offspring of the crisis of *négritude,* its exhaustion and super-session as conceptual paradigm and exemplar, Creolization is sensitive both to that movement's historic achievements as well as to its critical and political limitations, no less than to the dubious premises that under-lie our more traditional and orthodox conceptions of *mestizaje.* More conscientiously dynamic, it is also less unilaterally constrictive, meta-physically inclined, or reductively homogenizing. It, in addition, more deliberately allows a wider space for the specificity, variously unique cultural and regional complexities of our many negritudes and other socio-ethnic American identities. What is more, Creolization places the emphasis on the unfixed, unfolding *process* of their continual change and mutation. For all that, and despite the growing interest it has re-cently awakened, its general impact on the Spanish-speaking world is, to all appearances, still rather limited.

These, then, in broad strokes and in all too summary fashion, are the general historical coordinates that have placed us where we are at the dawn of our new millennium. Though some retain a greater continuing vitality and power than others, each of these currents is still very much with us. None has yet entirely disappeared from the scene. Thus we need, for ourselves, for our communities, for the Americas as a whole to work toward and develop genuine alternatives to their negative weight of inheritance and history.

An Antillean Afro-Latino American born and raised in Spanish Har-lem and so one in whom many histories, regions, and peoples inelucta-bly converge, I am not in the least disposed to renounce any part of the strength and legacy of riches that come of that convergence. Neither pa-trician nor racial nationalist, my intent here is like to that which, more than seventy years ago now, prompted the poet whose words serve as this essay's opening epigraph. In an earlier, 1929, article in which he revealed to his compatriots the little flattering realities about the general family's racial attitudes, their social corrosiveness and terrible long-term threat, Nicolás Guillén concluded, as I do now, by observing that "All of these things are true, and in saying them I am moved by no other wish than to bring many of our faults out into the open, dust them off and expose them to the sunlight before us all, blacks and whites alike, to see if, becoming convinced that we do not always love each other as much as we say we do, it is also possible that we might apply ourselves to the beautiful task of acting a little more [as authentic people of our Americas], replacing the false embraces and little flag waving articles with a mutual respect and a definitive understanding."[32]

Notes

1. Anthony Pagden, *The Fall of Natural Man: The American Indian and the Origins of Comparative Ethnology* (Cambridge: Cambridge University Press, 1986), 24.

2. As Mary B. Campbell effectively demonstrates, the earliest written accounts of Christian pilgrimage to the Holy Lands before Islamic conquest blocked European passage (beginning with Egeria's Diary of visits to Aculf and Adamnan) offer only meditative itinerary *de locis sanctis* which, as the site of Christ's passion and a topography charged with allegorical import and made sacred by God's own presence, were not documents of cultural or anthropological curiosity. Consciousness of the quotidian existence of any indigenous sensibility, culture, or individuals had no central place in their tableau. Their organizing metaphor, as she emphasizes, was the image of a museum "in which the occasional darting appearance of a native of the Levant comes to seem like a glimpse of a derelict loiterer in the lobby" and "in which there is simply no human reality but that of the amazed and alienated traveler himself." Mary B. Campbell, *The Witness and The Other World: Exotic European Travel Writing, 400–1600* (Ithaca: Cornell University Press), 41–42.

3. Maxime Rodinson, *Europe and the Mystique of Islam* (Seattle: University of Washington Press, 1987), 10.

4. Donald F. Lach, *Asia in the Making of Europe* (Chicago: University of Chicago Press, 1965), vol. 2, book 2: *The Literary Arts,* 86. George H. T. Kimble also notes as characteristic "the misuse of the name India to designate Ethiopia, [as] a common practice of Greek and Latin writers from the fourth century." See his *Geography in the Middle Ages* (London: Methuen, 1938), 12.

5. Thus Duarte I (1391–1438) of Portugal, petitioning the Pope with regard to the Canaries in language worthy of any conquistador, of a Gonzalo Fernández de Oviedo or a Juan Ginés de Sepúlveda *avant la lettre,* writes: "They are inhabited by untamed, wild, hardly human men who are not united by any religion or restrained by any kind of law and who, unconcerned with civil intercourse, pass

their lives like animals in a state of paganism." See Peter Russell, *Prince Henry 'The Navigator': A Life* (New Haven: Yale University Press, 2000), 264.

6. Gomes Eannes de Zurara, *Chronicle of the Discovery and Conquest of Guinea,* trans. Charles Raymond Beazley and Edgar Prestage (London: Hakluyt Society, 1896–1899), vol. 1, 54. See also Ronald Sanders, *Lost Tribes and Promised Lands. The Origins of American Racism* (New York: HarperCollins, 1992), 62.

7. Cristóbal Colón, *Textos y documentos completos,* prólogo y notas de Consuelo Varela, (Madrid: Alianza Universidad, 1982), 31. English version in *The Log of Christopher Columbus,* trans. Robert H. Fuson (Camden, Me.: International Marine Publishing Co., 1987), 77.

8. Thomas Jefferson, *Notes on the State of Virginia.* In *Writings* (New York: Library of America, 1984), 268. For a detailed study of the changes made to Jefferson's original draft on its way to final approval, see Garry Wills, *Inventing America: Jefferson's Declaration of Independence* (New York: Vintage Books, 1979). Specifically referring to the Haitians and their revolution, John Adams was of the opinion, expressed as president in 1799, that "Independence is the worst and most dangerous condition they can be in, for the United States." As a consequence, the United States consistently denied full diplomatic recognition to the Black Republic until the 1860s, when, after entering into civil war over the issue, it had itself abolished slavery. The reasons for this were articulated plainly enough, on the floor of the Congress, by Missouri Senator Thomas Hart Benton: "We receive no mulatto consuls, or black ambassadors from [Haiti] . . . [b]ecause the peace of eleven [slave] states will not permit the fruits of a successful Negro insurrection to be exhibited among them. It will not permit black ambassadors and consuls to . . . give their fellow blacks in the United States proof in hand of the honors that await them for a like successful effort on their part." See Ludwell Lee Montague, *Haiti and the United States, 1714–1938* (Durham, N.C.: Duke University Press), 29 and 53, respectively.

9. *Selected Writings of Bolívar, vol. 1, 1810–1822,* trans. Lewis Bertrand; ed. Harold A. Bierck (New York: Colonial Press, 1951), 181. For the original text in Spanish, see Simón Bolívar, *Obras completas* (Caracas: Ediciones Cibema, n.d.), vol. 3, 677.

10. *Selected Writings . . . ,* vol. 2, 628–29. Original in *Obras completas,* vol. 3, 447.

11. C. L. R. James, *The Black Jacobins: Toussaint L'Ouverture and the San Domingo Revolution* (New York: Vintage, 1963), ix.

12. The expression has been variously attributed to, among others, Alexandre Dumas père and Napoleon. As regards the first, see Peter Yapp, ed., *The Travelers' Dictionary of Quotation: Who Said What, About Where?* (London: Routledge and Kegan Paul, 1983), 185. For the second, see Ivan Van Sertima, ed., *The Golden Age of the Moor* (New Brunswick: Transaction Publishers, 1992), 337.

13. Francisco Gracía Calderón, *Les démocraties latines de l'Amérique* (Paris: Flammarion, 1912), 327. See also Martin S. Stabb, *In Quest of Identity* (Chapel Hill: University of North Carolina Press, 1967), 25.

14. Robert Lawless, *Haiti's Bad Press* (Rochester Vt.: Schenkman Books, Inc., 1992).

15. See, for example, Joaquin Balaguer, *La isla al revés: Haiti y el destino dominicano* (Santo Domingo, R.D.: Editora Corripio, 1989).

16. Philip S. Foner, *A History of Cuba and Its Relations with the United States* (New York: International Publishers, 1962), vol. 1, 198; Louis A. Pérez, Jr., *On Becoming Cuban: Identity, Nationality, and Culture* (Chapel Hill: University of North Carolina Press, 1999), 90.

17. "Cuba's great problem," Antonio Saco would declare, "is the immovability of the black race, which retaining forever its color and primitive origin, is separated from the white [race] by an impenetrable barrier: but put it in motion, mix it with the other race, let it continue that [forward] movement and that barrier will then be gradually chipped away, until it [with a distinctly black race itself?] finally disappears. Were *mestizos* to be born from the union of black and white, it would be something much to be lamented, because by this decrease in our white population, it would, in every sense, weaken the latter. But since [as a consequence of the presumed superiority of the white racial stock and anticipated diminution of the population of blacks?] precisely the opposite occurs, far from looking upon this as an evil I consider it a good." See Manuel Moreno Fraginals, *El ingenio: complejo económico social cubano del azúcar* (La Habana: Editorial de ciencias sociales, 1978), vol. 1, 298.

18. Christopher Schmidt-Nowara, *Empire and Antislavery: Spain, Cuba, and Puerto Rico, 1833–1874* (Pittsburgh: University of Pittsburgh Press, 1999), 33.

19. José Martí, *Páginas Selectas,* ed. Raimundo Lida (Buenos Aires: Angel Estrada y Cia Editores, 1939), 261.

20. José Martí, *Obras completas,* ed. Gonzalo de Quesada (La Habana: Editorial Trópico, 1953), vol. 2, 999.

21. Ibid., 487.

22. Ibid., 276.

23. Foner, *A History of Cuba and Its Relations with the United States,* vol. 1, 198.

24. If, as Clair Healy notes, "Argentina is still recalcitrant in its refusal to acknowledge the crucial part that Africans and Afro-Argentines played in its colonial and post-colonial history," the seminal work of George Reid Andrews (*The Afro-Argentines of Buenos Aires, 1800-1900,* Madison: University of Wisconsin Press, 1980), Marvin A. Lewis (*Afro-Argentine Discourse: Another Dimension of the Black Diaspora,* Colombia: University of Missouri Press, 1996), Daniel Schávelzon (*Buenos Aires Negra: Arqueología Histórica de una Ciudad*

Silenciada, Buenos Aires: Emecé, 2003) and Alejandro Solomianski (*Identidades Secretas: La Negritud Argentina,* Rosario: Beatriz Viterbo, 2003), among others, has, in the years since 1980, much contributed to that acknowledgment, revealing and measuring the weight and substance of their presence, and effectively drawing that presence out of its more conventional obscurity and invisibility. See Claire Healy, "Review Essay: Afro-Argentine Historiography," *Atlantic Studies* 3, no. 1 (April 2006): 111.

25. Luis Lloréns Torres, "The Unknown Island," in Iris M. Zavala and Rafael Rodriguez, eds., *The Intellectual Roots of Independence. An Anthology of Puerto Rican Political Essays* (New York: Monthly Review Press, 1980), 166.

26. Tomás Blanco, *El perjuicio racial en Puerto Rico,* ed. and introduced by Arcadio Díaz Quiñones (Río Piedras: Ediciones Huracán, 1985), 132.

27. Ibid., 133.

28. Nicolás Guillén, *Obra poética* (Havana: Editorial Letras Cubanas, 1980), 106.

29. Luis Palés Matos, *Poesía, 1915–1956* (San Juan: Editorial U.P.R., 1968), 218.

30. Isabelo Zenón Cruz, *Narciso descubre su trasero: El negro en la cultura puertorriqueña* (Humacao, P.R.: Editorial Furidi, 1974), 24.

31. Ibid.

32. Nicolás Guillén, *Prosa de prisa 1929–1972* (La Habana: Editorial Arte y Literatura, 1975), vol. 1, 5–6.

Nationalism, Nation, and Ideology

Trends in the Emergence of a Caribbean Literature

But today I recapture the islands' bright beaches.
EDWARD KAMAU BRATHWAITE

READING DEREK WALCOTT'S (Saint Lucia, 1930) poetic meditation on the impact and legacy of the Enterprise of the Indies, "Origins," one is struck by the holistic sweep of a single line: "Lost animist, I rechristened trees."[1] Resonant with multiple reference, it synthesizes as it points to a critical dimension in the historical and cultural evolution of the Caribbean: the continuous process of inventive and creatively adaptive Creolization that, in spite of "those who conceive[d] of white cities in a raindrop / and the annihilation of races in the prism of the dew,"[2] ultimately gives the archipelago its very distinct personality, its polychromatic ethnic and cultural particularity.

Walcott's line similarly underscores the dramatic tension between alienation and opportunity, irresolution and resolve, defeat and victory at the heart of each successive "rechristening" of the local landscape. More subtly, it suggests the inextricable link of this dialectic to the problems—and possibilities—inherent in postulating a regional, "national," and literary identity that is an appropriate and genuine reflection of the varied complexity and vitality of Caribbean life. This is finally the poet's real subject. It is the recurring obsession which motivates and gives significance to everything he writes. As concept, esthetic creed, program, organizing metaphor, and historical commentary, moreover, Walcott's observation is virtually the signature of an entire generation. It echoes a sentiment that emerges—with varying emphasis, distinct focus, and nuance—in the work of writers as different in outlook, temperament, language, local origin, and circumstance as Jacques Stéphen Alexis (Haiti, 1922–1961), Edward Kamau Brathwaite (Barbados,

49

1930–), Alejo Carpentier (Cuba, 1902–1980), Édouard Glissant (Martinique, 1928–), Wilson Harris (Guyana, 1921–), John Hearne (Jamaica, 1926–1994), Pedro Mir (Dominican Republic, 1916–2000), Luis Rafael Sánchez (Puerto Rico, 1936–), and Simone Schwarz-Bart (Guadeloupe, 1938–).

The list could be extended to include nearly every contemporary Caribbean writer worthy of note. His contemptuous disdain and haughty dismissal of the area as bereft of future possibility notwithstanding, even V. S. Naipaul (Trinidad, 1932–) cannot avoid its eminence in and centrality to his fiction. His best work, *A House for Mr. Biswas* (1961), for example, compellingly offers the unfolding, among the heirs of East Indian indentured immigrants, of the social, cultural, and historic drama of Creolization Walcott's line so forcefully conveys. When one completes that line with the one immediately preceding ("Between the Greek and African pantheon"), its bearing on Naipaul's—and other writers'—work becomes all the more apparent. The pull of conflicting gravities, the synthetic result of this taut polarity, is an inescapable part of their common inheritance as Antilleans. The rueful impassivity and sense of perpetual displacement typical of Naipaul's preoccupations, protagonists, and narrators; that edge of besieged panic and negrophobia that laces and finally undermines the integrity of his later fiction especially, are so many signs of the peculiar effect the recognition of that inheritance and its immediate implications have produced in this unusually gifted Trinidadian of East Indian ancestry. This panic is what lies behind his own feelings of alienation, his restless and peripatetic "search for a center."

In their differences no less than in their similarities, these writers are joined by the consequences and vicissitudes of a shared history of colonialism, imperialist rivalry, inter-territorial isolation, and ethno-class confrontation. They are all equally the product of the combined force of these not yet fully reconciled contradictions. They are at once provoked, constrained, and challenged by a vivid appreciation of the enduring significance of their "origins." Like Walcott, they are inevitably drawn to a critical reassessment of that same patrimony of conflict. They are all, directly or indirectly, obliged to come to terms with the structures—of economic, social, and political interaction, of feeling and perception—that have emerged from that legacy. Though not the strictly axiomatic correlative of those structures, their writing is the expression, in esthetic terms, of their ideological tensions and current experiential contours.

Its thematic and formal characteristics are a testimony to that—evident or implicit—symbiosis. Whether in enthusiasm, uncertainty, indecision, or disapproval, these writers participate in, and their work effectively reflects, the crisis, reshufflements, and realignments that have been the substance of Caribbean reality during the last half century or more. Their reevaluation of and shared sense of urgency with regard to the past, the acknowledgment and positing of a uniquely Caribbean genesis, are inextricable from their commitment to the perceived exigencies of the present and from their hopes for the future.

History, unreconciled and pressing, is their natural element. Memory is their métier, *primum mobile* of their reevaluative posture, source of all prophecy. Édouard Glissant, in a passage as representative as Walcott's and which the latter would later use as an epigraph to his poetic autobiography *Another Life* (1972), speaks directly to this point. "On the day when I finally fasten my hands upon its wrinkled stem and pull with irresistible power," Glissant writes in *La Lézarde* (1958), "when my memories are quiet and strong, and I can finally translate them into words, then I shall perceive the unique and essential qualities of this place. The innumerable petty miseries, the manifold beauties eclipsed by the painful necessity of combat and birth."[3]

Caribbean literature has obviously reached this moment of maturity and conscious self-perception. These authors, among many others, have been instrumental in the process of its articulation. The coincidence of thematic preoccupation (if not always of specific ideological response) found in their fiction and verse also underscores the Pan-Caribbean scope of their defining experiences, without in the least diminishing the force of clearly manifest sub-regional identities. Against the power of a tradition of derivative, orbital perceptions of the area, it argues the presence of a broader Caribbean ethos—and esthetic—whose elements cohere beyond the restrictive colonial, specifically "national," or strictly linguistic borders and premises of those perceptions. This increasingly distinguishing feature of their "rendezvous with history" has its antecedent: it represents only the most recent phase in a centuries-long process of cultural and literary evolution. What follows is an effort, unavoidably cursory and synoptic, to place the achievement of contemporary Caribbean writing into the sharper relief and perspective an appreciation of its major stages can provide.

Occurring during the apogee of the system of slavery and in the most spectacularly profitable of the New World's colonies, the Haitian

Revolution (1791–1804) marked a pioneering watershed. It represented, in the collective person of those who carried it out, the threatening coincidence of every primary social, economic, and political contradiction in which both the Caribbean planter class—which came to include *affranchis,* propertied mulattoes—and mercantile imperialism were enmeshed. Its impact was profound, long lasting, and palpably felt throughout the region.

The creation immediately after emancipation (1834–1886) of an increasingly heterogeneous (though still caste-conscious and pigmentocratically divided) working class of now wage-earning ex-slaves, peasants, and indentured immigrants of largely East Indian and Asian origin was also a part of the attenuated fallout of the Haitian Revolution. As the ideological complement of its political independence, Haiti, finally, pioneered an entire cultural revolution. It opposed the notion of a *génie national* to a colonialist universalism that, at best, saw in the colonies so many inferior reproductions of European culture. It defined its historic originality in terms that focused on its ethnic and cultural uniqueness. It simultaneously sought to refute racist stereotypes of nonwhite inferiority and, giving it specific weight and content, accented its sense of a distinctively Creole national sensibility. The features of the Haitian state's particular pigmentocratic emphasis in this regard would, of course, remain a matter of unceasing dispute among the black and mulatto elites that, once the dominant minority of whites had been expelled, continued their contention for hegemonic control.[4]

The *prise de conscience* evident in their mutual affirmation of a Haitian identity and culture nonetheless once more implied a necessary rehistorizing of the past that endowed it with a novel—even, to some extent, mythic—ontological significance.[5] This represented a crucial shift in the locus of cultural authenticity—a relative change of context, audience, and intention—that opened a modest, formally tentative, but still significant breach in the uncritical imitation of French metropolitan culture. In matters literary and otherwise, it gave incremental pride of place to the legitimacy of *Creole* claims on the landscape, exposition of the characteristic facets of the nation's singularity, and exploration of the emerging possibilities inherent in the facts of Creolization—and conflict—from which that distinctiveness and promise derive.

"We are quite like the American, transplanted and stripped of traditions, but there is in the fusion of the European and African cultures which constitutes our national character, something that makes us less

French than the American is English," Emile Nau, one of the group of Haitian writers gathered around the newspapers *Le Républicain* and *L'Union*, declared in 1836. "This advantage," he went on to conclude, "is a real one."[6] Among the literary tasks it imposed, if it were not to remain an unrealized opportunity, was the need for "our poets" to "naturalize the French language in our culture." This, Nau averred, would "not be a question of taking the [French] language ready-made from [its] best exponents; it [would] be necessary [rather] to modify it and adapt it to our local needs."[7] The premises underlying Nau's observations were at once an echo and an anticipation of trends already evident throughout the region and that, in the long wake of the Haitian Revolution, reached a certain crystallization.

Ushering in a period of unrelieved crisis and change, the harbinger of things to come, Haiti initiated a new stage of radical anticolonial self-assertion, uneasy accommodation, and conservative reaction. Part of the evolving process of regional class formation, caste and demographic differentiation, it heightened consciousness of a distinctively Creole culture. Its features included a sharpening of the white elite's racist fears of the "Africanization" of the Caribbean and stimulation of a climate in which the goals of maximum local autonomy, affirmation of a sense of specific "nationality," and the articulation of the constituent elements of an esthetic adequate to its expression became linked and allied aspirations. The contrasting purposes of some of these tendencies were not necessarily always mutually exclusive. They frequently complemented each other; more often than not, they came together in an odd blend of contradictory impulses that found in the evolving forms of romanticism—*costumbrismo*, realism, naturalism, and indigenous forms of symbolism—a vehicle for holding them in effectively dynamic stasis.

The Cuban abolitionist novel (from *Petrona y Rosalia* [1838], *Cecilia Valdés* [1838, 1882], and *Francisco* [1839] to *Sab* [1841] and *El negro Francisco* [1875]) managed thus to combine close observation of the physical environment, the social texture, sexual mores, and racial oppression of insular experience with confirmation of the patrician bias and still racially exclusive assumptions of the white Creoles who constituted the primary public, producers, and dramatis personae of scribal fiction, poetry, essays, and plays. A strict typology was established—master, señora, black mistress, illicit offspring, impossible loves—whose bathos, exoticism, and melodrama were so many stereotypical tributaries of the lyric "primitivism" of romantic convention.

Documentation of the indignities associated with chattel slavery did not prevent its creators from narratively closing off the possibility of slave rebellion as a legitimate option in the struggle to end them. Indeed, despite the frequency of slave uprisings, slaves were invariably—wishfully—depicted as passively enduring their collective lot with stoic, if tragic, resignation. Historical veracity was less at issue than the requirements of internal security.

Calculated to emphasize the morally debilitating influence of slavery upon whites, narrative strategies made little attempt to examine the personality of the slave. When they did, they transformed him, culturally, politically, and psychologically, into a Creole white in blackface. Sympathy for the mulatto was emblematic of the hybrid the ascendant Creole ruling class felt itself to be—a people "neither European nor North American, but a mixture of African and the Americans who originated in Europe" as Simón Bolívar, in a similar context, had succinctly put it.[8] It was the metaphorical transposition of the need to ground, in an image of etiolating conciliation between extremes, its pretension, again in Bolívar's words, "to exercise an active domestic tyranny" and, through purposeful ideological manipulation of that image, effectively—fictively—to impose it.[9]

Exploration of the many layers of Cuban society, revealing both a will to define its distinctiveness and the problematic centrality of the black—or mulatto—protagonist within it, did not preclude a posture that, except as they might be "bleached" or made gradually to effectively "disappear," excluded the darker hues from any acceptable definition of Cuban nationality. "The task of all Cubans of hearts and of noble and sacred patriotism," Domingo del Monte, the liberal reformer who served as mentor, patron, and sponsor of much of this writing, argued, "ought to be, first, to end the slave trade [as replenishing source of the black population], and then go on little by little to the suppression of slavery without convulsions and violence, and, in the end, to clean Cuba of the African race."[10] José Antonio Saco, Del Monte's more conservative colleague and friend, was more emphatic still: "Cuban nationality," he declared, "is formed by the white race."[11]

The Ten Years' War (1868–1878) gave rise to a radically new context. It was in this new context with the de facto abolition of slavery that Antonio Maceo's and José Martí's more sympathetic recognition of the strategic importance and social potential of the nonwhite masses engendered the latter's more radical and cohesively inclusive formula of the 1880s and 1890s: "Cuban is more than white, more than black, more than mulatto."[12] Aiming to minimize both race and the internal tensions it produced, this formula was increasingly to become ideological common coin in more progressive liberal circles. Martí perceived something sui generis in the making and pointed to the problem of its creative, firmly rooted, and lasting articulation. "No nation on earth that turns from the way of life laid out by its origins, and follows a purpose other than that inevitable one presented by the elements composing it," he repeatedly insisted, "can live long or prosperously."[13] There had moreover to be a fundamental congruence between the spiritual and material. 'The problem of independence," Martí emphasized, "did not lie in a change of forms but in a change of spirit."[14] He thus did not stop short of a frontal attack on the tradition of Eurocentric mimicry and the tyranny of the model that remained an obstacle to the emergence of a genuinely original literary voice and sensibility. Informed by his resolute dedication to the revolutionary promise of a radically liberal vision of cultural efflorescence and social harmony, Martí saw each dialectically as an aspect of the other. A guiding premise of that outlook, concisely recorded in a journal entry of 1881 which points to a fully coherent *esthetica,* was the critical notion that

> To an irresolute nation, [an] irresolute literature! But as soon as the elements of a people approach some unity, the elements of its literature draw nearer together and condense into a great prophetic work. Let us now bemoan the fact that we lack this great work, not because we lack it but because it is a sign that we are not yet the great people of which it must be a reflection; for it must reflect, it must be the reflection.[15]

National independence, nation building, the ordering of the polity's social priorities, and the achievement of an autochthonous literary voice were all, in anticipation of the future, intimately related facets of a single imperative.

In Puerto Rico and the Dominican Republic, Del Monte's identification of national purpose with the ascendancy of the white Creole elite and paternalist liberal ideals produced, respectively, Manuel A. Alonso's *El Jíbaro* (1849, 1884) and Manuel de Jesús Galván's *Enriquillo* (1882). Like *Cecilia Valdés* and the novels mentioned above, each proved to be a work of foundational ideological and literary significance.

Alonso offers the reader a series of *escenas* or vignettes in prose and verse which seek to "give an idea of the customs of the island."[16] Keenly conscious of the hovering threat of the official colonial censorship which made him initially reluctant to publish his observations, Alonso intends discreetly, sometimes obliquely, but as unambiguously as possible to demonstrate the "lack of harmony" between Spanish educational policy and the demands of local needs and experience.[17] Central to this experience and its urgencies was the Creole elite's intensified commitment, its critical need, to promote the continued economic growth and expansion of an agricultural economy still at a distance of only a few decades from the two-centuries-long doldrums of officially sanctioned commercial isolation which the colony's function as a strategic *presidio,* or imperial military outpost, had traditionally imposed upon Puerto Rico. A trend away from the small independent peasant producer, incident to the privatization of land (1778) and its subsequent concentration within the ascendant class of sugar plantation owners and coffee plantation *patrones* between 1797 and the date of publication of *El Jíbaro,* forms the decisive backdrop of Alonso's preoccupation responsibly to record those features of rural life that have already been or are in the process of being historically superseded by a Creole-sponsored "progress." This is the subtext which gives force and meaning to the assumptions of value underlying Alonso's interwoven series of vignettes.

Alonso's choice of the romantic form of the vignette, he confesses, is itself related directly to both his consciousness of the censor and the didactic impulse of the prohacendado moralist's evocative, reforming nationalist focus on and critical evaluation of local custom and tradition. The form allows Alonso pithily to combine the ethnographic precision of his descriptions of "The Dances of Puerto Rico," "The Cockpit," "The San Juan Races," "The Saint Peter's Day Parade," and similar examples of a historically evolved, socially layered, and distinctively Puerto Rican culture with an expressly declared concern that his scenes "give a not too disagreeable exterior to disillusionment [*al desengaño*]," "always with a view to improving local custom as [he] entertains" his reader.[18]

These several angles converge in the symbolic image of the titular *Jíbaro* or rural *mestizo* peasant. Emerging as a metaphor for "Puerto Ricanness," the figure pointed to the country's racially mixed origins while still managing to glide discreetly past any actual inclusion or direct engagement with the social, political, and cultural presence of the slave and his mingled legacy of descendants. Indeed, except for an incidental, wholly secondary appearance of the protagonist's mulatto manservant in the short-story-like "Bird of Ill Omen,"[19] and Alonso's affirmation earlier on that the dances "of the African blacks and the creoles from Curaçao do not merit inclusion" in his discussion of popular national dance forms,[20] the population of "colored" Puerto Ricans does not enter significantly into the worldview of El Jíbaro.

Alonso's evocation of the jíbaro's way of life is not motivated, however, by any wish nostalgically to defend or symbolically idealize the rural peasant whose modes of speech and mores he faithfully, if humorously, strives to depict in pieces like "A Jíbaro Wedding" and "The Utuado Festival." Alonso's judgment about and even the depth of his identification with particular local customs are consistently informed by a perception of what he regards as their relative utility as a stimulus to the kind of economic growth on which the power and political future of the rising class of hacendados depend. Alonso is particularly sympathetic to and affiliates with that class's struggle to ensure that a formerly dispersed, perhaps still too "egotistically irresponsible" peasantry of subsistence farmers, agregados, and day laborers will be permanently transformed into the stable pool of reliable labor for hire with which contemporary (sugar and) coffee growers were then especially obsessed.

Thus, it is primarily "the deals, sales, and exchanges to which it gives rise," not any sentimental attachment to it, that finally vindicates "a custom so usefully pleasing and so pleasantly useful" as the Saint Peter's Day Parade.[21] The same premise allows him to note the value of the cockfight "as a form of communication between some towns . . . encouraging the circulation of money" while simultaneously condemning it as "a mere holiday pastime" which, being "highly prejudicial" to progress, is destined to disappear.[22] By the same token, neither Alonso's meticulous attention to folkloric detail in depicting forms of peasant culture nor the obvious pride of his more classically literate sonnet to "The Puerto Rican" Creole whose "love for the country none surpass" prevents him from finally concluding that it is

> The peasants [labradores], content with knowing how to govern their own homes as they please and limiting themselves to their town without caring what goes on in any other, [who] are promoting selfishness, which is the death of all progress, because confined within such narrow limits, they have given no thought to joining the merchants, manufacturers [industriales], and artisans in petitioning the government to create . . . [schools of agriculture] which are much more useful to the country than the dull routine which, with few exceptions, is still the rule in our country.[23]

Alonso's text thus combines the Creole elite's defense of a distinctively Puerto Rican national personality with condemnation of the traditionalism of the *jíbaro* who, to a large extent, emerges as its historic repository, embodiment, and symbol. To the extent that the image of the *jíbaro* actually corresponds to a historically specific and socially concrete class of people within the culture, it is that class's "selfish" refusal gracefully and patriotically to assent to the role reserved for it by its more favored fellow Puerto Ricans which ultimately proves to be the most formidable domestic obstacle in the way of the colony's future economic development. Ironically, to that extent, too, the *jíbaro's* recalcitrance is seen as impeding the island's cultural development. For, as Alonso argues in an *escena* devoted to "Puerto Rican Writers: D. Santiago Vidarte" (a commentary which incidentally initiates an insular tradition of self-consciously national literary criticism), only "when our agriculture finally emerges from its ancient routine, in a word, when we can without disadvantage compare ourselves with the [more plantocrat-dominated] island of Cuba, will the terrain [of literary endeavor] be prepared."[24]

Alonso's image of *El Jíbaro,* in sum, synthesizes the colonial, racial, and interclass drama at the core of a historically evolved Puerto Rican culture and society during a period of radical transition in which "the old is passing away and is being replaced by the new";[25] in which the contributions of the slaves and their descendants are minimized or ignored; in which the traditional independence of the peasantry is at once undermined and rejected as economically retrogressive; and in which the entrepreneurial spirit and emergent dominion of the native Creole ruling classes are at once the material and ideological measure of that culture and society's most advanced current state and best future prospects.

Less anti-Spanish in sentiment, Galván's *Enriquillo* invoked the cacique of an extinct population to the same effect. The Dominican Republic's proximity to Haiti, the complexion, annexationist inclinations, and general restiveness of the majority of its inhabitants, as well as a political atmosphere of unending internecine strife between different factions of the white Creole elite, made the Dominican ruling class particularly nervous and sensitive to the disquieting portent of this volatile complex of forces. Its anxiety about the possibility of "Africanization" was, in consequence, all the more acute. That the country had for a time actually been annexed by Haiti and, after the achievement of independence from both Haiti (1844) and Spain (1865), had known the ravages of civil war merely heightened its fears about the hovering specter of both. Under the circumstances, the lyric evocation of—and symbolic identification of Dominican nationhood with—the loyalist opposition to Spanish abuse of Guarocuya, the novel's orphaned, Christianized, and Spanish-educated Enriquillo, offered several advantages. It not only permitted the author to circumvent, by in effect ignoring, the actual presence and wider significance of a national majority of blacks and mulattos. As a conservative patrician alternative to the Haitian revolutionary solution, it had the additional merit of associating the origins of the republic with an aboriginal past. It provided its emergence with indigenous roots, a certain epic grandeur, enveloping in an aureole of historic authenticity the romantic excesses of Galván's *leyenda*. Interlacing the narrative with transcribed excepts from the writings of Bartólome de Las Casas, who as Enriquillo's mentor and protector serves as the ideological pivot of the piece, enhanced the effect of this documentary illusion. Galván thus invoked history itself to support an imaginative invention otherwise reminiscent of the exotic romances made popular by Chateaubriand's "Atala" and "René."

It proved a persuasive fusion. Dominicans, whatever their ethnic origins or color, could—would, and occasionally still do—identify themselves as descendants of Enriquillo and, hence, as in some sense "Indian." Blacks or darker-skinned mulattoes were, as a result of this double fiction, cast as "foreigners," "Haitians," or ceased effectively to exist. Enriquillo's eventual, grateful submission to the authority of Las Casas with which the novel concludes moreover redeems, in the person of one of its most enlightened and sympathetic representatives, the image of Spain's colonization of the New World. Like Del Monte, Galván emphasizes the social dimensions and political virtues of a policy of assimilation and intermarriage that (as a reluctant concession to the facts of cultural and biological *mestizaje*) both perceive as a strategic necessity. As a cultural process, however, he regards it, at best, as an intermediate stage on the road toward a "more normal and civilized," proto-European "whiteness." No less significantly, Galván's denouement resolves, if only symbolically, the contradictions between the former metropole and its antagonist(s), between the Creole elite and the masses over whom it would rule, in a self-flattering image of domestic tranquility and harmonious mutual accommodation that, ideally compelling as it appears, was as ideologically charged as it was wholly fictitious.[26]

The burden of adaptation and conformity on which this vision of concord and collaboration depends is, logically, predicated on the "lower orders'" acceptance of the terms and jurisdiction of the ruling elite.

One need hardly note that, like the protagonists of the Cuban abolitionist novel, Enriquillo is esthetically and ideologically the metaphorical surrogate of a white Creole consciousness. "His dress, air of self-confidence and manners, as well as the regularity of the young cacique's features, gave him the appearance of one more among any number of sons of rich and powerful Spanish colonists on the island."[27] In the final analysis, Galván is essentially concerned with how continued confrontation and civil instability negatively affect the fortunes of this class. The vision of cultural synthesis and restoration of domestic harmony which allegorically emerges in *Enriquillo* is related to Galván's perception of that class's need to consolidate its economic, political, and social position. A climate of greater internal stability, under its aegis, would simultaneously represent the indispensable prerequisite and necessary proof of that consolidation. Its absence would, in any event, prove a discouragement to the foreign investment that was a crucial element of Creole ruling class ideas of economic development. Successful incorporation of the Dominican elite into the world market system, which it properly regarded as the linchpin and guarantor of its domestic ascendancy, lay at the center of its notions of progress. This is the subsoil of uneasy preoccupation which informs the novel's movement away from social and political crisis toward peaceful reconciliation and (apparently) mutual accommodation. Consistent with the characterization of its protagonist, it is a movement that faithfully represents the program and perspective of the "sons of rich and powerful Spanish colonists on the island." A further token of the Creole elite's identification of its own interests with the authentic spirit of the "nation," whether figuratively embodied in the image of an assimilated "Indian," rural peasant, Creole black, or mulatto, it registers, as *fait accompli* and continuing patriotic project, the circumscribed sociopolitical horizon and ethnic bias of that identification.

In the Anglophone Antilles, where it was still the almost exclusive province of transients, sojourners, or expatriates such as Michael Scott (*Tom Cringle's Log* [1836]) and James Rodway (*In Guyana Wilds* [1899]), the novel remained a casual, more rudimentary and circumstantial affair whose narrative point of view, even when most empathetic, was primarily that of the outside observer. Not until the twentieth century would it reveal—structurally and esthetically—the level of self-conscious "naturalization," affinitive sense of literary continuity, and formal sophistication already evident in the Hispanophone islands. Memoirs, diaries, and poetry—with all the characteristics attributed to it by Edward Brathwaite—continued the predominant genres.[28]

The last half of the nineteenth century nonetheless witnessed the rise of a core of Afro-West Indian intellectuals no less nationalist than their Hispanic Creole counterparts. Its foundation lay, in significant part, in the impact of the ex-slaves' post-emancipation flight from the plantation. That flight brought with it the burgeoning of new communities and townships with demands to make upon the resources of the state. Together with its effect on the economy and demography of existing towns, it accelerated the already developing process of formation of an articulated, politically cohesive middle class of mulatto and black proprietors, professionals, petty merchants, skilled artisans, and teachers. It provided this class with an expanded population base of potential political support—a "new" audience to be instructed, wooed, and cultivated—as well as, to a lesser extent, a replenishing source of potential new members. Primary and secondary school teachers, along with journalists, ministers, and lawyers, crucially important to the ideological cohesiveness and continued viability of this class, were particularly well represented among this new corps of Afro-West Indian intellectuals. In the pivot between a colonial administration of foreigners and expatriates, an oligarchic minority of white plantocrats, and the growing number of indentured Asian immigrants, they struggled to advance their own alternative to the assumptions of white supremacy, planter dominance, and metropolitan empire. More conscious of their (racial) victimization by and historic roots in pre-emancipation society, they were perhaps even more sensitive to the urgency of the need for social reform, though not any less susceptible to the lures of liberal paternalism than their Hispanic Creole contemporaries. They, too, saw themselves as the legitimate representatives of what they regarded as the only authentically national majority. In contrast with the Hispanic Creoles, however, they identified this majority with the indigenous population of Creole descendants of the slave and, more specifically still, with the class of the more educated, prominent, and "competent" among them. Their reformist and anticolonial agitation laid the foundation for the populist alliances that set the stage for the achievement of formal independence in the next century.

The Trinidadian teacher and writer John Jacob Thomas (1840–1889) was a particularly striking example of this new breed of Afro-West Indian intellectual. His extraordinary career reflected the weight and larger implications of the changes described above, to which it was, more than partially, indebted. The son of humble parents of African descent, beneficiary of a newly inaugurated (1851) system of free secular primary schools and a partially subsidized Normal School education, he eventually became himself a rural village schoolmaster. The perspective given him by that focal position between the illiterate masses of black agricultural workers and the rising group of educated blacks and coloreds to which he himself now belonged, provoked Thomas— as pedagogue, autodidact scholar, writer, and organizer of the island's first literary society—to contest the governing assumptions of authority still dominant in his society. Its unconsidered mimicry of inappropriate models and "pernicious idolatry" of racist categories were particularly favored targets of his censure.[29] Anticipating the substance of later debates on the issue, in 1887 he noted that the curriculum in West Indian schools did not go beyond "a servile imitation of the now almost entirely exploded English fashions of instruction . . . in many particulars hopelessly inapplicable to the training of the children of the tropics"— an observation that, beyond its pragmatism, unequivocally pointed to his awareness of a peculiarly non-English "national" reality.[30]

Like his Hispanic and Francophone contemporaries, Thomas was keenly appreciative of the process of cultural amalgamation and differentiation that, in his region no less than in theirs, had produced a uniquely Caribbean species of person, with its own distinct national characteristics and style. As part of a larger argument in support of Creole—in this case, Afro-Creole—claims on the landscape and polity, he sought, like them, to materially substantiate and detail that self-assertive perception. *The Theory and Practice of Creole Grammar* (1869), Thomas's pioneering description of the structure, internal logic, cultural originality and significance of the primarily oral speech of the folk, was in fact a sustained vindication of the linguistic integrity of the Creole's language. A work comparable in motivation and intent, if not in the racial identification of its specific constituency, to the novels discussed earlier, it effectively proposed a reordering of the reigning linguistic paradigm by granting parity of cultural value to the local idiom. What others sweepingly dismissed as an inferior form of a presumptively "purer" and "more rational" European tongue, Thomas recognized as the manifestation of a dynamic process of confrontation, adaptation, and differentiation: prima facie evidence of a cultural distinctiveness and the palpable sign of an unmistakably decisive historical *achievement*. To the degree Thomas implicitly suggests the "literacy" of ordinary speech and its potential as an untapped reservoir of material and a vehicle for literary expression, one is reminded of the defenses of the creative vitality and insufficiently explored literary possibilities of the vernacular, as against Latin, written by, among others, Dante and Cervantes.

As conscious as the Hispanic Creole elite of the black population's increasingly strategic position, indeed more emphatically so, Thomas was at the same time more sympathetic to the social, political, and cultural challenge it represented to the white Creole ruling class. Like José Martí's, his political vision combined an emphasis on the greatest degree of national sovereignty with a cultural definition of the 'nation" that was more radically democratic and socioethnically inclusive. *Froudacity: West Indian Fables Explained* (1889), Thomas's rejoinder to the colonialist impertinence, national self-aggrandizement, and transparent negrophobia of James Anthony Froude's *The English in the West Indies* (1888), brings both these dimensions into dramatic focus.

The product of a tourist's brief visits by one of England's most distinguished historians presented as an objective, comprehensive assessment of the character and condition of the Caribbean and its people under British rule, Froude's book was actually an apologia in defense of the traditional plantocracy, with which he closely identified, an obliquely wistful excursus on the need to reinvigorate the metropole's imperial resolve in the face of changing conditions. More pragmatically, it sought to win over British public opinion to the cause of the minority of white planters, a continuance of the narrow or nonexistent franchise, and the centralization typical of the Crown Colony system. "I believe the present generation of Englishmen to be capable of that that their fathers were and possibly more," Froude writes, "but we are just now in a moulting state, and are sick while the process is going on. Or to take another metaphor. The bow of Ulysses is unstrung. . . . They [the empire's colonial subjects] cannot string the bow. Only the true lord and master [England and its "English" Creoles] can string it."[31] Full of the Social Darwinist clichés and conventions characteristic of the period, Froude's book is, finally, no more than a paean to the premise of the natural superiority of the English—and their overseas brethren—with which its author originally set sail.

Pointing to the sheer arrogance of drawing conclusions concerning the essential character of any people on the basis of a Cook's tour spent primarily among a minority of the privileged, Thomas immediately cuts to the heart of the matter, denouncing Froude's work as part of a "scheme to thwart political aspiration in the Antilles . . . by deterring the home authorities from granting an elective local legislature . . . to any of the colonies . . . [on the grounds that] it would avert definitively the political domination of the Blacks, which [Froude fears] must inevitably be the outcome of any concession of the modicum of right so earnestly desired."[32] He goes on systematically and in turn to expose each of Froude's "fables": his empirical failures of perception, the lack of sociological discrimination, analytical subtlety, and methodological reliability as well as the theoretical circularity and logical absurdities consequent upon his "singular contempt for accuracy" in support of the status quo.[33]

The result is far more than a critique of the casual effrontery and racial hauteur of an eminent metropolitan literary lion and man of affairs. *Froudacity* ultimately emerges as an adroit, passionate, and comprehensive nationalist reproof of the racist underpinnings of the colonial system itself. A vindication of the cultural singularity and self-directive capacities of each of the territories in question, Thomas's work is a catalogued enumeration of the historic basis and inescapable centrality of the Afro-Creole population's legitimate claims to full citizenship and direct and equal participation in the conduct of its countries' affairs. An example of the ideological articulation of the vanguard of the newly emergent black elite of professionals, *Froudacity* placed particular emphasis on the obstacles colonialism put in the way of this class, despite its demonstrable achievements. The tone and intensity of Thomas's attack on race ideology, however, make clear his wider identification with the frustrations of the masses of blacks. "Does Mr. Froude in the fatuity of his skin pride, believe," Thomas inquires, "that educated men, worthy of the name, would be otherwise than resentful, if not disgusted, at being shunted out of bread in their own native land, which their parents' labour and taxes have made desirable, in order to afford room to blockheads, vulgarians, or worse, imported from beyond the seas?"[34]

Thomas rejected Froude's postulation of an inherent or necessary antagonism between the races. He stressed instead the conflict between the class of intransigent Anglo-West Indian ex-slaveholders and the remaining sectors of the population throughout the West Indies. This, in his view, was the primary contradiction. "There is no government by reason of merely skins," he insists. He envisioned a society open to talent of whatever color and, as a means to that end, argued in favor of a confederation of the different castes and classes which, drawing together the most "eligible and competent" from each, would look to the interests of all. "We have hundreds of both races belonging to the class, competent and eligible," Thomas writes, "and hundreds of both races belonging to the class, incompetent and ineligible: to both of which classes all possible colours might belong. It is from the first mentioned," he concludes, "that are selected those who are to bear the rule, to which the latter class is, in the very nature of things, bound to be subject."[35] Thomas thus replaces Froude's pigmentocratic oligarchy with the gathering colored middle class's notion of a meritocracy, whose specific emphasis accentuates his conviction that blacks are "apt apprentices in every conceivable department of civilized culture."[36] His wording in each case is significant. It points to an essential paradox and characteristic ambivalence. Like that of the great majority of his equally liberal Hispanic and Francophone contemporaries, Thomas's incisive defense and contextualization of the "national" interests of an emerging domestic elite are only as democratic as rule by a patriciate of the "most competent and able" from among that elite will allow. He was definite, nonetheless, with regard to the ultimate meaning of what he recognized as a decisive change of context in the Caribbean. In this regard, Thomas, whose tone of historical optimism stands in sharp contrast to Froude's edge of anxious historical foreboding, finally minces no words: "the ignoring of negro opinion" by all those for whom Froude speaks, he warns, "though not only possible but easily practiced fifty years ago, is a portentous blunder at the present time. *Verbum sapienti.*"[37]

It was a prophetic warning. Its emphasis on the need for a rearticulating of "national' assumptions, guiding definitions, and priorities is unmistakable. Thomas's pointed notation of the crucial shift of axis implied by the growing consciousness, ever-looming presence, and portent of the anonymous majority of blacks was especially prescient. It framed the central thrust and challenge of dramas yet to come. Like José Martí's essays and commentaries, *Froudacity* presaged—as it was itself symptomatic of—the crisis of hegemonic white Creole dominion throughout the area. It prefigured the ideological exhaustion, political deterioration, and eventual eclipse of seigniorial society whose consummation would occupy the first four decades of the twentieth century and serve as the backdrop and milieu of the new literary outlook of the writing produced then and immediately after. An eloquent exemplar of liberal nationalist Afro-Creole opinion, Thomas's work, like Martí's, constituted a penetrating adumbration of some of the defining features, as well as the anticolonial tone and mood, of the world into which Walcott and his generation were born.

The expanding presence of the United States in the region after 1898 and its progressive displacement of the effective power of European colonialism there by force of its own neocolonial ambition were, undoubtedly, among the most distinguishing features of that world. By the 1940s, when the majority of that generation was on the threshold of its teens, the United States by a combination of political threat and maneuver (e.g., Roosevelt's "Big Stick" policy), increased economic penetration (e.g., Taft's "Dollar diplomacy"), direct intervention (in Cuba, Puerto Rico, the Dominican Republic, Haiti, Nicaragua), negotiation (e.g., "Lend Lease" agreements) or purchase (e.g., the Virgin Islands) had clearly established itself as first among imperial equals in the Caribbean. Its burgeoning economic predominance and ultimate political cultivation of a moderately reformist middle class only then coming into its own further eroded the conservative agricultural oligarchies' traditional dominance: tied to a system of seigniorial, personalist, or superannuated production techniques, they found themselves increasingly unable to compete with the "modernizing" aggressiveness of American corporate capitalism.

In the terrible, ruinous wake of World War I, Europe also began to lose much of its former luster as a model. With this accustomed paragon itself turning to new sources of revitalization and spiritual renewal, Caribbean intellectuals turned inward to a more sustained exploration of their own neglected reservoir of people and resources. They began not merely to highlight but increasingly to celebrate those characteristic features and populations that, though generally disdained, made their societies decidedly un-European. In response to the ebb of Europe and the disjunctures and dislocations that came with Yankee imperialism, a critical self-scrutiny and enucleating self-discovery became the order of the day. Where writers of the previous century typically regarded ethnocultural amalgamation (and its class associations) as something to be overcome or reluctantly tolerated as an "exotic" liability or, more benignly, as an unavoidable, strategic necessity, the facts—and forms—

of Creolization would now be pointed to in the context of a more positive vision of synthesis, on the one hand, and a heightened appreciation of the contributions of the African ancestor, on the other. It was the cultural reflection and complement of a more broadly based call for a radical change in the traditional social order.

The developing self-consciousness, new political importance, and increasingly militant discontent of the rural and urban working classes, resulting in uprisings, strikes, riots, stoppages, and the formal crystallization of an organized labor movement during the twenties, thirties, and early forties, gave revolutionary edge to the force of that demand. It became more and more difficult, without risk of alienating this now critical constituency, to entirely dissociate the long-standing aspiration to complete national sovereignty and a reinvigorated concern with ethno-historical self-affirmation from the popular felt urgency for the achievement of social justice. The push from below, as Martí had foreseen, J. J. Thomas had warned, and the proletarianism of such as the Puerto Rican Ramón Romero Rosa and the radical black nationalism of the Jamaican Marcus Garvey now made palpably clear, could no longer be ignored.

A new public was beginning to flex its muscles, and to precipitate a decisive realignment of forces. It led the advancing *mestizo,* colored, and black middle classes to forge, as part of their own assault on the traditional distribution of power, that uneasy alliance with the working class which, on terms generally more favorable to themselves, effected the political demise of the old hacendado and planter elites. The nationalist populism to which these middle classes recurred to achieve it had, by the late fifties, effectively transformed them into the new arbiters of the domestic Caribbean scene: new middle-class regimes of either liberal populist (e.g., Puerto Rico, Jamaica, Trinidad) or despotic right-wing outlook (e.g., Haiti, the Dominican Republic, Cuba, and Grenada) became increasingly characteristic. Though clinging demagogically to their earlier rhetoric, they were increasingly unable to deliver on promises to the working classes, save by encouraging their increasingly massive immigration abroad. Nor were they able to check—indeed their economic policies, growing political isolation, and defensiveness actually stimulated—neocolonial dependence on the United States and the systematic impoverishment of the unprivileged majority of their own people to which it contributed. The definitive collapse of those alliances, a feature typical of the decade of the sixties and after, made this reality all the more apparent. The general estrangement of "the dispossessed classes" and their supporters among the more liberal and radical wing of that middle class gave a renewed immediacy and vigor to the critique of the status quo and the defiant nationalism in which those alliances had, ironically, originated. It was precisely to those branches of the middle class that a community of writers struggling to establish its cultural and professional authority and demanding a functional and infrastructural recognition of the legitimacy and social value of their craft and calling, in the main, structurally belonged.

Beyond a common nationalist denominator and the generally shared perception of the need to engage or somehow come to terms with the masses, the initial critique was neither monolithic nor univocal. Those being displaced naturally sought nostalgic refuge in the past with which they identified. To prevent any further erosion of their class's traditional prominence, they defended the stability, cultural superiority, and "national" integrity of its values. Denied by American intervention the "right" to a domestic hegemony it was poised to assume upon the collapse of Spanish colonialism, the Hispanic Creole elite thus invoked, in the face of the cultural and economic threat of American imperialism, the alleged spiritual superiority of its Iberian heritage. To the more conservative among them, the refusal of the peasantry and emerging proletariat to rally to its patrician cause became, in the event, evidence of what they regarded as either an endemic inertia or proof of a lack of patriotic, familial solidarity, or both.

A radical Latinism, grounded in a platonic rejection of Yankee materialism and its putative lack of more transcendent virtues, became a symptomatic point of cohesion. It was a posture reminiscent of José Enrique Rodó's (Uruguay, 1871–1917) seminal essay *Ariel* (1898). Rodó shared an aristocratic repudiation of what he perceived as the era's tendency to an "inappropriately" democratic mediocritization to the lowest common denominator of society which his work shared with the Spanish philosopher José Ortega y Gasset's (1883–1955) equally influential *The Revolt of the Masses* (1937). José de Diego's (1866–1918) anti-assimilationist protest against the imposition of North American culture and its pragmatism in Puerto Rico reflected their underlying premises. "We do not know in these historic reversals," he writes in one of his better known poems of the period, "Hallelujahs to the Gentlemen from the North,"

The language and the meaning of English-speaking peoples.
We have another language, another way of thinking . . .

. . . .

Unhappy scions of that sapless trunk,
That flowered in the souls of Seneca and Hugo.
We know the mysteries of pure Philosophy
And of the art that reigns in Holy Poesy.
But nothing do we know, in the land of the sun,
Of the art of Government, as Tammany Hall's run.[38]

Conveniently disregarding the fact that Spain was the last of the colonial powers in the region to finally abolish it, and muting its less savory realities, a hyperbolic revision of the domestic history of slavery emerged that was calculated to demonstrate, as in the work of Tomás Blanco (1897–1975), an essential benevolence in comparison with the experience of the United States. It was another trope of the same ideologically charged claim to a certain moral superiority. The normative cultural paradigm for "the nation" remained, for all that, quintessentially white, eurocentrically Western. A reductive Hispanophilia, exaggerated Catholicism, and idealist transformation of the local agrarian past into a mythic national pastoral of cheerful *jíbaros,* enlightened landlords, and *hommes de lettres* were among its more distinguishing elements.

The (anti-Black) racialist determinism into which it could often degenerate, as in *Insularismo* (1934), Antonio S. Pedreira's (1899–1939) influential examination of the Puerto Rican personality, was another response to the crisis in which the Hispanic Creole elite found itself and the disquieting awareness, succinctly expressed by Pedreira, that "Given we're in the midst of a transition, we must take care to watch what belongs to us [*la propiedad*]."[39] The *francophonie* of the mulatto elite in the French Antilles and the Jamaicanism of a Herbert de Lisser (1878–1944) were rooted in a nationalism of a similarly conservative and genteel predisposition. This did not prevent de Lisser's novel, *Jane's Career* (1913), from being one of the first to focus on the displacement of the rural peasantry to the major cities and among the first by a native West Indian in which the central character is both black and a woman. It did, however, likewise texture his approach to the problem, and informed the patronizing attitude he took to the people and culture she represented.

Negrismo, in the Hispanic Caribbean, emerged as a more democratic liberal alternative to this dominant Hispanophile discourse. Drawing inspiration from an untapped cornucopia of popular custom and experience, it acknowledged the ubiquitous cultural influence of the black. Its literary celebration of the oral traditions, verbal inventiveness, and suasive power of that disdained and neglected patrimony thus represented a challenge to orthodox prejudice and dogma. It underscored the process of biological and cultural miscegenation which had taken place in the area. From the perspective of its recognition of the demands of a distinctly new context, and in only partial continuity with nineteenth-century liberal thought, it pointed to the ineluctably syncretic character of the national identity. Luis Palés Matos (1898–1959), whose initial "Afro-Antillean poems," "Pueblo negro" (1925) and "Danza negra" (1926), were among the first examples of the new modality, insisted "The Antillean is a Spaniard with the manner of a mulatto and the soul of a black."[40] The first of Alejo Carpentier's many novels, *¡Ecué Yambá Ó!* (1927), was a quasi-anthropological attempt at exploration of the world of *ñañigo* ritual and belief premised on similar assumptions. The movement's faddish transience—by the late 1940s, interest in "the black theme" as such apparently exhausted, it faded from fashion—was emblematic of the mediational and predominantly idealist posture that sustained it. The picturesque exoticism, uncritical susceptibility to an imagery of questionable racialist suppositions, and assumed formal distance from the world of their chosen protagonists evident in the work of some of the movement's most representative figures—Ramón Guirao (Cuba, 1908–1949), Emilio Ballagas (Cuba, 1908–1954), José Z. Tallet (Cuba, 1893–1955), Manuel del Cabral (Dominican Republic, 1907–1999) and indeed Palés Matos himself—revealed that an emphasis on the syncretic facts, congregational, democratizing, and reconciliatory virtues of *mulatez* or *mestizaje* were not always incompatible with confirmation of the conventional clichés of racist stereotyping. As in the conceptual redundancy of the term "Afro-Cuban" itself, it sometimes contained the latent suggestion that, for all its impact, the "Afro" contribution was effectively still an addendum affixed to an essentially inviolate national core that remained exclusively Hispanic.

Though he broadly shared their emphasis on the consolidating historical and cultural importance of *mestizaje,* Nicolás Guillén in this respect proved to be doubly exceptional. His affirmation of his country's *africanía* was neither temporary nor abstract. His identification with the concrete person of the black, moreover, evinced little of that ambiloquy and detached lack of internal consistency. "I deny the art that sees in the Negro only a colorful motif and not an intensely human theme," he demurred.[41] The notion of a constitutively Antillean *mulatez* is the guiding premise of an impressive corpus of poetry and prose covering more than a half century of sustained intellectual activity from which a concern with the specific material condition of the black, as barometer of a given society's overall health and situation, is never absent. "I am aware, of course," he notes with ironic audacity in the prologue to *Sóngoro cosongo* as early as 1931, "that these verses are repugnant to many people, because they deal with blacks and ordinary people. I don't care. Or more accurately: I'm pleased. That means that such fastidious spirits are not included in my lyrical agenda. They are, moreover, good people. They're risen with great difficulty into the aristocracy from the kitchen, and tremble as soon as they see a pot." "Someday," he reproaches his more priggish compatriots, "we will say: 'Cuban color,'" adding, "these poems wish to hasten its arrival."[42]

More than that of any other Hispanic contemporary, Guillén's work succeeded in dynamically grounding his *negrismo* in the socially concrete, effectively transforming the black into material embodiment and symbol of the nation's heterogeneous underclass as a whole. Regarding as that of the nation itself the collective aspirations of the latter, Guillén's affirmation of Cuba's ethnohistorical particularity and radical anti-imperialism are, in both form and substance, inextricable from a critique of the narrowly culturalist discourse of his more conventionally liberal compatriots and from the wish to see definitively overthrown an ignominious social system that is not without its homegrown defenders. "What the black must aspire to . . . everywhere," he writes in 1950, "is not that there be ten or a hundred rich and cultured brethren . . . [domiciled in gilded ghettos] but that thousands of destitute blacks do not rot in the misery, in the ignorance, in the pain . . . [of the nation's slums]."[43] Guillén rejects the more conventional elitist preference for moral and "cultural" solutions as evasive, ineffectual indicators of a limitedly defined class self-interest:

> The bourgeoisie falsely affirms . . . that that terrible condition [of economic inequality] will disappear with [the acquisition of] "culture," and is willing to throw a bit of its money to entertain the blacks, domesticating them in the process . . . [. T]he liberation of the black lies very far . . . [from that] program of racist cultural intensification . . . as well as from that patriotic

embrace that [Gustavo Urrutia] suggests between blacks and whites in the heart of imperialism . . . No: the future holds a more profound, more drastic, more revulsive, more historically just solution, [one] derived from a powerful revolutionary upheaval.[44]

At one with Luis Palés Matos in affirming the *mestizo* substance, historical and cultural unity of the Antilles, Guillén's nationalism reflects neither the disconsolate pessimism nor the quasi-existentialist angst which informs Palés Matos's work. The elegiac undertone provoked in Guillén by the nature of Cuban reality prior to 1959 is inseparable from the satirical, humorous edge of the national self-scrutiny and firm historical optimism that suffuse his

> . . . simple song[s] of death and life
> with which to greet the future drenched in blood,
> red as the sheets, as the thighs,
>   as the bed
> of a woman who's just given birth.[45]

It is in the direction of this fusion between circumstantial discontent and historical optimism that, striving in its own way to be "universal y cubano," the documentary compactness and expressionist historicism of Alejo Carpentier's later proposition of the "magical realism" of the Americas (in his preface to *the Kingdom of This World* [1949]) will evolve.[46] Guillén's embrace of socialism was as logically continuous with his realism and the subversive, holistic sweep of his version of *negrismo* as Palés Matos's more exotically metaphorical, "culturalist" evocation of a "Mulata Antilla," for example, was with the patrician populism to which his own sympathies inclined and as a result of which he was ultimately to become that populism's representatively democratic, canonical figure.

In no case did Hispanic *negrismo* ever imply any denial or outright rejection of the nation's Spanish inheritance. Its stress on *mestizaje* as both a syncretic and unique cultural fact and a creatively mediating historical force, indeed, came generally to be accepted as normative and became increasingly ideologically dominant. In the Anglophone and Francophone territories, the analogous nationalist reclamation and recuperation of the contemned African ancestor, though motivated by a similar set of anticolonialist perceptions, initially reflected a deeper sense of mutual estrangement and a much more immiscible temper.

There, save for Haiti, the traditional colonial power was a continuing and palpable presence.

Unlike Spain, it was something still to be immediately contended with. The inescapable influence of American imperialism, for all its impact, had not changed that. Long-standing policies of cultural dependency and assimilation, adjunct to the economic and political integration of the colony within the metropolitan orbit, added both ire and urgency to anticolonial declarations and aspirations of cultural and national independence. Idealization of the traditional metropoles, especially as travel to them increased and widened its class base, became all the more difficult to sustain.[47] The image of a historically achieved resolution of the kind suggested by *negrismo*'s convergent accent on *mestizaje* was, in this context, not always as immediately compelling. The mulatto as an image of mediating conciliation or national symbol of a syncretic ethos proved, under the circumstances, to be rather more precariously uncertain and problematic. The truth of biological and cultural amalgamation, though recognized as salient, did not by itself offer any comforting sense of resolution. An anguished consciousness of irresolution and continuing contradiction emerged, indeed, as recurring leitmotiv.

Léon LaLeau's (Haiti, 1892–1979) much anthologized "Betrayal," with its revelation of "This haunted heart that doesn't fit / . . . the words of France / this heart that came to me from Senegal,"[48] and Léon Damas's (Cayenne, 1912–1978) "Whitewash" ("they dare to / treat me white / though everything within me / wants only to be black"),[49] like Derek Walcott's later and still more tragically tormented "A Far Cry from Africa" ("I who am poisoned with the blood of both [Africa and Europe] / where shall I turn, divided to the vein?"),[50] are characteristic cases in point. Where (as in Martinique, Guadeloupe, and, to a lesser extent, Jamaica and Trinidad) mulattoes and propertied coloreds had themselves become identified with—or emerged as a discrete element of—a pigmentocratically sensitive and privileged native aristocracy, the difficulty was naturally compounded. Haiti, where after the revolution and prior to the American Occupation (1915–1934) there were no whites at all in positions of proprietorship or power, provided the most pristine example of just such a ruling mulatto elite. Inured to snobbery, cultural mimicry, like some autarchic protocol, remained pervasive within its ranks. "Crammed full of white morality, white culture, white education and white prejudices . . . a faithful copy of the pale-skinned gentleman," Etienne Léro (Martinique, 1910–1939) exploded in disgust; its members, he charged, took "a special pride in the fact that a white man can read [their] book[s] without ever guessing the color of [their] skin . . . [or ever coming upon] an original or meaningful accent . . . a trace of the black man's sensuous and colorful imagination or the echo of the hatreds and aspirations of an oppressed people."[51] His equally reform-minded Anglophone colleagues, with little ground to quarrel with Léro, certainly would have sympathized with his assessment. Criticizing the reigning, submissively derivative tendency to a Victorian exoticism and inversimilitude, one of them wrote: "We fail utterly to understand . . . why anyone should want to see Trinidad as a miniature *Paradiso,* where gravediggers speak like English M.P.s . . . The answer is obviously that the average . . . writer regards his fellow-countrymen as his inferiors, an uninteresting people who are not worth his while. He genuinely feels (and by this, of course, asserts his own feeling of inferiority) that with his people as characters his stories would be worth nothing."[52]

The combined force of these several factors gave point and substance to the more dramatically pronounced, specifically black, and militantly defiant sense of the need for a radical divorce from the culture and traditions of Europe that, in contrast with Hispanic *negrismo,* is discernible in the texture, tone, and thematic foci of *negritude* and its equally anticolonial counterparts in the Anglophone Antilles. Joined to the influence of more broadly international social and intellectual currents (Freudianism, Marxism, Nationalism, Pan-Africanism, Surrealism, Literary Realism), the catalytic impact of these factors also helps to explain the more intensely sustained concentration on the unique (double) alienation of the black in a racist environment. It accounts, too, for its focus on the complex psychological dimensions of racism, colonialism, and the process of decolonization which *negrismo* tended generally to slight or ignore altogether.

Reaching a kind of apogee in the critically penetrating and ideologically synthesizing commentaries of Frantz Fanon, this exploration of the internalized effects of colonialism on ego integrity proved to be enduring and influential well beyond the French- or English-speaking Antilles. Their retrieval and defense of the African ancestor nonetheless often evinced a general tendency, later empathetically reproved for its mystifying idealism by Fanon, René Depestre, and Walter Rodney among others,[53] to appeal to a virtually transhistorical Negro essence.

Beyond any recognition of a heritage denied or the simple affirmation of internationalist solidarity with a common experience of racial oppression, this essence seemed to take precedence over, to obscure, or otherwise absorb the black's specific contextual matrix. This oftentimes had the effect of diminishing the force of his or her national particularity, detaching it from its social and historical concreteness, even as it appeared to invoke it.

In a manner not unlike the more idealist versions of *negrismo,* it minimized or avoided as well the problem of internal class conflict in favor of a larger ethnic-ethos identification. Though by a more dissociative contrast of cultures, Anglophone and Francophone varieties of negritude served the same nation-defining and broadly convergent purpose as the Hispanic emphasis on *mestizaje.* Rhetorically invoked and ideologically manipulated by a François Duvalier, an Eric Gairy, the later Eric Williams, or a Forbes Burnham, this indistinctiveness of contours—albeit with indisputable elements of accuracy—could easily degenerate into the self-promotional, populist demagoguery which helped to secure, as it concealed, the nationally hegemonic ambitions of the rising black middle class that each came finally to represent. Like *negrismo,* though, it was initially aimed at and, like it too, succeeded in opening a significant breach in an until then complacently dominant, all too decorous Eurocentric discourse.

The opening salvos of this iconoclastic avant-garde sensibility were registered in the innovative, culturally rebellious little magazines and journals around which the vigorously nationalist temper of this new literary-political project crystallized. They served as a first launching pad which, in more than one case, would survive to offer a place of early apprenticeship for those, like many of the writers born in the thirties and after, destined to carry that project more critically forward: *Revue du monde noir* (1930), *Légitime Défense* (1932), *Tropiques* (1941–1945) in Martinique, and *Présence Africaine* (1947–) in Paris; *Trinidad* (1929) and *The Beacon* (1931–1933, 1939) in Port of Spain; *Bim* (1942–) in Barbados; *Focus* (1943, 1948, 1956, 1960, 1983) in Jamaica; *Kykoveral* (1945–1962) in Guyana; the BBC's broadcast review "Caribbean Voices" (1942–1962) in London; and *La Trouée* (1927), *La Revue Indigene* (1927–1928), *Le Petit Impartial, Journal de la Masse* (1927–1931), *Les Griots* (1938–1940), and *La Ruche* (1946) in Haiti. The names themselves are a testimony to their specific cultural intent or allegiance.

The completed version of what remains to this day perhaps the single most celebrated, sustained, and representatively compendious lyrical monument to négritude, Aimé Césaire's (Martinique, 1913–) *Cahier d'un retour au pays natal* (1939), in which the word itself made its most influential debut, was originally published in *Tropiques*. An apocalyptically visionary manifesto explicitly leveled at the hoary premises of the French concept and policy of *assimilation* ("accommodate yourself to me / I won't accommodate myself to you"),[54] it describes the poet's journey back from physical and spiritual exile, his rejection of "the sterile attitude of the spectator," his rediscovery, embrace, and cultural repossession of his own country. The conceit of European technical progress, nature-overpowering pragmatism and rationality, in an inversion of the value-meaning of ancient stereotypes, is mockingly played against the deeper authenticity of "those who give themselves up to the essence of all things / ignorant of surfaces but struck by the movement of all things / free of the desire to tame but familiar with the play of the world." Suggesting the universal identification of suffering, the *Cahier* expands outward beyond the landscape of Martinique eventually to encompass the whole of the black world. A journey in reverse across the Middle Passage made necessary by the consequences of the colonizer's *mission civilisatrice,* it is as an antidote to the pained recognition of a historic fragmentation, marginality, self-alienation, and inauthenticity, inextricable from a search for the source of cosmic harmonies. Infused with the imperative of this question of wholeness, the poem is, in effect, a lyrical catharsis. Evoking the word-magic of a surrealistic pantheism, Césaire "plunges into the red flesh of the soil [of Martinique, Africa and its Diaspora]," to break "the yoke-bag / that separates me from myself" and, in an effort "to proscribe at last this unique race free," becomes "the furious WE." If the contours of an irreducible individuality—personal, sociohistorical, geographic, or national—fade into as they illuminate one another during the course of its powerful and multifaceted dialectic, Césaire's programmatic thrust is never in any doubt. Repudiating the inveterate paternalism and omnifarious pretension to superiority of the West, he aspires, as his "Letter to Maurice Thórez," then Secretary General of the French Communist Party, put it in 1956, to "nothing short of a Copernican revolution, so deeply entrenched in Europe, in every party and in every sphere, from old guard right to red left, is this habit of making our arrangements, this habit of thinking in our behalf, in fine, this habit of contesting our right to initiative . . . which is ultimately the right to a personality of one's own."[55]

In Jacques Roumain (Haiti, 1907–1944), Césaire's allegory of the return, of communal integration, and of affirmation of this "personality of one's own" took the form, in *La montagne ensorcelée* (1931) and the more accomplished and influential *Gouverneurs de la rosée* (1944), of a critical celebration of the organic integrity of Haitian peasant culture. Skillfully handling a contrastive imagery, figurative and structural use of voodoo ritual, and the *combite* as symbols of a dialectic between despair and possibility, Roumain's exploration of peasant life, in its language and narrative posture, argued its intrinsic esthetic potential as it insinuated his awareness of the twin dangers of a slumming patronization and the diffusion, corollary to it, of intragroup and intraclass conflict.

Roumain had already earlier on, in his *Analyse schématique, 1932–1934,* taken issue with the "attitude sentimentale" of those among the mulatto and black middle classes who, in defense of Haiti's African identity, appealed, as Duvalier and *Les Griots* were to do, to a psychobiological cluster "of abstractions which contain the entire world, precisely because they are no more than abstractions without any root in reality and which in the end commit themselves to nothing at all (racial consciousness, verbal and utopian nationalism, etc.)."[56] It was a critique that, as the temporary alliance of the different classes began progressively to collapse, would gain increasing currency. Like Roumain's fictional engagement with the remarkable complexity of the Haitian cultural landscape, it also intimated the need for a less hazily reductive, more imaginatively comprehensive and scrupulously probing scrutiny of Caribbean culture and reality. His example would later inspire Jacques Stéphen Alexis's own notion of "Le Realisme Marveilleux Haitienne," and find echo in Édouard Glissant's complementary concept of *Antillanité*, as well as in Maryse Condé's (Guadeloupe, 1936–) critical appraisal of the achievement and limitations of *négritude*. *Négritude* in the Antilles, she writes in *Présence Africaine* in 1972, "was a total, passionate, blind, refusal, born of the assumption of an acute awareness of the condition of being an exploited person, economically and culturally underdeveloped. The *Antillanité* we want to oppose to it is no more than the second phase: that in which, after total refusal, the Antillean creates out of his complex inheritance and strives to express it in every one of its forms."[57]

It is to the challenge and esthetic exigencies of this program, with its more conceptually concentrated focus on regional specificity and its suggestion of a wider Pan-Caribbean resonance, that the writers of this generation have turned their attention with increasingly impressive verve and originality—and in sometimes uneasy recognition of their debt to the predecessors whose achievements their own work extends.

Césaire's contemporaries in the English colonies, though perhaps without so immediately spectacular a success and, as a more intellectually eclectic and racially heterogeneous cohort lacking any single so fortuitously definitive a label as *"négritude"* proved to be, were motivated by an identical concatenation of forces and pursued similar goals. They, too, spurned the values of the smug, claustrophobic society colonialism and an unctuously pretentious native elite had produced. They condemned its "ubiquitous cruelty," its poverty, the pernicious indifference and torporific propriety which permeated its social and spiritual environment. They thus determined to lay siege, as Albert Gomes, founding editor of *The Beacon,* recalls, to their society's "ancient incrustation of psychic mildew and cobweb."[58] "Our right to be ourselves," they were also convinced (the words, again, are Gomes's), "was sacred."[59] Like that of their Francophone colleagues, their esthetic program was informed by the commanding need to give material literary expression to these concerns. Ardent nonconformists, as Reinhard S. Sander points out, they demanded

> writing which utilized West Indian settings, speech, character, situations and conflicts. [They] warned against the imitation of foreign literature, especially against imitation of foreign popular literature. Local colour, however, was not regarded as a virtue by itself. A mere occupation with the enchanted landscape of the tropics did not fulfill the group's emphasis on realism and verisimilitude. . . . Realism combined with and supported by the Trinidadian's social and political ideology resulted in fiction [and poetry] that focused on West Indian characters belonging to the lower classes. [Though] the group around *Trinidad* and *The Beacon* consisted essentially of middle class people. . . . [t]he barrack-yard was of particular interest to . . . [them].[60]

Alfred Mendes's *Pitch Lake* (1934) and *Black Fauns* (1935), C. L. R. James's *Minty Alley* (1936), R. A. C. DeBoissiere's *Crown Jewel* (1952) and *Rum and Coca Cola* (1956)—whose authors all collaborated in those journals—were the products of this outlook and mood. Each reflected its writer's exploratory interest in the West Indian underclass, the peculiar formal tensions of a compassionate outside-narrator's view of it and, especially in DeBoissiere's novels, the intensity of the radically nationalist content of their proletarian sympathies.

James quickly emerged as one of the modern Caribbean's most prolifically pioneering and influential thinkers. Combining unorthodox Marxist with Pan-African ideas, he went on to write his seminal examination of the unfolding, wider consequences and enduring significance of the slave insurrection in Haiti, *The Black Jacobins: Toussaint L'Ouverture and the San Domingo Revolution* (1938, 1963). The impact of his provocative analysis and commentaries on politics, society, and culture—from *The Case for West Indian Self-Government* (1933), *World Revolution* (1937), and *A History of the Negro Revolt* (1938) to *Party Politics in the West Indies* (1962) and *Beyond a Boundary* (1963)—was later gratefully acknowledged to have been one of their major sources of inspiration by the succeeding generation of activist West Indian intellectuals.

The Beacon group's linkage of its promotion of a more genuinely West Indian literary culture to the political project of decolonization and the establishment of an independent nation-state by which James himself was encouraged, and to which he significantly contributed, was characteristic of its sister journals in the region. In the two decades immediately before formal independence from Britain and the breakup of the West Indian Federation in 1962, they established the national ground and pioneered the esthetic dominion of a distinctly Anglophone Antillean sensibility. Part of a progressive populist movement which, in the wake of universal suffrage and a political strategy of class convergence, eventually gave the middle class nominally representative control of the administrative apparatus of the state, this was one of their most lasting contributions to the process of formal independence. In the seventeen years of its existence its founder-editor, A. J. Seymour, tells us in *Growing Up in Guyana* (1976) that *Kykoveral*

> caught and focused in the first place the ideas and desires of a group of young Guyanese writers acting as an instrument to help forge a Guyanese people, making them conscious of their intellectual and spiritual possibilities, and then changed its form and pattern in response to the contemporary trends of writing in the region, to become a nursery for the expression of a West Indian literary cultural spirit, a new cultural sensibility which foreshadows a new nation, along with its contemporaries BIM in Barbados and the occasional FOCUS in Jamaica.[61]

These were the "nurseries" which, in addition to the work of those already mentioned, nourished, cultivated, or encouraged the precursory fiction of Roger Mais (Jamaica, 1913–1955). Mais's pessimistic realism, his bitter denunciation, in *The Hills Were Joyful Together* (1953), of "what happens to people when their lives are constricted and dwarfed . . . girdled with poverty" and victimized by the callousness and ineptitude of the larger society,[62] added dramatic vividness, an unsparing naturalistic quality as well as a systemic, panoramic scope and almost palpable sensual immediacy to Mendes's and James's comparatively more timid examination of life in the barrack-yard. Its tough-minded exposé "of the real Jamaica and the dreadful conditions of the working classes"[63] included, in defiance of conventional middle-class prejudice, a precociously empathetic portrayal of the Rastafarian which he went on to develop more fully and symbolically in *Brother Man* (1954).

Mais effectively fused social realism with a symbolically resonant probe of the tension-fraught dilemma of his own predicament as an artist in the allegorical portrait of a peasant blacksmith and sculptor he offered in *Black Lightning* (1955). An exceptionally gifted, self-absorbed visionary, his protagonist in that novel becomes the alienated victim of the exaggerated sense of self-sufficiency with which he protects himself against the uncomprehending community to which he is devoted. It was Mais's metaphor for the anguished feeling—shared by so many of his fellow West Indian writers at the time—of the sometimes unsustainable strain between their sense of loyalty and responsibility to a still underdeveloped colonial society and an equally consuming dedication to their own growth as artists that eventually compelled so many, including Mais, to temporarily emigrate to the metropole. Suggesting as it does the lack of an integral wholeness of anything short of a mutually sustaining interdependence between the artist and his community, the study of individual psychology *Black Lightning* presents put in still starker relief the overarching significance of the collective protagonist Mais had located at the center of his earlier works. The clearest forerunner of H. Orlando Patterson's (Jamaica, 1940–) *The Children of Sisyphus* (1964), a no less grimly unrelenting if more deliberately existentialist depiction of the fragility and desperation of life in the Kingston slums, *The Hills Were Joyful Together* brought an unprecedented intensity to the emerging literature of the barrack-yard. Taken as a whole, moreover, Mais's work intimated some of its still unexplored terrain. It widened the genre's repertoire of characteristic figures and, despite a sometimes too theatrical staging and occasional abuse of co-incidence, extended the scope of its formal, imaginative, and allegorical complexity.

Similarly, V. S. Reid's fictional celebration of the *New Day* (1949) inaugurated by Jamaica's new constitution and the coming of universal suffrage in 1944 captured the initial optimism inspired by the national movement and, in particular, Norman Washington Manley's People's National Party. Its formal structure, choice of narrator, and privileging of the demotic gave literary prestige and validation to the social and cultural centrality of the country's rural black peasant core.

By contrast, Edgar Mittelholzer's Kaywana trilogy—*Children of Kaywana* (1952), *The Harrowing of Hubertus* (1954), and *Kaywana Blood* (1958)—made its author's obsession with the violent clash of racial and sexual potentialities, with the white-identified mulatto's tormented sense of "impurity" and the inimical power of his "dual nature" and irreconcilable "bloods," the prime mover of his fictional reconstruction of Guyanese history from its initial settlement by Europeans to the mid-twentieth century. Like Reid's, however, it was a work of foundational ambition. For all their very different emphases, both novels sought to give specific definition, historical coherence, and national integrity to local experience; "creating a tale," in Reid's words, "will give as true an impression as fiction can of the way by which. . . . [their respective countries and] people came to today."[64] Among the desiderata of the esthetic vocation of Seymour's "new cultural sensibility which foreshadows a new nation," this conceptual framework reflected, too, the spirit which animated his heroic little journals.

As Seymour suggests, the magazines gave all these authors some impetus and a forum. They also provided the initial core of a sympathetic reading public, a mutually sustaining link, and the sense of a rising community of common endeavor to the efflorescence of major writers in the fifties and sixties whose work would extend that of Mendes, James, DeBoissiere, Mais, Reid, and Mittelholzer to include a likewise motivated scrutiny of the populist fraudulence of a neocolonial independence. Colonialism had also to be examined, in the words of George Lamming, as "a continuing psychic experience that has to be dealt with long after the actual colonial situation formally ends."[65]

The common presumption in all this multivalent anticolonial and self-defining literary ferment throughout the archipelago was a solidifying conviction, succinctly enunciated by Jacques Stéphen Alexis in

1956, that "the forms in a national culture must, before anything else, correspond to the character and tendencies of the people in question,"[66] and serve to define it. The essentials of that character came more and more to be seen as inseparable from the style, speech, unsung experience, and primarily oral traditions of the popular masses. Even if only tacitly, unwittingly, or in the context of a continued opposition to the wider implications of their historic emergence stage-center, the anonymous multitude increasingly assumed the role of clearly indicated or obliquely implied protagonist. Beyond a certain democratization of the Caribbean literary landscape, forcefully affirmed in the pointed declaration and unadorned realism of José Luis González's (Puerto Rico, 1926–1997) collection of short stories, *El hombre en la calle* (1948), no less than in the work of Mais, Lamming, Guillén, Césaire, Roumain, and others, this shift of focal perspective was tantamount to proposing, by rearticulating the locus of its subject, a fundamental reassessment of the history—*another* rehistorization—of the Caribbean. The classic epic, turned on its head, thus gives way to the oftentimes deliberate enunciation of a new epic: an epic of the wretched, the anonymous, the obscure and neglected—of those hitherto absent from History. Underscoring their part in the historical formation of a distinctively Caribbean culture, the writer identifies the fate and national authenticity of his society as a whole—the authority and allegiance any government can legitimately claim—with the relative fortunes of its rural or urban, primarily black underclass and the level of appreciation of its importance to the achievement of any credible sense of social health and spiritual integrity. The thematic forms and patterns of conception the artistic expression of this (re)appropriating, synthesizing epic assumes in the evolving canon of the region's most recent writers reveal the persistence and recurring prominence of several interrelated tropes.

As already suggested, the first of these involves an unavoidable engagement with History itself. "History," the Jamaican novelist John Hearne writes, "is the angel with whom all we Caribbean Jacobs have to wrestle, sooner or later, if we hope for a blessing."[67] A critical encounter with the past as both the prehistory of the present—active, unreconciled, unpropitiated, contradictory, continuing or permanent presence—and proper ground for establishing the entelechy, cultural and national, of a Caribbean ethos is indeed one of the premises and compositional principles of the current vogue of the historical novel in the region. "The constitution of History as it affects the Caribbean and the Guianas,"

Wilson Harris insists, requires its writers "to embrace the muse through an imaginative re-discovery of the past."[68] History must not only be confronted or—to the extent it has been neglected, ignored, denied, or remains enigmatic—revealed. It must, above all, be disinterred and (re)*constituted* as part of a larger effort to, in the words of Harris's preface to *The Whole Armour* (1962), "relate new content or new existences to a revised canvas of community. That new content ironically—on another level—is very old or eclipsed or buried material of consciousness which cries out for relief."[69] It is ultimately the haunting, only half-hidden specters that threaten a society born of genocide, conquest, slavery, and colonization. For Harris, vision lies in the retrieval of "those 'monsters' back into ourselves as native to psyche, native to a quest for unity through contrasting elements, through the ceaseless tasks of the creative imagination to digest and liberate contrasting spaces rather than succumb to implacable polarizations."[70] Beyond testifying to a fundamental lack of achieved resolution and the tenuous stability of an already fragile enough polity, such polarizations threaten to imperil the actual and future possibility of an intrinsically viable society.

It is easy enough, Harris tells us, "to pronounce on [our] 'historylessness,' oppression, etc. . . . once one does not creatively descend into the disorder of it: an escape route which may well prove the best of two worlds and permit a skillful shortcircuiting of real crisis or confrontation in depth."[71]

A creeping edge of unease and apprehension is part and parcel of Harris's idealist optimism. However, in its essential motivation, this "act of memory" is very close to the concept of "the backward glance" which informs George Lamming's work. Particularly as exemplified in the formal construction and unfolding of *Season of Adventure* (1960), it is clear that Lamming, with Harris, regards it as at once revelatory and unavoidable, cathartic, redemptive, and epigenetic. An encounter with the past remains preliminary to any lasting resolution of the conflicts inherited by a colonial or, as in *Season of Adventure*'s prophetic focus on the public and private failures of the fictitious San Cristobal's First Republic, neocolonial West Indian society this fictive island nation is meant to represent. Harris's poetic evocations of an exuberant, primal Guyanese hinterland, his experiments with time and Amerindian cosmology and legend—all of which are primary among his *spaces*—collapse the borders of Lamming's comparatively more "realistic" aesthetic to hover on the far edges of the phantasmagoric and mythical.

They also add a continental dimension to the more clearly insular con-centration of the majority of his island-born colleagues. The journey into the American interior of a racially representative crew of ill-fated conquistadors in *Palace of the Peacock* (1960) is, in consequence, orga-nized around "the odd fact" that its characters' "living names matched the names of a famous dead crew that had sunk . . . and been drowned to a man . . . But this in no way interfered with their life-like appearance and spirit and energy. Such a dreaming coincidence [our participant narrator tells us] we were beginning to learn to take in our stride."[72] Far from being dead, the past is a quite vital *presence*.

These living-dead, in the resonant title of one of Lamming's other novels, are *Natives of My Person* (1972) to Harris. One is more imme-diately reminded of the contrasting simultaneity of historical epochs, the fusion of documentary history and the only apparently marvelous—because *real*—typical of Alejo Carpentier's fiction after *¡Ecué Yambá Ó!*. The journey of Harris's crew is not unlike one of Carpentier's protagonist's attempt to (re)trace *The Lost Steps* (1959). Carpentier is similarly drawn, he tells us, by "the possibility of establishing cer-tain possible synchronisms—American and recurrent—outside of time, which would relate one thing to another, past to present . . . [so as] to convey our truths . . . to understand and measure them in their proper dimensions."[73] His work also shares Harris's overarching ambition to demonstrate that an area to which Hegel himself would deny any inde-pendent historic particularity "is not without history but in fact is," in Harris's formulation, "pregnant with a native constitution—the 'lost' ages of men."[74]

The "Muse of History," as Derek Walcott calls it, is also at the heart of the combination of fiction, history, and popular (oral) tradition that Édouard Glissant seeks to synthesize in his work. It is a way of reclaiming—giving continuity, a distinct spiritual "itinerary" and form to—his *Antillanité*. "The child that I was and the man that I am," he writes in *La Lézarde*, "have this in common: they confuse legend and history."[75] In *Le Quatrième Siècle* (1964) that melding, evoked in the evolving relationship between Mathieu, the young "urban" intellectual and Papa Longoué, the maroon-descendant *quimboiseur* who gives him a greater confidence in himself, is the source of a knowledge more true than the superficially logical "reporting in minute detail of dates and facts [that] masks the [subterraneous] continuous movement of our past."[76] Pointing to "a land of tremblings, of extinguished or forbidden truths," it is, most crucially, "profoundly rooted in the drama of West Indian soil . . . expresses *another* reality, *another* style of life."[77] As a principle of composition, Glissant's "confusion" embodies a mode of historical reassessment, of national authentication, an act of faith in "the open, collective swelling and creative fertility of a culture which has been chosen,"[78] a registry of its contending divisions and the projection forward of its distinct future possibilities.

The prologue to Andrew Salkey's epic poem, *Jamaica* (1973), significantly entitled "I into history, now," pithily condenses the different general aspects of this epochal obsession. Situated in the present, its anonymous speaker's speech denotes an ordinary, undistinguished member of the working class or rural peasantry. Invoking the authority of the mocking, cunningly inventive spiderman of West African and Caribbean folk tradition, he introduces his subject with the following self-affirming declaration:

> I into history, now.
> Is not'ting but song I singing
> an' name I callin'
> an' blood I boilin'
> an' self I raisin'
> in a correc' Anancy form,
> a t'ing I borrow
> an' makin' me own
> wit'out pretty please
> or pardon.

The ground from which it issues is an unpostponable question. "I sittin' down," he goes on,

> scratchin' me 'ead
> an' watchin' the scene,
> an' I ol' as Anancy
> but wit'out f'rim brain-box,
> an' I say to me self,
> "Is how the *mento* music go?"[79]

A question that is analogous to Edward Brathwaite's "Where then is the nigger's / home?"[80] Like Brathwaite's more broadly encompassing New World Trilogy—*Rights of Passage* (1967), *Masks* (1968), and *Islands* (1969)—the poem that follows this prologue is an extended response to the gravid, deceptively simple query on which it concludes.

Organized to highlight the historical evolution and collectively representative moments that culminate in the present, it is simultaneously a summation of the very process of articulation and primacy of the question.

The assumption of a collective voice and condition—an expressed or implied "we" already seen in Césaire and inextricable from the work of nearly every contemporary Caribbean writer—is generically corollary to the narrative unfolding of this epos. The postulation of the claims of this "we" as against those of the constrictive, individualist "I" achieves a particularly transparent formulation in Pedro Mir's *Viaje a la muchedumbre* (1972; Journey to the Multitude), especially in what are perhaps its two most celebrated poems: "Hay un país en el mundo" (There Is in the World a Country) and "Contracanto a Walt Whitman (canto a nosotros mismos)" [Countersong to Walt Whitman: A Song of Ourselves]. Drawing together the cultural and esthetic burden of both, Mir writes in Canto 9 of the latter poem:

> For
>> what has a great unflagging poet ever been
>> if not a limpid pool
>> in which a people discovers the precisions
>> of its face?
>
> . . . . . .
>
> And what
>> if not a string on an infinite guitar
>> on which the fingers of nations play
>> their simple, their own strong
>> and true and innumerable song?[81]

Mir's intertextual evocation of *Leaves of Grass* effectively places the failed promise of Whitman's democratic vistas and the deterioration, in the contemporary United States, of nineteenth-century liberalism into the rigorously individualist egotism demanded by modern capitalism, in critical counterpoint to the collective ethic and vision of a historically awakening Latin America. Thus, in Canto 15, Mir adds:

> And now
>> the word is no longer
>>> I
>> the word fulfilled
>> the touchstone word to start the world anew
>> And now
>> now the word is
>>> we.[82]

As the above examples suggest, the engagement with history is intimately related to the search for an appropriately comprehensive metaphor in which to distill the essential elements of the Caribbean experience and condition. It is part of the quest for an archetypal symbol, a prototypical image, one that embodying the communal aspiration to a future whose promise remains unfulfilled might, by honest recognition and acceptance of the facts of continuing sociocultural conflict and contradiction, absorb and articulate as it strives to transcend the legacies of the past.

The figures most recently and frequently proposed—Ariel, Crusoe, Caliban—are, to some extent, a relative barometer of the ideological faith and wider programmatic outlook of those that invoke them. As the personification of the patrician middle-class, classically literate Creole intellectual whose self-proclaimed mission is properly to educate the masses to an acceptance of its leadership as civic-minded representative of an aristocracy of the spirit, Ariel has lost much of the power of the appeal it originally commanded. It has joined Prospero in increasingly being identified as the outdated emblem of a fundamentally conservative vision.

Those of more liberal, individualist predisposition made uncomfortable by Marxist or black nationalist politics, by a too radically absolute insistence on the claims of any one class or racial group, regard the isolate Crusoe as a more persuasively compelling symbol. They see in his isolation, in his struggle to impose order and give meaning to his new insular environment, in his impulse to (re)create a society almost from scratch, the simile of their own predicament, the image of its anguish and the extent of its opportunity. In Derek Walcott, for example, Crusoe is the personification of "a truly tough aesthetic of the New World [which] neither explains [n]or evaporates in pathos."[83] He emerges as the image of a new Adam whose task, like the artist's, is that of "rechristening" the landscape and giving things their names. It is, at the same time, the oblique expression of Walcott's unresolved feeling of being "wrenched by two styles."[84] It has about it an element of the utopian. In John Hearne, whose novels disenchantedly record the deterioration and ultimate untenability of any alliance between the liberal mulatto middle class and the black proletariat as a consequence of what he regards as the "irremediably anarchic" response of the latter,[85] it is Crusoe's isolation and a sense of being out of sync with the times which emerges most forcefully.

In Naipaul, however, the image of the shipwreck achieves its most nihilistically conservative extreme. Token of his peculiar situation as "the late intruder, the picturesque Asiatic, linked to neither [white ex-master nor black ex-slave],"[86] which he shares with the narrator of *The Mimic Men* (1967), it is also a distillation of his vision of the inherent disorder and stasis of the West Indies, and of his antipathy for "this romanticism [which] begins by sympathizing with the oppressed and ends by exalting their values."[87] In Naipaul the image of the shipwreck, one of his favorite conceits, is an image almost wholly of abandonment and alienation, of a marginality the only answer to which is flight, recurrent and unending. It is the complement of his view of islands and colonies as crushingly insular enclosures "incapable of supporting large events."[88]

As a symbol of the anonymous masses and the full scope of the battle against a (neo)colonial condition, Caliban, the Antillean slave mocked but ceaselessly struggling for his freedom in Shakespeare's *The Tempest* (1623), has, on the other hand, emerged as the emblem of those more unambiguously identified with the black and *mestizo* underclass. In the cultural vindication and social challenge of that underclass, they see the revolutionary potential for a genuinely egalitarian *Caribbean* society. Specifically invoked by Césaire, Brathwaite, Lamming, Roberto Fernández Retamar (Cuba, 1930–), and Anthony Phelps (Haiti, 1928–), among others, this trope is also kindred to the spirit which informs the work of Jacques Stéphen Alexis, René Depestre (Haiti, 1926–), Édouard Glissant, Martin Carter (Guyana, 1927–1997), and Luis Rafael Sánchez.

Whatever the emphasis in the choice of overarching metaphor (Andrew Salkey's almost protoplasmic "Caribbea" and José Luis González's description of Puerto Rico as an Afro-foundationed "four-story country" are another two),[89] its function is that of crystallizing, in a single synthetic image, the perceived tensions and traumas of a context and repertoire of preoccupations these writers all share.

As primary instrument of the writer's craft and part of the problem of how best to give holistic expression to an authentically Caribbean *voice,* language itself is an inescapable leitmotiv of contemporary Caribbean writing. It is at the crux of the effort to forge a genuinely indigenous literary idiom The essence of that idiom, beyond recording the region's linguistic personality, is a deliberate avoidance of even implicit apology, condescension, or narrative and linguistic distance from its subject. It must itself be a dramatic example of the dynamic process of Creolization, of cultural confrontation and inventive creation the writer aims faithfully to examine and reflect.

The essence of this project is a continuing pursuit of internal consistency, of the confirming cultural complementarity between *what* is said and *how*. This is of course the sign of an enhanced recognition of the linguistic complexity and rich diversity of Caribbean life and culture. But, beyond any semiotic appreciation of its multiple layers or any possible analytical reduction of them to fetishlike exaltation of literary language for its own sake, this concern with language is reflective of its crucial role as a vehicle for directly engaging the problem of *who is* and speaks for the Caribbean. It is meant to convey the importance of a (re) consideration of who is speaking and being heard—and who *should* be. The choice of idiom(s) and inflection(s) as a central element of this question of literary authenticity, then, is at once a choice of *person(s)* as well as *persona(s)*. It is, in addition, a way of signaling what in the lives and cultural experience of the people who are its subject is specifically unique and critical. In that context, the concern with language is part of a challenge to the officious, aristocratic pretension of a too narrow perception of Antillean culture, especially one premised on a strict, hierarchical divorce between its oral and scribal traditions—between a superficial "folkloric realism" of surfaces and one more deeply textured by the contagious "magic" of popular practice and belief—to which even some of the most immediate predecessors of this literature made some obeisance. The establishment of what Glissant openly refers to as *Le Discours Antillais* (1981) requires, in consequence, the creative superseding of the restrictive and ahistorically purist negation these rigid dichotomies, sometimes unwittingly, ratify. "The era of Languages which are proud of their purity," Glissant writes, "must end for man: the adventure of speech (of the poetic theories of the diffracted but recomposed world) begins."[90] An exploration of the intersecting middle ground between social realism and an art which, in Stéphen Alexis's words, "is indissolubly linked to the myth, the symbol, the stylized, the heraldic, even the hieratic"; that "achieves a diction, a wholly internal grace, born of singularity and synthesis" is one of the facets of that adventure.[91] But it is especially the shared space between the oral and scribal traditions, originally hierarchically separated, which emerges as its most indisputably proper literary terrain. Beyond its national or regional appropriateness, as an aspect of the above balance, it is regarded as the space that holds the potential for a genuinely "universal" projection of the particular and the reconceptualization even of exhausted conventional notions of what is literature. "My language," Glissant says of his own work, "tries to place itself at the limits of writing and speaking, which seems to me something rather new in the literary enterprise. I am not talking about writing and speaking in the sense that one says a novelist imitates ordinary speech, that he has a style at writing degree zero, etc. I mean a synthesis, a synthesis of the syntax of the written and the syntax of the spoken, which I am interested in creating."[92]

Despite Derek Walcott's characteristic emphasis on his own "schizophrenia," the similarity of his comments on the issue is striking in its corroboration of a common modality, its intent, and aspiration. In "What the Twilight Says: An Overture," one of his most eloquently revealing statements about the sources and foundations of his art, he recalls his early struggle to *find a voice* truly reflective of a colonial reality in which "both the patois of the street and the language of the classroom hid the elation of discovery." He concludes his recollection by noting the young writer's ultimate apprehension that

> What would deliver him [the New World Negro] from servitude was the forging of a language that went beyond mimicry, a dialect which had the force of revelation as it invented names for things, one which finally settled on its own mode of inflection, and which began to create an oral culture of chants, jokes, folksongs and fables . . . a new melodic inflection meant a new mode, there was no better beginning. It did not matter how rhetorical, how dramatically heightened the language was if its tone were true, whether its subject was the rise and fall of a Haitian King or a small island fisherman, and the only way to recreate this language was to share in the torture of its articulation. This did not mean the jettisoning of "culture" but, by the writer's creative use of his schizophrenia, an eclectic fusion of the old and the new. So the people . . . [he concludes] awaited a language.[93]

In the evocatively lyrical novels of Simone Schwarz-Bart (Guadeloupe, 1938–)—*Pluie et vent sur Telumée Miracle* (1972) and *Ti Jean L'horizon* (1979)—the lore of the folk, this culture of oral storytelling, of proverbs, "chants, jokes, folk-songs and fables" is thus no longer limited to and *contained* in dialogue sequences, to the quasi-anthropological commentary of an aloof third-person narrator, or explicative footnotes. Infused into the very linguistic fabric, narrative posture, and tone of the text, it is at the compositional heart of the tale. Linguistically poised between the oral and scribal traditions, Schwarz-Bart's novels also blend and move smoothly between the "two worlds" of African cultural retentions and European empiricist convention, of a cyclical and lineal cosmology, of the seemingly fabulous and the "real," of the peasants of Font-Zombi's here and now and their easy familiarity and sense of enduring connection with "The Bridge of Beyond." The fundamentally Creole texture—and intent—of these novels is as evident in the spaces they bring together in elegant synthesis as in the details of the Lougandor women's story of heroic endurance or Guadeloupe's unregarded "long history, full of wonders, bloodshed and frustrations, and of desires no less vast than those that filled the skies of Nineveh, Babylon or Jerusalem" to which they pay tribute.[94] As sign and chronicle of that, Schwarz-Bart, too, regards that synthesis as the true emblem of her "unbroken and unbreakable" black peasants' Caribbean identity, proof of a "victory in the heart of darkness, and [evidence of their] . . . inexhaustible patience longer than all future defeats."[95]

In Luis Rafael Sánchez's La guaracha del Macho Camacho (1976), it is the dramatic juxtaposition of class and cultural languages, rather than any achieved synthesis, which allows its author to heighten our awareness of their continuing confrontation and, simultaneously, to "liberate the language [from] academic finickiness or social anxieties" and "make space for a kind of language [that of the 'lower' classes] that having been branded as crude had no real place in our literature."[96] The synthesis of self-consciously rhetorical speech or literary performance and the immediacy of the oral tradition, indeed, emerges by way of a kind of fused polyphony. The novel's contrapuntal structure accentuates "the need to transform colonial reality in all spheres—political, moral, even in the realm of the physical" to which the sensuous, percussive rhythms of its overarching musical motif are directly related.[97] The speech of Sánchez's characters, including that of his narrator(s), its relative communicative efficacy and intrinsic authenticity, becomes the linguistic mirror of their moral or political outlook as well as the measure of the paucity—or untapped richness—of imagination and spiritual resource available in their universe of meaning. Language itself thus becomes the contested terrain of a national ethos exposed to both internal and external assault. What finally emerges is a book whose idiom requires it, in the words of one critic, "to be read in Puerto Rican."[98] Sanchez's declared concern, like that of his Antillean contemporaries, is "to corrupt the traditional text, to redefine the form [in this case, the novel] from the inside out."[99] The ubiquitous presence of the figure of the guaracha, moreover, is calculated to emphasize the national character and communicative power of the (oral, Afro-Hispanic) traditions from which the irrepressible popular dance tune draws its pervasively subversive authority.

The idea that "forms in a national culture must, before anything else, correspond to the character and tendencies of the people in question," which informs the full range of all this creative ferment and experimentation, naturally received a considerable impetus from the insurgent nationalism of the Cuban Revolution. The revolution marked a crucial juncture in the Caribbean's perception of itself. Cuba's radical refusal of the neocolonial arrangements which, in the decades immediately preceding, had become the status quo revivified as it redefined the terms of the anticolonial movement throughout the archipelago. Its early successes in health, education, and welfare, in the face of all attempts to isolate the island's example and "destabilize" its social experiment, dramatize the failures of "The Puerto Rican Model of Development" and the limits of the liberal populist vision that inspired it.

Like the Haitian Revolution before it, the revolution in Cuba gave new dimension and vitality to the cultural articulation of the area. Encouraging new confidence in the region's capacity to achieve a genuine independence, it, at the same time, drew attention to the value and necessity of relying on one's own reservoir of native resources, courage, and imagination as essential guarantors of that independence. Among its demonstrable achievements was, precisely, the inauguration of what amounted to a cultural renaissance, an enthusiastic and multifaceted blossoming of cultural, creative, and intellectual activity. Extending the compass of their vision and the commitments of their publication programs to include the nonhispanophone areas of the region, institutions like Casa de Las Americas also gave renewed vigor and currency to a Pan-Caribbean outlook which the collapse of the West Indian Federation and a long tradition of mutual isolation between and among imperial zones and subsectors had prevented from emerging more forcefully. N. D. Williams (Guyana, 1957–) is only one of the several young and not so young talents its annual prize revealed or introduced to the Hispanophone islands and a wider international audience.

Guyana's inauguration, in 1972, of a Caribbean-wide Festival of the Arts of changing venue, Carifesta, is a tribute to the growing attraction of that outlook and its contribution to a broadly regional cross-fertilization in the creative—popular and scribal—arts. The Grenadian Revolution, up to the moment of the United States invasion of 1983, gave further encouragement to these initiatives. Quickly becoming a magnet of attraction for the Caribbean, particularly for the West Indian, intelligentsia, the two conferences of Intellectual Workers for Regional

Sovereignty of the Caribbean Peoples (1981, 1983) which it sponsored ratified the trajectory of already evident trends. Like the work of so many of the region's writers, they called for "a more comprehensive definition of culture,"[100] one more consonant with the character of the region,

In all its infinite variety, this challenge continues to lie at the heart of the literature the Caribbean produces. It is evident in the sorrow, sense of outrage and resolve, of Nancy Morejón's (Cuba, 1945–) *Cuaderno de Granada* (1984) and Miguel Barnet's (Cuba, 1940–) sustained commitment to the recuperative power of the "documentary novel." It is equally apparent in the provocative historicism of Edgardo Rodríguez Juliá's (Puerto Rico, 1946–) fictional probings of *La renuncia del héroe Baltasar* (1974), *La noche oscura del Niño Avilés* (1984–) and *La crónica de la Nueva Venecia* (1986), and in his keen interest in the contradictory vitality of popular thought and feeling which emerges in his volumes of essays *Las tribulaciones de Jonás* (1981) and *La muerte de Cortijo* (1983). It is there in the piquant vibrancy of the *salsa*-peppered language of Ana Lydia Vega's (Puerto Rico, 1946–) short stories, *Encancaranublado y otros cuentos de naufragios* (1982–), no less than in her feminist Pan-Caribbeanism. It is evident in Michael Thelwell's (Jamaica, 1939–) reimagining of Jimmy Cliff's character in *The Harder They Come* (1980) and in N. D. Williams's exploration of the familiar theme of the school in a colonial setting and in his protagonist's pilgrimage among the Rastafarians in *Ikael Torass* (1976). It is what compels Earl Lovelace's (Trinidad, 1935–) defense of the world of the calypsonian against the encroaching corruptions of its commercialization. Indeed, it is there in the most recent work of nearly all his equally well established colleagues through the region.

One is everywhere struck by the enduring aptness of José Martí's shrewd observation of 1891, in "Our America." "Nations stand and greet one another," he wrote. "'What are we?' is the mutual question, and little by little they furnish answers." "The youth of America are rolling up their sleeves," he went on, "digging their hands in the dough, and making it rise with the sweat of their brow. They realize that there is too much imitation and that creation holds the key to salvation. 'Create' is the password of this generation."[101] It remains still a critical watchword.

The ongoing evolution of the region's diverse, multilingual literature also reveals just how compelling the salients of its historic trajectory remain. The common ground of its evolving foci and convergent lines of force, moreover, serve to illustrate the demonstrable reality and continuing aptness, insofar as literary expression is concerned, of the French abolitionist Victor Schoelcher's (1804–1893) striking observation of the 1850s:

> Examining the position of the Antilles in the middle of the sea, looking at the map where they can be seen nearly touching each other, one is taken by the thought that they might well, one day, together constitute a social body apart in the modern world. . . . They would be united in a confederation by a common interest and have a navy, industry, arts, a literature that would be their own. That will perhaps not happen in one, in two, in three centuries, but it will happen because it is only natural.[102]

A prophetic, incisive and visionary thought, it, in addition, eloquently speaks to what is at once the de facto achievement and continuing promise of the literature of the Caribbean.

Notes

1. Derek Walcott, *Selected Poems* (New York: Farrar, Straus, 1964), 52.
2. Ibid., 55.
3. Édouard Glissant, *The Ripening* (New York: George Braziller, 1959), 207.
4. For a detailed analysis of the various and complex dimensions of this continuing confrontation of the Haitian black and mulatto elites—its historical and class roots, social content, political impact, and ideological articulation as "Noirsime" and a competing "Mulatto Legend," see David Nicholls, *From Dessalines to Duvalier: Race, Colour, and National Independence in Haiti* (Cambridge: Cambridge University Press, 1979), esp. chaps. 2–4 and, by the same author, *Haiti in Caribbean Context: Ethnicity, Economy, and Revolt* (New York: St. Martins Press, 1985), esp. 21–60. The ongoing consequence and legacy of what Michel-Rolph Trouillot refers to as "the Returning Crisis" is given still more structural, class, and political depth in *Haiti: State against Nation. The Origins and Legacy of Duvalierism* (New York: Monthly Review Press, 1990).
5. "Once more" because it significantly displaced the previous rehistorization of the Caribbean carried out by its "discoverers," conquistadors, settlers, and clergy, their various overseas governments, and patrons. An epic assumption and narrative vision regarding the heroic scope of their collective mission in the New World filled the *wilderness* and *tabula rasa* indigenous culture and the landscape it inhabited were presumed to be. The primary function of this earlier reconstitution of history was to rationalize, legitimate, institutionize, and give transcendent importance to "the Enterprise of the Indies." As paradigmatic trope, this epic notion proved to be a powerfully cohesive, figuratively elastic, and

especially adaptable image, which served equally well the very distinct and not infrequently opposing interests of crown, conquistador, metropolitan investor, clergy, and settler.

6. *Le Républicain,* October 1, 1836. Quoted in Michael J. Dash, *Literature and Ideology in Haiti, 1915–1961* (Totowa, N.J.: Barnes and Noble, 1981), 9. On the ideas of Nau and his colleagues, see also Nicholls, *From Dessalines to Duvalier,* 74ff.

7. *L'Union,* November 16, 1837. Quoted in Dash, *Literature and Ideology in Haiti, 1915–1961,* 9.

8. *Selected Writings of Bolivar,* comp. Vicente Lecuna (New York: Colonial Press, 1951), vol. 1, *1810–1822,* 181. See also 110–11.

9. Ibid., 176.

10. Quoted in Raúl Cepero Bonilla, *Azúcar y abolición: Apuntes para una historia crítica del abolicionismo* (Havana: Editorial Cenit, 1948), 99–100, and Philip S. Foner, *A History of Cuba, vol. 1, 1492–1845, vol. 2, 1845–1895* (New York: International Publishers, 1962 and 1963), 1: 198.

11. José Antonio Saco. *Contra la anexión* (Havana: Cultural, 1928), 1: 224. Quoted in Foner, *A History of Cuba, 1492–1845,* 1: 198. Saco was equally unambiguous as to the underlying concern of the class for whom he spoke: "In our present circumstances," he emphasized, "the political revolution is necessarily accompanied by a social revolution and the social revolution is the complete ruin of the Cuban [white] race" (47).

12. José Martí, *Letras fieras* (Havana: Editorial Letras Cubanas, 1981), 101.

13. José Martí, *On Art and Literature: Critical Writings,* ed. Philip S. Foner (New York: Monthly Review Press, 1982), 307.

14. José Martí, *Our America: Writings on Latin America and the Struggle for Cuban Independence,* ed. Philip S. Foner (New York; Monthly Review Press, 1977), 90.

15. Martí, *On Art and Literature,* 306.

16. Manuel A. Alonso, *El Jíbaro* (Río Piedras. Puerto Rico: Editorial Cultural, 1968), 3.

17. Ibid.

18. Ibid.

19. Ibid., 115. It is only in the expanded 1884 edition, a decade after the decree of emancipation, that slavery emerges as a theme in the work—and then only to record, and to applaud post factum, its legal abolition as a historic event, not to indicate or examine the substance of its larger social and historical significance, cultural legacies, or the continuing challenge of the now ex-slave's presence to any reductive, nonexclusive definition of the "national" identity.

20. Ibid., 40.

21. Ibid., 19.

22. Ibid., 53.

23. Ibid., 97.

24. Ibid., 62.

25. Ibid., 113. See also 161–66 which includes "1833–1883. Perdemos o ganamos," his generally favorable retrospective on the period added to the expanded edition of 1884.

26. For a perceptively sustained examination of the workings of this process in Galván's novel, particularly as it relates to his "patriarchal" assumptions about the "Motherland," see Doris Sommer, *One Master for Another: Populism as Patriarchal Rhetoric in Dominican Novels* (Boston: University Press of America, 1983), 51ff. Sommer's examination of this "The Other Enriquillo," is more analytically sound and comprehensive in its appreciation of Galván's programmatic outlook and ideological loyalties than that of any of his more conventional liberal and conservative commentators. It is also more sensitive to the concrete historical context out of which his novel emerges than is Selwyn R. Cudjoe's oftentimes anachronistically radical "materialist" critique. Ironically ignoring precisely the actual material circumstances to which Galván's novel is a response, Cudjoe misperceives the work as "an almost literal retelling of the resistance of the Indians in precise historical details, in which Galván's sympathy seems to lie with the Indians," whose primary intent Cudjoe vaguely, rhetorically specifies as "to remind the people of the constant need to resist foreign oppression." Neither "the people" nor the "foreigners," as Galván understood these terms and their programmatic implications, are convincingly delineated or defined. See Selwyn R. Cudjoe, *Resistance and Caribbean Literature* (Athens: Ohio University Press, 1980), 83–89, 146.

27. Manuel de Jesús Galván, *Enriquillo: Leyenda histórica dominicana* (New York: Las Americas Publishing Co., 1964), 267. My translation.

28. See his "Creative Writing of the West Indies during the Period of Slavery," *Savacou* 1 (June 1970): 48. Those writing then, Brathwaite observes, "were Englishmen or English-oriented creoles" and "the work they produced was not 'West Indian' but 'Tropical English.' Their models were the metropolitan masters. . . . Their limitations stem from the fact that few of them were able to record a truly convincing experience [of the genuinely local]."

29. J. J. Thomas, *Froudacity; West Indian Fables by James Anthony Froude Explained* . . . (London and Port of Spain: New Beacon Books, 1969), 16. With caustic irony, he also spoke of the "ineffable privilege of whitemanship."

30. Ibid., 18.

31. James Anthony Froude, *The English in the West Indies or the Bow of Ulysses* (London: Longmans, Green, 1888), 14.

32. Thomas, *Froudacity*, 51.

33. Ibid., 75.

34. Ibid., 114.

35. Ibid., 155.

36. Ibid., 179.

37. Ibid., 120.

38. José de Diego, "Hallelujahs to the Gentlemen from the North," *Revista de las Antillas* 5 (August 1913): 118–19. My translation.

39. Antonio S. Pedreira, *Insularismo: Ensayos de interpretación puertorriqueña* (San Juan: Biblioteca de Autores Puertorriqueños, 1934), 112.

40. Quoted in Arcadio Díaz Quiñones, "La poesía negra de Luis Palés Matos: Realidad y conciencia de su dimensión colectiva," *Sin Nombre* 1 (Septiembre 1970: 23.

41. Ángel Augier, *Nicolás Guillén: Notas para un estudio biográfico-crítico,* vol. 2 (Las Villas: Universidad de Las Villas, 1964), 286.

42. Nicolás Guillén, *Obra poética, 1920–1958* (Havana: Instituto del Libro Cubano, 1972) vol. 1, 113–14.

43. Nicolás Guillén, *Prosa de prisa, 1929–1972* (Havana: Editorial Arte y Literatura, 1975), vol. 2, 70.

44. Ibid.

45. Nicolás Guillén, *Obra poética* (Havana: Instituto del Libro Cubano, 1973), vol. 2, 19.

46. Alejo Carpentier, *El reino de este mundo* ([Caracas, Venezuela:] Organización Continental Festival del Libro, n.d.), 5–11.

47. As its class base dramatically widened to become increasingly defined as the near-to-inevitable journey of the economically marginal, displaced, or unemployed lower classes, the experience of emigration to the metropolitan centers, which had played so signal a part in the emergence of Pan-Africanism, *negritude,* and the work of the Anglophone Antillean writers of the fifties, would by the late sixties and seventies produce a much more genuinely "settled" migrant/emigrant—as opposed to transient students, middle- or upper-class sojourners—literature of Caribbeans in the metropolis to which Claude McKay (1889–1948) had already pointed. The writing of the Puerto Ricans Pedro Pietri, Edward Rivera, Nicholasa Mohr, and Caryl Phillips's (Saint Kitts, 1958) novels (*The Final Passage* [1985], *A State of Independence* [1986], and commentary [*The European Tribe,* 1987]) are only some among the several more recent examples of a "new," if still theoretically "unlocated," nor as yet fully examined, dimension of Caribbean writing.

48. Ellen Conroy Kennedy, *The Negritude Poets: An Anthology of Translations from the French* (New York: Viking Press, 1975), 15.

49. L. G. Damas, *Pigments* (Paris: Présence Africaine, 1962), 57. The translation, by Ellen Conroy Kennedy, is included in ibid.

50. Walcott, *Selected Poems,* 4.

51. Etienne Léro, "Misère d'une poésie," *Légitime Défense* (1932). Reproduced in L. Kesteloot, ed., *Anthologie négro-africaine: panorama critique des prosateurs. Poètes et dramaturges noir du XXe siècle* (Verviers, Belgium : Editions

Gérard, 1967), 77. English translation by Norman Shapiro, whose more extended excerpt appears in Norman Shapiro, ed., *Négritude: Black Poetry from Africa and the Caribbean* (New York: October House, 1970), 70.

52. Reinhard Sander, ed., *From Trinidad: An Anthology of Early West Indian Writing* (New York: Africana Publishing, 1978), 5.

53. The pertinent texts in each case are: Frantz Fanon, *Peau Noire, Masques Blanc* (1952), English translation *Black Skin, White Masks* (1967), *The Wretched of the Earth* (1968) and, in *Toward the African Revolution* (1967), his essays "Racism and Culture" and "West Indians and Africans"; Walter Rodney, *The Groundings with My Brothers* (1971); René Depestre, *Bon jour et adieu à la négritude* (1980); and "Jean Price-Mars y el mito del Orfeo negro," in *Por la revolución, por la poesía* (Montevideo: Biblioteca de Marcha, 1970), republished as "Jean Price-Mars et le mythe de L'Orphée Noir ou les aventures de la négritude," in *Pour la révolution, pour la poésie* (Ottawa: Lemeac, 1974)

54. Aimé Césaire, *Return to My Native Land* (Baltimore: Penguin Books, 1970).

55. Aimé Césaire, *Letter to Maurice Thórez* (Paris: Editions Présence Africaine, 1957), 12.

56. Jacques Roumain, *Analyse schématique, 1932–1934* (n.p.: Editions Idées Nouvelles, Idées Prolétariennes, n.d.), 28.

57. Maryse Condé, "Autour d'une literature antillaise," *Présence Africaine* 81 (1972): 175. See also her "Order, Disorder, Freedom, and the West Indian Writer," *Yale French Studies* 2, no. 83 (1993): 121–35, where, placing a more specific emphasis on what she regards as *négritude*'s formal attributes, narrative limitations, too-narrow thematic focus and repertoire of characters as a model, she takes it to task for its too male-centered rules of order, conventionally normative treatment of sexuality, and proper procedure.

58. Albert Gomes, *Through a Maze of Colour* (Trinidad: Key Caribbean Publications, 1974), 17.

59. Ibid., 77.

60. Reinhard S. Sander, ed., *From Trinidad: An Anthology of Early West Indian Writing.* (New York: Africana Publishing, 1978), 7.

61. A. J. Seymour, *Growing Up in Guyana* (Georgetown: Labour Advocate Printers, 1976), 53.

62. *The Three Novels of Roger Mais* (London and Kingston: Sangster's Book Stores and Jonathan Cape Ltd, 1970), 197. "They make animals without hope of the men who pass through here," as one of his characters muses in prison (211), emerges as a metaphor for that larger society's treatment of its marginalized, poor, and destitute citizens.

63. *John O'London's Weekly,* May 1, 1953. Quoted in Kenneth Ramshand, *The West Indian Novel and Its Background* (New York: Barnes and Noble, 1970), 35.

64. V. S. Reid, "Author's Note," *New Day* (Kingston and London: Sangster's Stores, Ltd. with Heinemann Educational Books, 1970), n.p.

65. George E. Kent, "A Conversation with George Lamming," *Black World* 22 (March 1973): 92. Quoted in Sandra Pouchet Paquet, *The Novels of George Lamming* (London, Kingston, and Port of Spain: Heinemann, 1982), 1.

66. Jacques Stéphen Alexis, "Of the Marvelous Realism of the Haitians," *Présence Africaine* 8–10 (June–November 1956): 265. This is a special issue devoted to the proceedings of the First International Conference on Negro Writers and Artists.

67. John Hearne, ed., *Carifesta Forum: An Anthology of 20 Caribbean Voices* (Kingston, Jamaica, 1976), vii.

68. Wilson Harris, "The Unresolved Constitution," *Caribbean Quarterly* 14 (March–June, 1968): 44.

69. Wilson Harris, "Author's Note," *The Whole Armour and The Secret Ladder* (London; Faber and Faber, 1973), 9.

70. Ibid., 8.

71. Wilson Harris, "The Unresolved Constitution," 44.

72. Wilson Harris, *Palace of the Peacock* (London: Faber and Faber, 1960), 23–24.

73. Alejo Carpentier, "Tientos y diferencias," trans. Stephanie Merrim, *Latin American Literature and Arts Review* 28 (January–April, 1981): 28.

74. Harris, "The Unresolved Constitution," 46.

75. Glissant, *The Ripening,* 103.

76. Edouard Glissant, *L'Intention poétique* (Paris: Editions du Seuil, 1958), 19.

77. Edouard Glissant, "Note sur un 'poésie nationale' chez les peuples noirs," *Les Lettres Nouvelles* 4 (1956): 395.

78. Glissant, *L'Intention poétique,* 24.

79. Andew Salkey, *Jamaica* (London: Hutchinson, 1973), 10–11.

80. Edward Brathwaite, *The Arrivants: A New World Trilogy* (New York and London: Oxford University Press, 1973), 77.

81. Pedro Mir, *Viaje a la muchedumbre* (Mexico City: Siglo XXI Editores, 1972), 50.

82. Ibid., 62.

83. Derek Walcott, "The Muse of History," in *Massa Day Dead? Black Moods in the Caribbean,* ed. Orde Coombs (Garden City, N.Y.: Anchor Books, 1974), 2.

84. Derek Walcott, *The Gulf* (New York: Farrar, Straus and Giroux, 1970), 32.

85. John Hearne, *Land of the Living* (London: Faber and Faber, 1961), 84.

86. V. S. Naipaul, *The Mimic Men* (New York: Macmillan, 1967), 93.

87. V. S. Naipaul, "What's Wrong with Being a Snob?," in *Critical Perspectives on V. S. Naipaul,* ed. Robert D. Hamner (Washington, D.C.: Three Continents Press, 1977), 37.

88. V. S. Naipaul, *The Middle Passage. Impressions of Five Societies: British, French and Dutch in the West Indies and South America* (London: Andre Deutsche, 1962), 29. See also *The Mimic Men*, 160.

89. José Luís González, *El país de cuatro pisos* (Río Piedras: Ediciones Huracán, 1980).

90. Glissant, *L'Intention poétique*, 41.

91. Stéphen Alexis, "Of the Marvelous Realism of the Haitians," 265.

92. Quoted in Wilbert J. Roget, "Edouard Glissant and Antillanité" (Ph.D. diss., University of Pittsburgh, 1975), 166.

93. Derek Walcott, *Dream on Monkey Mountain and Other Plays* (New York: Farrar, Straus and Giroux, 1970), 17.

94. Simone Schwarz-Bart. *Between Two Worlds* (New York: Harper and Row, 1981), 4.

95. Ibid., 294.

96. Helen Calaf Aguera, "Luis Rafael Sánchez Speaks about *Macho Camacho's Beat*," *Latin American Literature and Arts Review* 28 (January–April 1981): 40.

97. Ibid.

98. Efraín Barradas. *Para leer en puertorriqueño: Acercamiento a la obra de Luis Rafael Sánchez* (Río Piedras: Editorial Cultural, 1981).

99. Ibid., 41.

100. General letter of invitation to Second Conference of Intellectual Workers for Regional Sovereignty of the Caribbean Peoples, 1983.

101. Martí, *Our America*, 92.

102. Victor Schoelcher, *Les colonies français* (1852). Quoted in Daniel Guérin, *The West Indies and Their Future* (London: Dennis Dobson, 1961), 174. See also Roget, "Edouard Glissant and Antillanité," 155.

Seeing Fragments/Whole

NOT SO very long ago Caribbean literature and literary criticism, inclusively considered, looked a fractured, balkanized, "orbitally" segmented affair. In keeping with what historian Franklin Knight aptly describes as the "fragmented nationalism" evident in the archipelago's diversity of political arrangements, states, territories, regional subdivisions and cultural zones, critical study of the area's literary output was (and all too often remains still) typically partitioned in an eclectic array of isolated, mutually self-insulated linguistic blocs, cultural enclaves, and literary exclusives. Routinely more than just geographically positioned—analytically, discursively, and categorically—on the insular pivot and seaboard rims of the continental Americas, on the one hand, and on the ultramarine periphery of various erstwhile European hubs, on the other, Antillean literature has most often been approached and commanded sustained critical attention outside its own local confines only as a distantly affiliated branch, outlying province, or exotic frontier satellite in the orbit of ostensibly more compelling canons and constellations. Incorporated as a division in the unfolding literary history of "Latin America," the "Hispanic Antilles" are most commonly privileged as the introductory chapter of our foundational New World beginnings quickly left behind for the riches of *tierra firme* and thereafter of a somewhat fitful and irregular interest which has left literatures like that of the Dominican Republic to suffer an all-too-conspicuous critical neglect; and, with that of Cuba and Puerto Rico, equivocally poised in that fugitively protean and polymorphous "hammock swung between Americas": at once on the island fringes of "Spanish" America and part of the multilingual core of its own distinctively Caribbean matrix. The "English-" and "French-" speaking zones, whose literatures emerged to the wider world's notice only in the three decades after 1939, had all they could do to give proper authority and inflection to their own evolving voice(s) and tradition(s) in the face of (neo)colonial conventions which persist(ed) in seeing them as so many distant wards, facsimile replicas, or derivative cultural extensions of places other and presumptively more worthy than themselves.

Locally, too, Caribbean literary history and criticism, its boundaries conventionally drawn along the edges of once imperial lines of force, tended rather to the centrifugal then the centripetal. Its most perceptively arresting and influential practitioners, for all their penetration and originality, were not, in some sense, *Caribbean* critics at all. Those who, while properly rooted in the soil of their own national or sub-regional context and cultural settings extended their compass, conceptually and methodologically, beyond its customary limits comparatively to engage the Antilles, writ large, as their singularly appropriate critical domain were very few indeed. If historians—C. L. R. James, Eric Williams, P. M. Sherlock, Juan Bosch, Franklin Knight, and David Watts, among others, come readily to mind—were out in front of the curve in envisioning the Caribbean as an integral and distinctive totality, the more conventional work of most still revealed the abiding effects of a powerfully centrifugal pull, hierarchic paradigms, and a patrician bias. The clash of exogenous nation-states *acting upon* the region, some sub-regional sector, the nationalist discourse and paternal ascendancy of local elites, or the exemplary lives of admirably heroic figures were usually still the primary focus of attention. Gordon K. Lewis's *Main Currents in Caribbean Thought: The Historical Evolution of Caribbean Society in Its Ideological Aspects, 1492–1900* appeared, as late as the early eighties, to be exceptional in the uncommon sweep, comparative heft, and integrative assumption of its engagement with the subject. The particular stress of his insistence that "The history . . . of Caribbean culture in its anthropological sense (and on which, in the nature of things, much of its literary culture is based) is the history of forms created by the masses . . . who . . . originated, and defended, their own art forms against the sterile and borrowed pseudo-European culture of the educated classes," in addition, captured the insurgent mood and tone of a fresh attitude whose maverick emphasis and vernacular accent had, long before, begun to effect a noticeable change in the traditional panorama.

Early prefigured in the work of many of the region's writers themselves, by the seventies a broad concatenation of forces was giving impetus to a cross-pollination of previously insular terrains and territories. The growing literary prestige of popular experience and shift of stress to accentuate the cunning inventiveness of Creolization, its progenitive and reinflective originality, was certainly one of those forces. Prompting an increasingly Antillean-centered self-assertion, they together encouraged an unprecedented creative audacity and discursive recognition of an assorted population of the traditionally marginalized, disregarded, or forgotten, including indigenous Creole minorities, women, communities of unorthodox custom or (religious) belief, and of those who, in Caryl Phillips's titular phrase, had made *The Final Passage* to become part of the region's burgeoning diaspora. The cultural, no less than political, impact of the Cuban Revolution was another, which palpably contributed the invigorating energy of its own initial promise and momentum. The initiation, in 1972, of a regular Caribbean Festival of the Arts (Carifesta) of region-wide scope and changing venue gave an even broader integrative will and Pan-Caribbean dimension to that energy and creative, cross-pollinating ferment. The failures and disillusionments which came in the wake of postcolonial regimes that everywhere led to the deepening crisis and final disintegration of the carefully forged populist alliances of the forties and fifties, by contrast, ominously revealed the impassioned intensities of a generalized popular disenchantment. The process of increasing economic globalization, further aggravating that crisis, at the same time made some form of regional integration at once more urgent and more appealing. The neologistic, paradoxically congregational effects and demographic gravity of Caribbean (im)migration to the major cities and urban capitals of the West, a crucially swelling procession of displaced labor, transnational commuters, temporary sojourners, and permanent settlers which invariably included a significant representation of the region's better known artists and writers, similarly exposed the attenuated credibility of official local authority and the daily more porous borders of our conventionally "imagined" national communities' territorial limits, reach, and extension. The media revolution, and the emergence of postcolonial, feminist, cultural and multicultural studies, all of which gave a chic cachet and currency to a dizzying boutique of fashionable (post)modern(ist) literary trends and theories, too, were among the several forces at work, playing their contributory part.

Altogether they further whetted and sharpened the widening appeal of a Pan-Caribbean outlook. Each strengthened appreciative awareness of the creative distinctiveness and autonomy of a polyglot and transnational Antillean esthetic modality, as well as of the need for a materially grounded criticism of more broadly comparative scope and sensibility. From the earliest assays of a wide spectrum of poets and novelists—George Lamming, Edward Brathwaite, José Luis González, René Depestre, Sylvia Wynter, Édouard Glissant, Marysé Condé, among others—to the more recent work of critics such as Selwyn R. Cudjoe (*Resistance and Caribbean Literature* [1980]), Peter Hulme (*Colonial Encounters: Europe and the Native Caribbean* [1986]), Silvio Torres-Saillant (*Caribbean Poetics* [1997]), J. Michael Dash (*The Other America: Caribbean Literature in a New World Context* [1998]), and Belinda J. Edmondson (*Caribbean Romances: The Politics of Regional Representation* [1999]), the effort to articulate the imaginative and historic coordinates of that esthetic has grown in extent and intensity.

Response to, embodiment, and something like preliminary culmination of the cumulative weight of those forces and the gathering exigency of that project, A. James Arnold's impressive three-volume *History of Literature in the Caribbean* is also one of its moments of signal achievement. The first collaborative endeavor of its kind, scope, and ambition, it both breaks new ground and offers the reader a broadly synoptic view of the current state and varied range of scholarly dialogue, opinion, and practice. Originally undertaken at the behest and under sponsorship of the International Comparative Literature Association as one in its series of Comparative Literary Histories, its contours initially mooted in exploratory colloquia devoted to "Caribbean Literary Historiography" held at the University of Virginia and at universities in Puerto Rico between 1986 and 1988, this *History* brings together perhaps the most richly diverse and distinguished international corps of literary Caribbeanists yet assembled in one work and admirably succeeds in its primary encyclopedic, reconfigurative intent. Their combined efforts effectively gives us the first genuinely comprehensive literary history which attempts to engage with all the literatures of the Caribbean as a single, unified—neither homogenous nor univocal—field. "Our goal from the earliest stages of preparation," its editor writes in the first of these volumes, "has been to create a history of Caribbean literature that could be read across the linguistic divisions both for commonalities and for regional cultural differences. We hoped thereby to present a contrastive view of how literature emerged as a social institution in the several areas of the Caribbean region." The map of its critical precincts is, thus, necessarily extensive and generously inclusive. It stretches beyond the Greater and Lesser Antilles to encompass the Caribbean rimlands of French Guiana, Guyana, Surinam, Colombia, Venezuela, and the enclaves and work of West Indians and their descendants in Central and North America. In yet another departure from conventional practice, it also extends to include sustained and thoughtful examination of the historical emergence and present state of the area's different Creole language literatures. A major contribution to our apprehension and ongoing re-envisionment of the Caribbean as a literary region, its conscientious charting of the territory, so far unequaled in its breath of reach, significantly advances our cartographic depiction of its manifold, vari-textured topography. Laying an ample foundation for still further explorations, it demonstrates, promotes, and authoritatively advances the prospects and practical viability of a burgeoning Pan-Caribbean criticism. Regarding nothing Antillean as alien to their concerns, Professor Arnold's three substantive volumes mark an important watershed in our consolidated scholarly engagement with its proper domain.

The first of these volumes, published in 1992 and devoted to the Hispanic and Francophone Regions, is organized initially to consider the general—social, economic, political, cultural-historical—context and the particular conditions out of and within which their respective literatures emerge to assume their uniquely Caribbean character. Informative essays on "The History of Literary Language," "The Formation and Evolution of a Literary Discourse: One, Two, or Three Languages?," "Education in the Hispanic Antilles," and "Literature and Folklore in the Francophone Caribbean" directly address the formation and process of maturation of a differentially Caribbean universe of language(s) and literature(s), its(their) various literate, popular, and ethno-cultural expressive registers and zones of activity; their infrastructural supports (or historical lack thereof), and current literary positioning. Summary chronicles of sub-regional and nationally specific literary experience from the earliest foundational period(s) through the nineteenth and early twentieth centuries are also provided. The reader is, in addition, alerted to areas where the available record suggests an insufficiency of historical or critical investigation: to those realms where, in effect, the history is still to be written. As sub-editor responsible for the section devoted to Francophone Literature and someone who in separate studies has already significantly contributed to our fuller understanding of pre-twentieth-century Francophone literary protocols, J. Michael Dash thus appropriately points, in his introduction to that section, to the century before *négritude*'s spectacular dawning in the "French" West Indies. "Surely," he notes, "nineteenth century [French Caribbean] writing as a whole needs to be reassessed." The place of the enigmatic and long eluded St. John Perse in the literary history of Martinique and Guadeloupe, he also suggests, demands serious critical study. If, as a daily widening consensus makes clear, there is a "need to resist the temptation of seeing the francophone Caribbean as simply an extension of global *francophonie* or of the Neo-African diaspora," Dash finally concludes, "the mythification of literary expression by an embattled Caribbean elite as a privileged cultural code [that negritude to some extent confirmed] also needs to be examined."

Of these summary chronicles, Silvio Torres-Saillant's examination of "Dominican Literature and Its Criticism: Anatomy of a Troubled Identity" is especially welcome for the layered density of its précis, the uncommon candor of its engagement with a vexed and prickly legacy of anti-Haitian racism, and as antidote to that tradition of critical neglect previously mentioned. Efrain Barradas's look "North of the Caribbean: An Outline for a History of Spanish-Caribbean Literature in the United States," Ian I. Smarts's review of "West Indian Writing in Central America," and Regis Antoine's brief on "The Caribbean in Metropolitan French Writing" add a still more unaccustomed dimension to the comparatively more familiar synopsis of literary history offered, for example, by Raquel Chang-Rodriguez, Carlos J. Alonso, and Ivan A. Schulman. Extending and recasting more traditional views of the canon, each points to the pertinent existence of a broader transnational Caribbean cultural sphere than more orthodox definitions allow for, documenting the compound and continuing impact of our many Diasporas on writing both "at home" and "abroad." The complexity of the historical framework and setting thus established, the volume moves on to concentrate on the unfolding development, defining concerns, literary practices, aspirations, overall reverberation, and general fortunes of various genres—fiction, poetry, the essay, and drama—in the latter half of the twentieth century.

A similar organizational format and procedure inform the second volume, devoted to the Caribbean's Anglophone and Dutch- and Papiamento-speaking regions. The unprecedented capaciousness of its coverage of the latter two, certainly, will almost immediately make it the most extensive and authoritative source of critical commentary on those literatures yet available in English. Ineke Phaf-Rheinberger and Mattias Rohrig-Assunção's report on the ultimate (racially suffused) meanings given independence in fictional treatments of the life of a mulatto Creole caudillo from Curaçao in Venezuela, Colombia, and Curaçao, included in the third volume of "Cross-Cultural Studies," further amplifies and complements that coverage. Allowing an atypically composite, global view of the region's variegated literary landscape, these first two vòl-umes together offer the reader a panoramic omnibus lit-crit caribbeana.

The recent publication of that final volume of "Cross-Cultural Stud-ies" brings to conclusion a formidable enterprise, which has for nearly fifteen years consumed the combined energies and attention of its editor, his editorial collaborators, and their well over fifty contributors from around the world. The one with the most obviously theoretical inflec-tion and a broadly (post)modernist bent, this capstone volume is also perhaps the trilogy's most methodologically eclectic and contrastively polemical. Focused primarily on the "task of [conceptually and com-paratively] framing our literary history and identifying prototypes and recurring motifs," it aims simultaneously "to bring together the best cur-rent work representative of the principal directions that are shaping our understanding of Caribbean literature today." The result is a provoca-tive and revealing, if critically disparate and on occasion oddly pitched, probe of those syntheses, representative themes, tropes, and organizing metaphors contemporary writers—and their critics—most generally invoke—or interrogate—as emblematic of the Caribbean's multifaceted universe and the varied forms of literary expression meant to dramatize and transmit its particulars. The nature, role, place, meaning, and impli-cations of "Creolization" for a Caribbean poetics thus necessarily has a certain pride of place as one of its major foci. Even before the Barba-dian poet-historian Edward Kamau Brathwaite's *Contradictory Omens: Cultural Diversity and Integration in the Caribbean* (1974) theoreti-cally mobilized the concept for the Anglophone Antilles as a less static, multivalent, non-hierarchical, lexically localized, and "indigenous" alternative to the deficiencies of the Cuban ethnographer Fernando Ortiz's influential notion of "transculturation" and the less adequate, even tendentious analytical terms—assimilation, acculturation, inter-culturation, pluralism—then long in conventional vogue, "Creolization" had already begun moving progressively to the center of contemporary Caribbean Studies and discussions of a Caribbean aesthetic. No reader of this volume, certainly, will be in any doubt that it will remain there for some time yet. "The Caliban Complex," by contrast, would appear to be receding from its once privileged position of allegorical authority in the era of the "postnational"; in the face of a sharpened critique of its masculinist inflection; and what, in the "Spanish" Caribbean at least, Vera Kutzinski trenchantly calls "its problematic validation of *mestizaje* as a cultural discourse and national ideology. . . ." The intricacies and connotations of race, racism, and racial discourse in so pigmentocratic, polychromatic a region, not unexpectedly, continue to be the inevitably central issues they have always been. A more broadly embracing idea of hybridity than the dyadic or triadic imagery which *négritude, negrismo, mestizaje,* or *marronage* usually conjures up seems, at the same time, to be winning increasing favor as it simultaneously corroborates the constitutive centrality of black, white, and mulatto and yet argues for extension of the traditional—ethnic and gender—range of inclusions in our discussions of Caribbean culture and identity. It is, in any event, evident that, though not wholly shared by all of its contributors, the overarching consensual "vision of Caribbeanness that structures this volume assumes that multiple ethnic and cultural strains have contributed to the formation of contemporary literatures in the region and that they are indissociably and inevitably connected." The splendid efflorescence of women writers throughout the region in the last quarter century has, obviously, brought novel and provocative nuance to the literary models inherited from *négritude* and, in the "Spanish" Caribbean, the Creole nationalist allegory, whose prescribed formal and thematic boundaries their writing often transgresses and seeks to transcend. The complacency of what, in "Hispanic" echo of Guadeloupe's Maryse Condé, Puerto Rico's Ana Lydia Vega has described as "the messianic vocation that weighs heavy on the shoulders and the heads of . . . [male] writers of all [previous] generations" has been permanently disturbed by the vigor of a feminist prose and poetry now less focused on the epic and heroic than on the quotidian, ordinary lives and psychic landscape of their female protagonists, and which, with Vega, very often asks, "And what if *machismo* should turn out to be one of those so often proclaimed National Values that every Creole writer must defend on pain of ceasing to be such?" That efflorescence has encouraged and given rise to an equally flourishing feminist criticism of Caribbean literature that has already re-articulated our established notions of the canon. Its influence, now beyond question, will almost certainly increase. It is, in varying degrees, attested to here in essays on female identity, Caribbean autobiography, forms of popular culture in the novel, and Derek Walcott's Don Juan authored by, respectively, Kathleen Balutansky, Gillian

Whitlock, Iris M. Zavala, Lizbeth Paravisini-Gebert, and Josephine V. Arnold. The classic European paradigms from which "the cannibal as a cultural synecdoche" was drawn for later Americanization, a masterfully concise presentation of Creole languages as "prismatic refractions of a single set" and, with less concentrated thoroughness, the difficult complex of relations between the region's scriptural and oral traditions are among some of the other major issues and themes of immediate moment to which this substantive volume turns its comparative attention.

These several lines of force all most synthetically converge around the representative primacy of Creolization which, in different guise, with varying emphasis and accentuations, suffuses the whole. The writer and *pensador* Édouard Glissant's sustained activation of the concept—as critical instrument, as descriptor of cultural process, as empirical outcome, and as still dialectically unfolding future possibility—in his own vision of *Le Discours Antillais* (1981; *Caribbean Discourse* [1989]) and a *Poétique de la relation* (1990; *Poetics of Relation* [1997]) enlarges and amplifies an earlier notion of *Antillanité*. Juxtaposed and contrasted to Antonio Benítez Rojo's turn to chaos theory for explanation of the Caribbean's complexities in *La isla que se repite* (1989; *The Repeating Island* [1992]), it is Glissant's more rhizometic model that ultimately presides as paradigmatic exemplar over the text. The work of a number of its contributors is more than just casually informed by its insights, figures, imagery, and Antillo-centrically canny appropriations of contemporary literary theory. For all its tantalizing postmodernist dash and theoretical ambition, Benítez Rojo's study of the Caribbean "as a turbulent system, beneath whose disorder . . . there are regularities that are repeated," a "meta-archipelago: a Chaos that returns, a detour without purpose," though it has lately met with more than passing favor in the American academy, seems perhaps too "chaotic" and incorporeal, too evasive of history, too predictably "orbital," provincially Cuban-centered, and intimately pessimistic effectively to theorize a broader Caribbean; or, as Keith Alan Sprouse's sympathetic examination of it points out, to suggest "how Caribbean peoples might make productive connections with other [postcolonial] peoples." At the core of the radical skepticism and fatalistic aura which hover poignantly about Benítez Rojo's conception of Chaos, more than the luminescence of wider vision, lie, one suspects, the unreconciled disenchantments of the Cuban émigré. Glissant's inquiry into the Caribbean's particularities, which, if not without its own elements of ambivalence, has a demonstrably broader compass, is less deferentially confining, more concretely grounded and panotopically fruitful.

Emerging as one of this volume's leitmotifs, the juxtaposition of the Cuban novelist and the Martiniquen poet becomes emblematic of the not always uncontentious polemic about the comparative applicability and relevance of postmodern constructs to a contemporary Caribbean poetics and criticism. It thus crystallizes the terms and stakes of a controversial dialogue whose amplitude, tacitly and explicitly, emerges in the conflicting emphasis, premises, methods, and ideological outlook which distinguish the Antillocentric, panotopic "modernity" of native intellectuals like Torres-Saillant, Ramón de la Campa, and Emilio Jorge Rodríguez from the Afrocentrism of a Femi Ojo-Ade, and the "postmodernity," abiding "orbitalism," or "neo-Europeanist" slant of some of their other colleagues. De la Campa's expert "unpacking" of the different contexts and ramifications of this debate in his lucid exploration of "Resistance and Globalization in Caribbean Discourse," like Saillant's welcome call for a centripetal perception of "The Cross-Cultural Unity of Caribbean Literature," makes clear that what they find most compelling about Glissant's cartography is the ways in which it "revolts against both identitarian myths of origin *and* [my emphasis] deconstructive dismissals of the Caribbean's stories of dispossession, decolonization, and other brushes with modernity" to reveal "a global awareness that is richly informed by specific [local and] international contrasts, not just synchronizing abstractions." The attentive reader will glean more than a little about the current state of our critical scene from the tensions and occasionally spirited clashes evident in such contradictory omens.

An undertaking of this magnitude and scope is bound to have its blemishes. The editor is himself cognizant of the risk of a certain loss of concentrated focus and sustained theoretical cohesion that, in a project of this scope, can only be unevenly managed: it is the inevitable risk that any such collection must run. The definition of "Caribbean" with which at least some contributors appear to be working can on occasion strike one as either overly elastic or unduly elusive, a given critic's "commitment to literature as a cross-cultural artifact, stopping nowhere, belonging to no one domain" as more conventionally comparative than comparatively *Caribbean*. For all its critical novelty, "obital" points of individual departure tend still to predominate. One also can't help but notice the odd contradictions of at least one examination of Caribbean popular culture which habitually refers the reader (and itself defers) to a nearly full pantheon of *au courant* European thinkers and, concluding with self-referential circularity, ultimately leaves one with more certainty about the primacy of what (or who) the critic has read than about the materially informed persuasiveness of its readings of the *vox populi*. I, in any event, confess myself unpersuaded that, as the editor intimates, it offers any effective response to the native intellectual's suspicions of the postmodern turn. It seems, on the contrary, almost deliberately to confirm them. There may be those who will wish for an even wider representation of writers and scholars permanently resident in the Caribbean. The inclusion of a briefly descriptive "Note on Contributors" would surely have been helpful to those less familiar with or coming entirely new to the field.

These, though, are so many quibbles, which detract neither from the achievement this *History* represents, its pioneering stature, nor from its indispensability to anyone seriously interested in the literature of the Caribbean. The reader is more than well served by the generally high caliber of the contributions and by the integrative singularity and deeper congruities which, like those of the archipelago itself, inhere in the discernible coordinates of even their disparities and fragmentations: by its general insistence that "The idea," as E. K. Brathwaite succinctly put it in 1974, "is to see the fragments / whole." And, also with Brathwaite, in the encouraging transparency of its diver's conviction that in matters Antillean, "The unity is submarine."

NOTES OF A
'NOTHER RICAN

Dweller and pilgrim live this same exile
ÉDOUARD GLISSANT

There is a sense in which every[one] . . . is bilingual,
and those of us who are more overtly so are only
living metaphors for the condition that applies to us all.
RHINA P. ESPAILLAT

We have come to the end of a language and are now
about the business of forging a new one.
JAMES BALDWIN

Sojourners, Settlers, Castaways, and Creators

Of Puerto Rico Past and Puerto Ricans Present

For Maceo and Gabi, outriders and legatees

I

"I came here to get gold, not to till the land like a peasant."
HERNÁN CORTÉS on arriving at La Española

THE HISTORY of Puerto Rico and Puerto Ricans in the Post-Indigenous Era, the peculiar character of their association with Europe and with what, with provocative imprecision, the nineteenth-century Cuban writer José Martí liked to call "the Other, Anglo-Saxon America," properly begins with the second, 1493, voyage of Christopher Columbus. The first of his expeditions actually conceived and organized as a full-fledged colonizing mission, it was, perhaps even more than the Admiral's historic landfall of the year before, a signal harbinger of the nature and content of things to come.

That armada of seventeen ships bound, with eager cupidity, for the beachhead island of La Española, loaded down with provisions, seeds, plants, and animals enough for its sizable company of six priests, a cannibal-haunted fleet surgeon, and almost fifteen hundred assortedly skilled sailors, colonists, and soldiers of fortune firmly set in place the already emerging terms and pattern of Europe's military, economic, ideological, demographic, and cultural invasion of the homelands, social and cosmological universe of the native inhabitants of the Caribbean.

It continued, in its coastings, the Commander's initial practice of conferring new names, names consistent with European cultural and theological proclivity, on the several territories encountered. Islands of the Lesser Antilles whose indigenous names are now generally forgotten or barely remembered were henceforth to be known as Santa María Galante, Dominica, Guadalupe, Santa María La Antigua, San Martín, and Islas Vírgenes. Also sighted for the first time during the course of this second passage, the island of Borikén, as Puerto Rico was then locally known, was rechristened San Juan Bautista. This genially impertinent act of onomastic appropriation sanctioned, without debate, Europe's proprietal yearning after dominion and ratified its self-bestowed authority to rehistorize the unfamiliar, disregarding as immaterial a part of the region's heritage of recollection of more than five thousand years of previous human settlement and independent historical development. History, thence forward, begins with the newcomer's arrival.

The disingenuous supposition that these territories' sumptuous panorama of natural abundance and tropical fecundity, their varied and "marvelous" reality as Columbus himself often rhapsodized, made them, not so much the exotic site of an ongoing social life, as a privileged venue of choice real estate brimming with unsuspected treasure, unwonted commercial possibility, and the promise of an extraordinarily accelerated upward mobility for audacious and imperious strangers was even more fully confirmed.

It was during and in the aftermath of this second voyage too, beginning with an offshore skirmish in now American St. Croix and Michele de Cuneo's brutal rape of a staunchly uncompliant female captive, that the comforting utopian image of docile and generously accommodating "noble savages" began giving way to the equally convenient "Bad Indian" myth of the recalcitrant, menacing, man-eating Carib. Enslavement and extinction were thus made increasingly palatable as both the reward for resistance to European intrusion and the necessary price of incorporation into the world market of heterogeneous societies and polytheistic peoples more or less efficiently adapted to the conditions and multiple hazards of their environment; and for all of whom land and labor remained an inalienable communal resource rather than a strictly income-producing private asset. The ambience and milieu of the Arawak-Taino and Carib, as regarded by the arriving colonists and conquistadors, was barely more than a *factory* in embryo, so many mines for the extraction of bullion, colonial plantations for the production of profit-yielding exportable crops, personal estates for the complacent enjoyment of a domestic privilege and social power one could not otherwise dream of achieving. Adaptive conformity and a prudent assimilation, through the obligation of labor tribute and religious conversion, were the only real alternatives to marginalization, erasure, or annihilation offered the locals, a Hobson's Choice they often chose to reject.

The decimation of the "Indian," which in the Antilles clearly preceded the introduction of the deadly smallpox virus, produced as early as 1531 a demographic profile in which Africans already constituted a majority of the population in the former Borikén.[1] By 1582 a summary of the history, current state, and general condition of the now definitively renamed island of Puerto Rico commissioned of the Governor by Phillip II, the *Memoria de Melgarejo,* soberly reported: "there are today no original inhabitants left here, save for a very few descended from Indians brought here from Terra Firma, numbering perhaps twelve or fifteen . . . [They] do not speak in their [original] language because the majority of them were born on this island; they are good Christians."[2]

The pagan denizens of a once *conuco*-centered society presided over by *caciques* and *nitainos* had, in the argot of our own time, been effectively "disappeared." "The blame for this punishment" wrote the Crown's then official chronicler of the Indies, "lies in the derelictions and abominable customs and rights of these people."[3] Their polities had been unceremoniously dislodged by the ill fortunes of a lost self-defensive war, demographic catastrophe, the facts of biological intermingling and, in the context of a remorseless colonial order, the mutually creolizing process of a broadly multicultural syncretism. Their sometimes matrilineal social structures were absorbed and superseded by the consolidation of a newly created social hierarchy, one directed by the invader and that, radiating outward from its pivot outpost at La Española, tended to conflate and confuse categories of caste and class, social rank, economic function, and ethnic identity.

An inevitably blended Creole population of whites, *mestizos,* blacks, mulattos, and the legion of their variously commingled descendants emerged, in the course of time, to give this society a singular, polychromatic distinctiveness. Any claim, however tenuous, to an untainted ethnic or racial pedigree remained for all that, and remains to this day, tantamount to unveiling the heraldic family shield of a presumptively less ignominious origin, more ennobling southern European lineage: in the words of the contemporary Puerto Rican poet Luis Palés Matos(1898–1953), the haughty antics of an "aristocracia macaca," or bogus aristocracy,[4] all too anxious to deny "the Antillean is a Spaniard with the manners of a mulatto and the soul of a black."[5]

Genocide, concupiscence, Eurocentrism, disdain for the working majority, and a pigmentocratic pretension: not, to be sure, an auspicious beginning. It persists, for all that, in greater or lesser degree, as the common heritage and a still essential reality of both "Our" and "the Other America." It is, in consequence, doubly part of the charged legacy of uninterrupted colonialism with which Puerto Ricans, and among them most dramatically those now living in the United States, have continually to contend.

II

*"I do not want us to be a colony: neither a colony of Spain
nor a colony of the United States."*
RAMÓN EMETERIO BETANCES, from exile, in 1898

Among the captains traveling with the First Admiral in 1493 was one Juan Ponce de León. It was this native of San Servas del Campo who, after several years' involvement in the *pacification* of eastern La Española and as conquistador and first governor of San Juan Bautista, was most directly responsible for the state of affairs recorded by his grandson in the *Memoria de Melgarejo*. It was this same Juan Ponce de León who, more than a century before the establishment of the first permanent English settlement at Jamestown, Virginia, came upon a land he called La Florida. It was this "discovery" that precipitated Spanish penetration of North America which, after further expeditions by Pánfilo de Nárvaez, Alvar Nuñez Cabeza de Vaca, Hernando De Soto, Francisco Vásquez de Coronado, and Hernando de Alarcón, extended as far north as Nebraska, as far west as California, and, by 1565, had already established the first colonial European city in the territory of the future United States at St. Augustine. Hardly a recent phenomenon, a Hispanic presence has ever since been an inextricable component of the historical and cultural reality of this "other America." It might even plausibly be said, with some justice, that the process of its post-indigenous colonization and settlement, no less than the continental barrios of present-day Boricuas, all began with the uncertain journey of a roving refugee from the island of Puerto Rico.

In the wake of the colonizer's expansion further north and south beyond Mexico, the island would, for nearly two and a half centuries, be relegated to the role of a *presidio,* or strategic military outpost, in defense of the larger empire. English, French, and Dutch challenges to

Spain's New World hegemony were not limited to military incursions, economic encroachment, and territorial acquisition. They included, too, wide circulation of self-promotional images of the savagery and brutality of Spain's conquests, the nationalistic diffusion of a *black legend* of Spanish barbarity. This comprehended the equally self-serving myth of a comparative Hispanic racial inferiority. These are among the historical antecedents of some still conventional perceptions of Latinos within the United States and of the condemnatory reverberations of the word "minority" as generally applied to them.[6] The motif of the Latino who travels everywhere with a blade for his American Express Card was not, in truth, invented yesterday.

Assigned to the periphery, Puerto Rico entered a long period of officially sanctioned commercial isolation, the domestic scarcity of practically everything, and the temporary loss of its former attraction for any incoming migration. Ostensible homesteaders occasionally become no more than temporary people in transit. Colonists who had not already migrated further on were left to make do on an unreliable subsidy from Mexico, a variable agriculture, and an increasingly lucrative contraband trade that, as a matter of necessity, did not exclude clandestine transactions with the colonies and representatives of Spain's imperial rivals. Offering his sarcastically dismissive first impressions of the island's capital early in September 1644, Fray Damían López de Haro, appointed Bishop of Puerto Rico, informs a curious correspondent from Santo Domingo:

> This, Madame, is a tiny isle
> bereft of foodstuffs and of any coin;
> the blacks, as there, don't cover any loin;
> and you'll find more people in Sevilla's jail
>
> Escutcheons common in Castilla
> are on few houses here, but many gents,
> dealers all in hides and ginger's rents:
> the Mendozas, the Guzmans, and Padilla.
>
> There's water in our cisterns when there's rain,
> a Cathedral Church, few priests to offer psalms,
> beautiful women lacking every grace.
>
> Envy, ambition were born here to complain;
> there is much heat, some shade beneath the palms,
> and a little breeze the best thing in the place .[7]

The settlers' subversive and profitable proficiency as smugglers revealed the colony's officially unexploited commercial prospects. This encouraged a change in Spain's policy of not-so-benign neglect. Revenues lost to the island's bustling hidden economy encouraged legislation intended to prevent this financial drain and convert the colony into a higher-yield imperial investment. By 1765, such measures included some relaxation of the monopoly ban on direct trade with foreigners and foreign ports. Stimulation of domestic export sugar production and immigration to the island of "men of means who might establish plantations"[8] were also promoted. There were, in addition, provisions for grants of land to prospective settlers, and the duty-free entry of slaves and agricultural implements. It was an early Spanish imperial antecedent of later American-controlled, post–World War II Puerto Rico's more well-known "Operation Bootstrap."

Trade and economic relations with the United States, already a gathering constant of insular commercial experience, were also formally tolerated for a time. From the days of the contraband trade, in consequence, merchants and their agents became a prime source of intermittent commuters between Puerto Rico and the American mainland. As early as 1828 their number was sufficient to sustain two New York periodicals, the *Mensajero Semanal* [Weekly Messenger] and *El Mercurio de Nueva York* [The New York Mercury] and, two years later, to justify the existence in that city of a Sociedad Benéfica Cubana y Puertorriqueña.[9]

These earliest migrants, however, were never more than transient sojourners for whom the continent was almost exclusively an emporium of exchange or, with the sharpening of moderate Creole nationalist sentiment, a place where sons of the island's rising mercantile and planter classes might spent some brief period getting an education relatively more in keeping with their pragmatically reformist outlook and "modernizing" ambitions.

Steady increase in the legal trade was accompanied by a domestic trend away from the small independent peasant producer that was the direct result of the privatization of land (1778) and its growing concentration, between the 1770s and the 1840s, in an ascendant class of sugarocrats and coffee hacienda *patrones*. A formerly dispersed and heterogeneous mix of subsistence farmers, *agregados,* and day laborers was, at the same time, permanently transformed into the stable pool of reliable labor on which the fortunes of these plantocrats and hacendados depended.[10]

This process of material transformation and internal class differentiation included the first paradoxical literary appearance of the hallmark
figure of the *Jíbaro*. The iconic metaphor of a bucolically rustic peasant
farmer is still nostalgically, if often uncritically, invoked as emblematic
embodiment of a historically evolved and distinctively Puerto Rican national character. Its initial appearance was not so charged with romantic
longing after the pastoral. The idealist texturing would, characteristically, come only after a genuinely *jíbaro* economy's historic passing. Its
context was the inland emergence of coffee to first place over sugar
and tobacco within the national economy in the last decades of the
nineteenth century and a sentimental revival of the rural vignette, or *es-
tampa*, provoked by the Creole elite's nationalist response to American
intervention after 1898. This elite's often unspoken assumption is nicely
expressed by the medieval Spanish poet Jorge Manrique's classic line:
"Cualquier tiempo pasado fué mejor." [Whatever time is past was best.]

For Manuel A. Alonso, whose 1849 collection of ethnographic
sketches, *El Gíbaro*, gave that figure its original emblematic currency,
the traditional independence of the rural *mestizo* peasantry represented,
on the contrary, a stubborn obstacle to the Creole elite's notion of national "progress." His foundational text's entrepreneurial celebration
of "the deals, sales, and exchanges"[11] stimulated by what he saw as
the island's more sympathetic local customs did not prevent him from
regarding the typical peasant of the interior as, on balance, an anachro-
nism and retrogressive force.

> Content with knowing how to govern their own homes as they please and
> limiting themselves to their town without caring what goes on in any other,
> [the *Jíbaros*, Alonso assured his readers, are] promoting selfishness, which
> is the death of all progress; [This] because . . . they have given no thought
> to joining the merchants, manufacturers [*industriales*], and artisans in pe-
> titioning the government to create . . . [schools of agriculture] which are
> much more useful to the country than the dull routine which, with few
> exceptions, is still the rule in the country.[12]

Alonso's complaint accurately reflected the emerging Creole elite's
identification of its own interests with the "genuinely" national spirit of
the "nation." Discreetly eliding the impact of their social and cultural
presence,[13] that notion of nation did not extend to include the caste of
slaves in the cities and coastal plains or the scattered mass of their darker-
hued descendants, except as an ignorable class of the subservient. This

at a time when those of mixed race, and notably mulattos, constituted a recognizable and demonstrably significant element of the population.

The hacendados' "imagined community" of insular patriots for which Alonso's construction of the island's interclass drama primarily spoke was, nonetheless, real enough. Creole aspirations to a domestic dominance of their own, their increasing restiveness under the Spanish colonial rule which effectively precluded it, inevitably pitted moderate nationalist home-rule liberal reformers—autonomists—and more radical *independentista* insurgents against status quo conservatives and peninsular *inconditionales*. The autonomists' failure to make any lasting headway against local and metropolitan colonialist intransigence had, by the 1860s, given independentistas a certain moral edge and political advantage. More fully committed to a total break with Spain, they spoke quite plainly. "Without schools, without books, whose importation is banned by the Customs, without metropolitan newspapers whose circulation is suppressed, without political representation, without municipal self-government . . . ," one prominent intellectual from the southwestern cane country of Cabo Rojo protested, "the physical and mental energies of our people are exclusively absorbed in the production of sugar to sell to England and the United States."[14]

Internecine conflict between coffee growers from the mountainous interior and coastal sugar planter factions of the Creole ruling class was a significant, ultimately never fully resolved, dimension of the process of articulating a sense of specifically Puerto Rican nationhood which is the central burden of our history before the Spanish-Cuban-American War. The writer José Luis González, indeed, goes so far as to argue that in characteristically Latin American fashion, the emerging nation "was so racially, socially, economically, and culturally divided, that it would be more appropriate to speak of two nations. Or more precisely, perhaps, of two national formations that [at the moment of American Intervention in 1898] had not yet had time to fuse into an authentic national synthesis."[15] The impact of this internecine division is evident still in our unrelieved oscillation between the rural *jíbaro* and (for those less inclined to *Hispanophilia*) the coastal or urban-based mulatto as the figurative representation best suited to personify our culturally syncretic national personality. Each, in any case, embodies different aspects of a single but protean Puerto Rican reality.

Creole radical nationalist agitation erupted into insurrection at Lares on September 23, 1868. The years between this *Grito de Lares* and

1898, which include Spain's too late concession of a Charter of Autonomy in 1897, led ultimately to the definitive collapse of Spanish colonialism in Puerto Rico. The epoch marks the decisive preeminence and political consolidation of the island's aspirants to Creole hegemony. It also witnesses the emergence of a looming American imperial presence in the Caribbean and, with the United States' defeat of Spain in the "splendid little war," the eventual acquisition of Puerto Rico as a part of the victor's spoils. The colonial power was now to be the United States. On the very verge of its imminent achievement, then, the historical project of a patrician-governed independent Puerto Rican republic is thus abruptly frustrated, though hardly abandoned or forgotten.[16]

III

"I am new. History made me. My first language was Spanglish.
I was born at the crossroads and I am whole."
Aurora Levins Morales and Rosario Morales, somewhere in the U.S.A.

Suppressed and outlawed by the Spanish, the politics of independence becomes the backdrop against which authentically self-contained enclaves, or *colonias,* of Puerto Ricans resident in the United States are initially established in the final third of the nineteenth century. Committees in support of Puerto Rican independence begin forming there as early as 1867. Creoles of liberal or revolutionary conviction subsequently found, primarily in the Lower East Side and Chelsea sections of New York City, that the United States offered a strategically located refuge from Spanish persecution and a privileged locus for vital planning from which to organize their political education campaigns and insurrectionary projects. Exiled patriots as well known, peripatetic, and influential as Eugenio María de Hostos and Ramón Emeterio Betances had intermittent periods of politically active residence in New York City. Others like José Julio Henna, Roberto H. Todd, Manuel Besosa, and Sotero Figueroa, founders of a Puerto Rican Revolutionary Junta established there on December 22, 1895, enjoyed more fixed and continuous stays. In concert with exiled Cubans ably led by José Martí, it was in the United States that their developing vision of a liberated federation of Hispanophone Caribbean islands—the notion of a *federación antillana*—achieved a fuller programmatic precision.

The formation, in 1892, of the Partido Revolucionario Cubano y Puertorriqueño, of which the New York Junta soon became the officially constituted Puerto Rican branch, gave it a certain tangible institutional materiality. Political and social clubs like Los Independientes (1888), Las Dos Antillas (1890), and Borinquen (1894) and a variety of pro-independence periodicals gave this *colonia* both infrastructural cohesion and collective purpose. They also created the atmosphere of a palpable, participatory sense of unbroken civic and cultural continuity with life on the island. That "political interlacing" of geographic and national spheres to which Professor Clara E. Rodríguez, among others, points as one of the distinct features of the experience of present-day *Puerto Ricans Born in the U.S.A.* is, at least in part, a heritage of the relative congregational efficacy of this multifaceted revolutionary activity.[17]

By criteria of race, education, social standing, and partisan inclination, these earliest migrants, with several notable exceptions, tended to a comparative class homogeneity. A majority of them belonged to the literate and patrician, progressive white Creole middle and upper middle classes. Directly reflective of the character of a leading sector of the island's Creole elite, this social complexion helped effectively to cushion it against the (racist) charge of cultural degeneration with which insular co-nationals would condescendingly stigmatize later generations of their overseas barrio brethren.

Their general outlook and worldview, still that of the transient sojourner, was that of political exiles. Their affective sense of audience and proper place remained in crucially significant ways that went beyond mere language, unequivocally, structurally extraterritorial. The literature they produced and the polemics they engaged in were, but for the locale, almost seamlessly continuous with Creole traditions and with what then absorbed the general attention of similar groups on the island. *In,* but most emphatically not *of* the United States, they were, the many anguishes of exile notwithstanding, relatively untormented by either divided national loyalties or any agonizing personal crisis of cultural identity.

As the century came to a close, their effort effectively to consolidate a multiclass revolutionary coalition, the associations, social clubs, and publications of this community of émigré Creoles increasingly

> appealed not only to the political founding exiles instrumental in their creation, but to the trickle of skilled and unskilled Puerto Rican workers who began to make their homes in the city during the first decades of the twentieth century. Among the latter group, some individuals had come as

contracted agricultural or factory workers; others as skilled artisans; still others had followed a pattern of migration originating within the island's internal population movements from rural to urban sectors, which culminated in migration.[18]

The annexation of Puerto Rico to the United States was a crucially significant factor, providing an important further stimulus to that emerging pattern of migration.

This more recent group of economic exiles, among whom unemployed, but skilled, literate, politically active cigarmakers and *tabaqueros* were well represented, gave their *colonia* a certain social-class heterogeneity and, gradually, a greater feeling of relative permanence.

As early as 1901 official experiments with a policy of "surplus labor" migration had already gained some currency among island annexationist politicians. Such operations, one witness tells us, "had the support of the [American-appointed] governor and were encouraged by the leadership of the [pro-statehood] Partido Republicano, which considered it the best solution to the problem of unemployment and so-called overpopulation."[19] American investment, in the meantime, poured into the island. American capital and the Puerto Rican population began increasingly to move in opposite directions. This early intimation of the theoretical underpinnings of the central structural role immigration was to assume as an "escape valve" for the insular economy and its politics in the two and a half decades after 1940 further contributed to the growing number of these economic exiles.

As they took jobs in the city, had families, set up an infrastructure of modest neighborhood businesses and, however reluctantly, set down roots, they textured communities of Puerto Rican nationals with the burgeoning signs of a more clearly identifiable (im)migrant consciousness. They were the eddying, exploratory edge of a great tropical cascade destined shortly to create of their asphalt atolls in Manhattan, Brooklyn, and (later) the Bronx richly layered, syncretized replicas of the island(s) of their eviction. These pioneers are our barrios' most indisputably founding settlers.

Arturo Alfonso Schomburg is at once a representative and signally precursory figure. Leaving behind his job in a San Juan stationary shop, he arrives in New York in April 1891. Almost immediately he becomes an energetic participant in the then flourishing independence movement, rising to Secretary of the revolutionary club Las Dos Antillas. Firmly settled in the city, he goes on, after 1898, to establish close ties with the local African American community, helping to found the American Negro Academy (1911), later becoming its president. The coordinates of his new milieu, no less than those of his insular Puerto Rican experience, become an increasingly undismissable point of reference.

Schomburg brought to New York a passionate interest in the history and culture of the New World Negro. His notable, but still insufficiently studied participation in the early phases of the Harlem Renaissance movement was entirely consistent with this interest. It was, at the same time, tinged with a Caribbean mulatto's suspicion and wariness of the snares and pitfalls of a rigidly dichotomous racial environment. He rejected both "the blatant Caucasian racialist with his theories and assumptions of race superiority and dominance" and his "Ethiopian counterpart—the rash and rabid amateur who glibly tries to prove half of the world's geniuses to have been Negroes and to trace the pedigree of nineteenth-century Americans to the Queen of Sheba."[20] Schomburg's localized use of "Americans" in this passage already suggests the measure of his progression from a sojourner to a settler-(im)migrant consciousness. Schomburg's collegial association with Alain Locke, Carter G. Woodson, and W. E. B. Du Bois would also permit him, in his own work and thinking, to articulate arguments that, for a later generation, would lead to the formation of Black Studies and, almost immediately, Puerto Rican Studies programs.

It is, nonetheless, for the impact of his activity as bibliophile, book collector, and curator for the New York Public Library that Schomburg is popularly remembered. The impressive private collection of books and materials on Negro history of this self-educated historian became the core of the world-celebrated, Harlem-based Center for Research in Black Culture, which now bears the Anglized version of his name. At his death, in 1938, Schomburg, a transitional figure if ever there was one, had endowed his fellow residents with a legacy of self-assertive achievement to which the Puerto Rican and African American communities might both point with some pride.[21]

Bernardo Vega and Jesus Colón, both of whom arrive in the states within a year of Puerto Ricans being all declared American citizens in 1917, further mark the fluid point of transition between sojourners and (im)migrant settlers. The first, a thirty-year-old "white" *jíbaro* from Cayey then already active in the organized workers' movement, arrives as a semi-skilled *tabaquero* on the steamship *Coamo*. The second, a darker-skinned sixteen-year-old *trigueño* from the same town, comes as a stowaway and busboy aboard the S.S. *Carolina*. These similarities and differences are themselves subtle registers of something of the shifting social character of the migration.

The reception that as Puerto Ricans each received on arrival was equally unwelcoming. Vega remembers that "For the majority of Yankees, Puerto Ricans were an expendable species—an ignorant, juvenile and uncultured people."[22] Both set down deep and determined root in the Latino community then gradually taking shape. They worked to expand its institutional and pragmatic political base and, against the lingering force of a sojourner mentality, to safeguard its cultural integrity in this new setting. As founding members of the Workers' Athenaeum in 1925, Vega tells us,

> We were interested in setting up an educational center which would counteract the widespread tendency among Puerto Ricans in New York to consider their stay a temporary thing and to continue to believe that they would eventually return to the island. We were well aware that a new generation of Puerto Ricans was being born and raised in the city, and that they demanded our close attention. It was important to help them learn their cultural origins. And . . . [he is clearly happy to report] we did accomplish some of this.[23]

Vega, whose *Memoirs* of more than three decades' residence is our most vividly detailed eyewitness account of these formative years in the city, was of the two the one whose consciousness and experience remained most unambiguously continuous with that of the earlier sojourners. He would eventually retire to Puerto Rico. Jesus Colón never permanently went back, but remained to become, in weekly columns and essays later collected as *A Puerto Rican in New York and Other Sketches* and *The Way It Was and Other Writings*, the chronicler of a generation that, well into the fifties, remained "unsung, unheralded and practically unknown to their fellow New Yorkers, except through the filter of an assiduously cultivated hostility, distrust, and ignorance."[24] Writing in a standard English already lexically and culturally accented with the signs of his Spanish language background, Colón, not incidentally, also became the precursor of a distinctively inflected, syncretic mainland branch of Puerto Rican letters.

The very modest seminal nucleus of which these individuals formed a part had, by 1930, grown to over 100,000 souls, nearly 60,000 of whom made their homes in the stretch of East and South Central Harlem now normally modified by the prefix "Spanish." In the five decades after, spreading outward beyond Brooklyn, the Bronx, and the Eastern corridor to establish at least some token presence in almost every state of the Union, the (im)migrant community resident in the United States would grow eventually to include approximately half of the total Puerto Rican population. By 1980, a majority of that number would, in fact, be living outside of New York State. In the twenty or so years running from the end of World War II to the early sixties, they would, in their thousands, convert the clippers of *La Pan American, La Eastern,* and *La TransCaribbean* into the Puerto Rican Airbuses which they quickly became. By 2000, their number had reached the 3.4 million the census of that year recorded. Still more recent estimates note that more than half (58 percent) of this number were born within the precincts of the continental United States, and still further observe that this Diaspora looms fair soon demographically to outnumber the 3.8 million inhabitants of its ancestral island homeland.[25]

IV

¿En qué lengua me entiende, en que lengua por fin te podré hablar . . . ?
Nicolás Guillén

To the insular architects of The Great Migration, this massive population transfer was part of a broader general strategy. That strategy's ostensible purpose was to promote development and reduce extensive poverty and unemployment through the rapid transformation of Puerto Rico from an agricultural into an industrialized society. Offers of economic and political incentives to potential overseas investors—among them tax holidays of up to seventeen years, what amounted to the creation of "export enclaves," and an officially harnessed labor movement—were all designed to attract what proved to be primarily capital-intensive American enterprises. Like Puerto Rico's official assumption of the shibboleth of "Free Associated State" in July 1952, this program ultimately only aggravated the island economy's structural weaknesses, further solidifying its colonial dependency on the United States.

The almost deliberate disgorgement of a significant portion of the Puerto Rican population was a pivotal element of this vision of development. It was also an unacknowledged measure of the magnitude of the insular government's failure to effect any growth with social equity.

Regarded as an expendable and problematic excess, Puerto Ricans of modest, little, or no means received the proverbial push from behind. Those receiving this push, it merits mentioning, were, compared to previous migratory waves, generally less skilled, from rural areas or the margins of capitoline urban centers, and of darker complexion. It all accentuated the fact that this migration, like that of contemporary Francophone islanders to Paris or Anglophone West Indians to London (and in contrast with more conventional European migrations to the United States), was intimately related to the terms of a specifically colonial relationship.

The need for labor in the United States and patrician Creole acceptance of the fabled theory of an American Melting Pot provided insular planners an apparently face-saving *raison d'être*. "We reasoned," Governor Luis Muñoz Marín himself confessed in an interview shortly before his death, that "after two generations the problem of the Puerto Ricans in New York would no longer exist, simply because by then they would no longer be Puerto Ricans."[26] They would, that is, no longer be "our" problem. In this, History proved him, rather dramatically, to be a poor prophet.

Probable (im)migrants for such patricians were, in the economic, social, and presumptively cultural sense of the term, so many potential castaways. Outcasts or castaways, they proved an impressively resilient, resourceful, and regularly returning lot. Cleaving to their Antillean singularity, they would ultimately forge of their experience and adversities a Puerto Rican identity which, moving sinuously and with ever greater knowledgeable ease, between the various coordinates of their bicultural universe, would effectively sabotage, "at home" and "abroad," any statically fixed, reductive and proprietal or narrowly patrician notion of "authentic" Puerto Ricanness. In this, too, Muñoz, to his chagrin, proved a dubious oracle.

The founders of the Workers' Athenaeum were more prescient. The generation of those raised, if not always born in the United States that they foresaw was, indeed, taking shape and, by the later sixties, would come increasingly into its own. In 1941 Piri Thomas, whose autobiographical *Down These Mean Streets* (1967) bore spectacular testimony to its literary debut, was a fourteen-year-old youngster registering the fact that it took a war to produce a job for his father, taking his freshman courses in that "sort of science" of hanging around on the block.[27] His fellow barrio school classmates Humberto Cintrón, the creator of

Frankie Cristo (1972), and Lefty Barreto, becoming conscious he was *Nobody's Hero* (1976), were also ragged-edged adolescents. Nicolasa Mohr, then only six, was just beginning to acquire her many memories of a Bronx to be remembered. Ed Vega, only a year younger and still eight years from leaving Ponce for New York, had not yet begun to dream his mocking *Mendoza's Dreams* (1987) of *The Comeback* (1985). Miguel Algarín, poet, "juggler," and "philosopher of the sugar cane that grows between the cracks of concrete sidewalks,"[28] had barely seen the first light of day; Pedro Pietri, whose *Puerto Rican Obituary* (1973) would with mordant compassion memorably capture the underside of our "American experience," was only three years old; and Julio Marzán, the scrupulous, keen-eyed, and subtle, only five.

The Puerto Rican community in New York had assumed its defining contours. For this new generation, then, it was this community and its eventual branchings to other cities that provided, as much as any memories of the flamboyant-scented precincts of Santurce, Cayey, Ponce, or Mayaguez, the spaces of their experience. Fixed in memory or allegiance, experienced oftentimes only briefly, at a distance, or at second remove, in the images of parents, family, and friends, Puerto Rico was simultaneously *nuestro país* and an ideal or imagined landscape: *la isla soñada*. As a place beyond immediate accessibility, it oftentimes assumed the utopian proportions of a paradise lost. It was as though, biting into our madeleine, one experienced all the remembrance of things past it provoked, with its sharp poignancies and longing, but without the immediate sensory impression of having bitten into *un delicioso pastel*.

The urban and concrete landscapes of the United States, its itinerant labor farms and fields, were, beyond any possible denying, now part of our milieu and defining singularity. It was certainly not, in the usual sense, an exile's refuge, or sojourner's furlough; nor were these "new" Puerto Ricans any longer, like Schomburg, Vega, and Colón, properly described as pioneering "Newcomers." The most neophyte among us was taken into the bosom of already fairly well defined and thriving communities.

Finding ourselves at the white-hot center of a clash within and between distinct histories and cultures—both now also, in some very real sense, our own—and in the equivocal, polymorphic interstices in which multiple worlds contend, cities like New York, Patterson, Newark, Philadelphia, Boston, Chicago, Hartford, Miami, San Francisco, Los Angeles, and, not so paradoxically the island locales to which we all insistently return, now become the places where history compels us to affirm, (re)establish, form, and articulate our individual and collective claims to a hybrid, distinctively plural, at once continuous and *not "Other,"* Puerto Rican new Creole singularity.

V

. . . punishing with
Their absence, or much too present, re-
Minding us our labor is a product of small parts:
With, by, for, in, on, against.
JULIO MARZÁN

For a people reflecting a kaleidoscopic range of "color," the absolutism of the American racial system would, in the event, prove especially incomprehensible, corrosively disruptive. Paradoxically too, a vexing spur to the need for more adequate definitions. The relation between race and nationality, and nationality as a predicate of geographical location, a given form of language, or an inherited and willingly embraced cultural affiliation, would almost immediately have to be examined. All the available categories simply proved insufficient to the contours of our reality. Tempered in this crucible, Alonso's emblematic figure had yet again to be boldly reimagined, in Felipe Luciano's subversive, doubly defiant affirmation, as a "Jíbaro, mi negro lindo, jíbaro, my pretty nigger."

Manifestly both black and white, we could turn our back on neither without heavy cost. It bordered on a form of suicide. In Thomas's words, "It wasn't right to be ashamed of what one was. It was like hating Momma for the color she was and Poppa for the color he wasn't."[29] Identification with African Americans, our closest friends, neighbors, and sometimes too our most intimate antagonists, with whom we share(d) more than then just a common social condition, came rather more naturally but sometimes merely sharpened, without resolving, the tug of war between race and nationality. "In the middle of a crowd of American Negroes [marching for their civil rights], fighting like them [against the police]. And for the first time in his life . . . [feeling] glad that he was a Negro and an American," one of the characters in Manuel Manrique's *Island in Harlem* feels compelled to ask himself, "But am I really an American? I'm black—no doubt about that. But an American?"[30] This charged and pregnant question, with which nineteenth- and early twentieth-century "settlers" and sojourners were not particularly troubled, is one of the central dramas in the lives of this newer generation of Puerto Ricans in the United States. Black, white, or brown, it could not be indefinitely avoided. The fact and particular tensions of being Puerto Rican in America imposed its centrality.

> If in Puerto Rico there was no need to put into question the actuality of being Puerto Rican because there, after all, everybody was Puerto Rican and lives in a place that is "their own" called Puerto Rico, here the Puerto Rican was called a Spic, and was not in his own house. If there it was [comparatively] no big deal to be more or less dark of skin, here one was confronted with a new racial definition that separates him [sometimes literally] from his brothers: *White, Black, Puerto Rican,* which makes him [or her] the intermediate point in the struggle between the dominant white society and the African American community. And one was [thus] no longer Puerto Rican as a consequence of belonging to a [particular] cultural community but as the result of having "a certain color," whose hue is never quite known. The North American will say to the "lighter" ones: "But you don't look Puerto Rican." Many who had taken for granted their Puerto Ricanness began to start thinking about it, to analyze it in order to understand it. Ironically, [a] racist North American society [thus] contributes to their having [assertively] to define themselves as Puerto Ricans in order to survive.[31]

One does not have to share what seems to me Victor Fragoso's rather oversanguine view of insular racial (and class) relations to grasp the importance and comparative accuracy of the particular paradox to which he points. Puerto Ricans' stubborn refusal to relinquish their Antillean identity, fade, "blend in," and disappear unproblematically into the "American Mainstream," moreover, directly undermines traditional images, conventional expectations, and previously customary guidelines for all immigrants to the United States. The presumption of the subaltern's cultural deficiency which has informed the "civilizing mission" of all assimilationist theory from Christopher Columbus to Nathan Glazer, Daniel Moynihan, Oscar Handlin, Oscar Lewis and beyond, is at once resisted and turned on its head: it is American categories of perception, not the (im)migrant's experience that are, socially and analytically, ultimately found wanting. Our assumptions of what we took to be "home," and why, are likewise, and unavoidably, subjected to closer scrutiny and interrogation.

Controversies about language and nomenclature, about articulating the noun(s) and adjectives properly descriptive of our cultural background and historic experience—Puerto Rican, Nuyorican, or "Am e Rícan, with the big R and the accent on the i!"[32]—in a language— Spanish, English, Spanglish— proper to and consistent with that experience are another facet of this same dialectic. For all the dissension and anxiety they can still arouse, such controversies have nonetheless also led to a creative, exploratory, and generally fruitful reconsideration of outdated premises and inadequate perceptions of our historical and cultural process. They effectively dramatize the fact that the usual categories of appropriateness and "authenticity" in language use, culture, and national definition, in Puerto Rico no less than in the United States, are in need of some revision. They challenge equally the condescension of American assimilationists, the ahistorical linguistic purism of language conservatives, and the not-so-latent Hispanophilia, class (and yes, racial) prejudices of certain insular nationalist patricians.

What emerges from all this is the bicultural and binationally problematic, inventive, intrinsically challenging nature of this "new" Puerto Rican (im)migrant who, in a very important sense, is in fact no longer an (im)migrant at all, but the unmistakable historical product and extension of the "old" Puerto Rican (im)migrant, and clings as fiercely to his island roots and legacy. No less inveterate commuters, these Puerto Ricans' "place" is now both "here" and "there" and, as invariably, neither "here" nor "there." Between "one" and "the other," it is no longer the pole points or patrolled borders but the syncretic results of constantly moving between and beyond them that increasingly emerges as central. It is the oscillating intensities of that being "in-between," at once rooted, fixed, and in constant motion, that nourishes a common, creatively defiant endurance and dynamic vitality.

The splendid assembly of contributive creators that collective energy has produced, in the last several decades, moreover, has been neither monotonal nor univocal. It represents a chorus of different voices, each with its own timbre, each adding its enriching texture to the larger communal song. Nor is it limited to a large, daily growing number of literati which, in addition to those already mentioned, includes, among others, Jack Agueros, Sandra María Esteves, Martín Espada, Edward Gallardo, Victor Hernández Cruz, Luisita López Torregrosa, Carmen de Monteflores, Rosario Morales, Judith Ortiz Cofer, Luis Reyes Rivera, Edward Rivera, Abraham Rodríguez, Jr., and Edwin Torres. It embraces the work of an impressive array of re-evaluative historians, sociologists, educators, political scientists, cultural critics, and general commentators that, among many others, includes Edna Acosta Belén, Samuel Betances, Frank Bonilla, Juan Flores, Sonia Nieto, and Virginia Sánchez Korral. The better known roster of actors, artists, and popular musicians, to name only those perhaps most immediately familiar, includes folk like Miriam Colón, José Ferrer, Juano Hernández, Raul Juliá, Rita Moreno, and Jimmy Smits; Elroy Blanco, Nick Quijano, and Juan Sánchez; Ray Barreto, Joe Bataan, Willie Colón, Joe Cuba, and Charlie and Eddie Palmieri. The emergence of Puerto Rican and Latino Studies Programs, no less than the burgeoning explosion of journals and reviews, as well as archival institutions of art and culture such as the Museo del Barrio, and of research and documentation such as the Center for Puerto Rican Studies at Hunter College, New York, likewise testifies to and adds still further dimension to this rich and daily expanding repertoire of creative ferment and vitality. The sustenance they all draw from, and the energy they each return to, the communities which are the ultimate source of their arts and endeavor are so many encouraging affirmationsof our individual and collective assumption of the right and obligation variously and independently to engage with and look critically at our past, and its not unmixed legacies, as well as at the evolving lively new contexts of our shared, communal responsibility to the future. Secure in the integrity of our syncretic, still unfolding Puerto Rican originality, distinctiveness, and singularity, we can, at the same time, confidently assert,, with Aimé Césaire: "I am of no nationality ever contemplated by the chancelleries."[33]

Notes

1. Fernando Picó, *Historia general de Puerto Rico* (Río Piedras: Huracán-Academia, 1986), 143.

2. Aida R. Caro Costas, *Antología de lecturas de historia de Puerto Rico (siglos XV–XVIII)* (San Juan: Editorial Universitaria, 1989), 167–68.

3. Gonzalo Fernández de Oviedo y Valdés, *The Conquest and Settlement of the Island of Boriquen or Puerto Rico,* trans. and ed. Daymond Turner (Avon, Conn.: Limited Editions Club, 1975), 63.

4. Luis Palés Matos, *Poesías 1915–1956* (San Juan: Editorial U.P.R., 1957), 213.

5. Cited in Arcadio Díaz Quiñones, *El almuerzo en la hierba (Lloréns Torres, Palés Matos, René Marqués)* (Río Piedras: Ediciones Huracán, 1982), 94.

6. For a review-summary of how such attitudes influenced romantic, social Darwinist, and Pan-Americanist North American scholarship and historiography

on Latin America, see Benjamin Keen, "Main Currents in U.S. Writings on Colonial Spanish America, 1884–1984," *Hispanic American Historical Review* 65, no. 4 (1984): 657–82. Phillip Gleason offers an interesting, though not wholly unpolemical, examination of the more recent history of the term "minority" among social scientists and sociologists in his "Minorities (Almost) All: The Minority Concept in American Social Thought," *American Quarterly* 43, no. 3 (September 1991): 392–424.

7. Caro Costas, *Antología,* 316. The translation is my own. The complete Spanish language text reads:

> Esta es Señora una pequeña islilla
> falta de bastimentos y dineros,
> andan los negros como en esa en cueros
> y hay más gente en la cárcel de Sevilla,
> aquí están los blasones de Castilla
> en pocas casas, muchos cavalleros
> todos tratantes en xenxibre y cueros
> los Mendoza, Gusmanes y el Padilla.
> Ay agua en los algibes si ha llobido,
> Iglesia catedral, clérigos pocos,
> hermosas damas faltas de donaire,
> la ambición y la embidia aquí an nacido,
> mucho calor y sombra de los cocos,
> y es lo mejor de todo un poco de ayre.

8. Ibid., 462.

9. Virginia E. Sánchez Korrol, *From Colonia to Community: The History of Puerto Ricans in New York City, 1917–1948* (Westport, Conn.: Greenwood Press, 1983), 12.

10. Dislodged from the comparative autonomy of their former status, these workers might be said to be, structurally speaking, the distant historical relatives of the peasants and modest landholders who, in the twentieth century, were similarly displaced and transformed into the unemployed pool of surplus labor produced in the long wake of American intervention.

11. Manuel A. Alonso, *El jíbaro* (Río Piedras: Editorial Cultural, 1968), 19.

12. Ibid., 97.

13. As late as 1788, noting that already "mulattos . . . constitute the majority of the island's population," the historian Fray Iñigo Abbad y Lasierra emphasizes that "for all that, there is nothing so shameful on this island as being Negro or one of their descendants: a white person can with impunity insult them with the vilest expressions." *Historia geográfica, civil y natural de la isla de San Juan Bautista de Puerto Rico* (San Juan: Porta Coelli Ediciones, 1971), 202.

14. Gordon K. Lewis, *Puerto Rico: Freedom and Power in the Caribbean* (New York: Monthly Review Press, 1963), 61.

15. José Luis González, *El país de cuatro pisos* (Río Piedras: Ediciones Huracán, 1980), 25.

16. In the face of its disillusionment and a frequently crass Anglo-Saxon ethnocentrism, nationalist sentiment shifts to a focus on the disruptive, dismissive impact of the American presence in Puerto Rico. This retrenchment necessarily includes a sustained, spirited, and abiding defense of Puerto Rico's national culture and patrimony against all attempts to assimilate the island to the needs— economic and political—and the cultural norms of the new colonialism.

17. Clara E. Rodríguez, *Puerto Ricans Born in the U.S.A.* (Boston: Unwin Hyman), 15.

18. Sánchez Korrol, *From Colonia to Community*, 12.

19. César Andreu Iglesias, ed., *Memoirs of Bernardo Vega: A Contribution to the History of the Puerto Rican Community in New York*. (New York: Monthly Review Press, 1984), 89.

20. Elinor Des Verney Sinnette, *Arthur Alfonso Schomburg: Black Bibliophile and Collector* (New York and Detroit: The New York Public Library and Wayne State University Press, 1989), 115.

21. Sinnette notes that invitees to a service in his memory a year later "read like a 'Who's Who' of black literati and scholars in the United States." Ibid., 192.

22. Iglesias, *Memoirs of Bernardo Vega*, 91.

23. Ibid., 144.

24. Jesús Colón, *A Puerto Rican in New York and Other Sketches* (New York: International Publishers, 1982), 10.

25. Edna Acosta-Belén and Carlos Santiago, *Puerto Ricans in the United States: A Contemporary Portrait* (Boulder, Colo.: Lynne Rienner, 2006), 1.

26. Edgardo Rodríguez Juliá, *Las tribulaciones de Jonás* (Río Piedras: Ediciones Huracán, 1981), 39.

27. Piri Thomas, *Down These Mean Streets* (New York: Vintage Books, 1991), 14.

28. Miguel Algarín and Miguel Piñero, eds., *Nuyorican Poetry: An Anthology of Puerto Rican Words and Feelings* (New York: William Morrow, 1975), 10.

29. Thomas, *Down These Means Streets*, 121.

30. Manuel Manrique, *Island in Harlem* (New York: John Day, 1966), 196.

31. Víctor Fragoso, "Notas sobre la expresión teatral de la comunidad puertorriqueña de Nueva York," *Revista del Instituto de Cultura Puertorriqueña* no. 70 (enero–marzo 1976), 22.

32. Tato Laviera, *AmeRican* (Houston: Arte Público Press, 1985), 95.

33. Aimé Césaire, *Return to My Native Land* (Middlesex, England: Penguin Books, 1970), 68.

One Boricua's Baldwin

For Luis, Ralphie, Cookie, Clara, and, in memoriam, Joe

WHEN THE word finally came, it was already dimly half-expected. He had been ill and, the bulletins of *radio bemba* (word of mouth) had it, the illness was serious, quite possibly life-threatening, nothing to be toyed with. Reports from Amherst—where until recently we had each found a relatively compatible, putatively temporary home—had lately turned elliptically intimate, tellingly vague: at once discreetly circumspect and cautiously allusive. The implications of only half-informed rumor and the details offered by more reliable sources had become gradually almost indistinguishable from one another. Those of us among that vast constellation of his many admirers, teaching colleagues, fellow writers, and friends were becoming increasingly uneasy, and, it was obvious, our anxiety and apprehension were starting to show. A shadow hung ominously in the air. Our worst fear was turning, by degrees, into an open family secret, suspended on the brink of an imminent and terrible general disclosure. It would eventually come in a cable from St. Paul de Vence by way of Paris, with its mists and greys, in the early hours of the first morning in December 1987.

All of our premonitions ultimately did not prepare us or mitigate in the least the immediate jolt of astonishment produced by the actual news. They did not lessen in any meaningful way our bewilderment and sudden perplexity, or the staggering sensation of utter disbelief before the startling announcement: *James Baldwin is dead.* The most conscience-stinging, prophetic, prodigally *loving* of our native sons would no longer shake our dungeons with new notes. He had served his time, and the witness and uncommon dignity of his passion down at the cross were now all that we had left. A recurring awareness— anonymous and grateful—of the offering and signal blessing that had been his *wrassling* recoiled instinctively against the knowledge of this

137

fall. That phenomenon of almost saintly innocence and righteous fire, in which a whole generation of people like myself found grace, warmth, and a decisive light, had this time left us definitively to check out the evidence of things not seen. The confident, pop familiarity of our ordinary routines was abruptly, inexorably penetrated by the sharp-edged melancholy of our own versions of Sonny's Blues; and, in the unsettled sanctuary of our own private amen corner, they reverberated with the harsh, piercing intensities of a lone saxophone echoing through Central Park, at once unmistakably communal and strictly personal.

Spoken with grave terseness in a measured, muted voice indicative of the speaker's thorough appreciation of the tangible weight and reverberation of his words, the full resonance and import of this loss, the stark simplicity and unyielding finality of the sentence was stunning. *Tell me how long the train's been gone.* The shock of it would find my sense of incredulity and confusion surprisingly intact, the intensity of our shared sorrow entirely undiminished. By some ancient, possibly even necessary, sleight of mind against the force of any intuition, the news was an affront, and so simply inadmissible.

The Basque philosopher novelist Miguel de Unamuno would have understood. It was precisely what he had in mind when, after Pascal and with Antonio Machado, his Sevillian colleague and compatriot, he stubbornly maintained that, in the face of the self-evidently unjust and cosmically irrational, the heart denies and adamantly resists the fateful truth of what the head already knows. Like Unamuno, James Baldwin had a keen sense of *The Tragic Sense of Life*.[1] They shared, too, a historically concrete, intensely personal sense of national crisis and a courageous advocacy of the collectively hygienic requirement and ethical urgency of always choosing honor before personal security and safety. In the face of Franco's minions, Unamuno also knew that "sometimes to be silent is to lie"[2] and that, as Baldwin put it, "people who shut their eyes to reality simply invite their own destruction, and anyone who insists on remaining in a state of innocence long after that innocence is dead turns himself into a monster."[3] An unsparing dealer in paradox and conundrum—one of Baldwin's favorite words—Unamuno surely would have applauded the obstinate integrity of the Afro-American's best prose, its incontrovertible potency and surgical efficiency. With Machado—had he too lived long enough to read it—Unamuno would have vigorously celebrated what the creator of *Juan de Mairena* would have instantly recognized: the aristocracy of its roots in the experience of average and ordinary folk; the communal idiom of its cadences and rhythms; the elegant asperity and subversive authority derived from its exacting lack of cant or condescension; and Baldwin's attentive, steady struggle as an artist to be at once honest with himself and fully worthy of the promise of those roots. The worldly burden and ordeal, though certainly not the triumph, of his furious passage had now ended: James Baldwin was dead. Like every other death, this one too came hapless and untimely; but, *Lord, didn't he ramble.*

In the days and weeks that followed the rituals of release, public eulogy, and tribute, my mind kept coming back to the security of James Baldwin's special place in my own private pantheon. Sorting out my memories intermittently, I fixed especially on the revitalizing elation of discovery in that first reading of his work; on the subtle shifts of context, emphasis, and sympathetic—though not uncritical—response that were the stuff of later reading or experience; and, of course, on those precious few moments when—almost in ironic corollary to our common origins in Harlem—our lives fleetingly, almost anonymously, touched, or intersected.

Initial discovery was quite casual and serendipitous. It was the summer of 1959. I was on the verge of seventeen. With my older ace boon coons, Luis and his brother Ralphie, I was contriving with secret determination to nourish my nascent intellectual enthusiasms while still hanging out, swaggering, hip, and fly; and—with the canny Machiavellian wariness that comes with the territory—trying quite literally to stay alive, maneuvering between a meager, sometimes spirit-maiming schooling and a materially impoverished, but still beguiling if unforgiving, street. Luis was the first to come upon and introduce me to a copy of *Notes of a Native Son.* The most immediately striking feature of the Beacon paperback number thirty-nine was, I vividly remember, the conspicuous unconventionality of its cover. Against a plain white background, a solitary, unmistakably black, and street-seasoned face filled nearly every inch of space. Candid and searching, it looked out at the reader. Like the tormented Christs crucified on a thousand tenement walls, its glistening, protruding eyes—hurt, sensitive, and set—appeared simultaneously to fix and slowly to follow as one moved.

The advertising clichés of the day were already dominated by the garish, the lascivious, or sensational. Blacks on book jackets—save as figures of amusement, archetypical threat, or enticing sexual menace— were a nearly complete *absence.* This cover, then, was something of a novelty and, whether by coincidence or by design, made a statement as subtle as it was arresting and dramatic. Its contrast with convention made the fact of that *absence* immediate, all the more palpable and apparent. It was the first thing about *Notes* to catch my attention. As he held the book with cool nonchalance during the course of one of our habitual walks—through Harlem to a then comparatively "upscale" South Bronx and back that had become our improvised, spontaneous colloquium and my first real college—Luis's excitement about it became contagious. His enthusiasm for the unknown author effectively quickened the curiosity and interest the book's cover had provoked. Luis's recommendations over the years—James Weldon Johnson's *Autobiography of an Ex-Colored Man,* the work of E. Franklin Frazier, the tales of Poe, the *Post* columns of Langston Hughes, and of Max Lerner—had invariably proved more pertinent and stirring than anything offered by my airplane mechanic's curriculum. And so, intent, still intellectually unanchored, inchoately groping, I read my first James Baldwin.

It was, as I said, the summer of 1959. Eisenhower was on the eighteenth hole of his presidency. McCarthy, though neither his influence nor his legacy, had died only two years before. Fidel Castro, unorthodox and unpredictable enough for the times, was not yet absolute anathema to the Ugly American. "Hispanics" were still "spiks" and Ricans not yet "Neo." *Salsa,* confined to the ranks of our native cognoscenti and the dance floor of the Palladium Ballroom, was still a gourmet's delight. Black people were officially called "Negroes," whose major tactical focus was the Jim Crow laws, with all that they implied, and whose strategic compass, almost everyone anxiously or piously assumed, was fixed on the harbor of full integration and the ineffable privilege of a naïve emulation. The Civil Rights Movement, catalyzed by the Montgomery Bus Boycott of 1954, was still generally regarded as a *southern thing* and Martin Luther King as a primarily regional, if not entirely local, leader. Orval Faubus's defiance of the Supreme Court order to desegregate Arkansas's Central High School in 1958 had made Little Rock the symbol of American apartheid and the southern way of life.

In the more liberal, smugly complacent North, Robert Welch's John Birch Society, growing to more than sixty thousand strong, had already begun peddling its candymaker's correlative dogmas as the proper canons of *American Opinion.* Vance Packard's status seekers, dreaming of *La dolce vita,* were the still unnamed, silent majority. Their white young lions, the defiant ones, lost as poor Charlie on the MTA, fought off the loneliness of the long distance runner and, barely two years on the road, gathered for a naked lunch. Some came running to the vertigo of Elvis Presley or "Pop Art." Lady Chatterley's lover, beating the obscenity rap, moved into Peyton Place with Sleeping Beauty and The Man With the Golden Arm, while the rest of us said our goodbyes to Columbus. Gigi continued to breakfast at Tiffany's, as the man in the grey flannel suit, feeling the seven year itch, ravished Lolita's lust for life. Bigger Thomas was more or less forgotten on death row. After a last delivery of fine clothes to the Jew, Jesse B. Simple, always the invisible man and nobody's hero, returned to his own edge of the city. Watching his own festering raisin in the sun, Frankie Cristo, trying to avoid the cops, escaped into the subway, as the Senecas turned social and the Viceroys and Enchanters, succumbing to heroin and smack more than ever they did to the Dragons or the Italian Redwings, formed a brother club. Jesus Colón was still writing to his grandmother, telling her not to come, while his fellow *Boricuas* in *Nueva York*, dreaming of finally paying off their family installments, wrapped *Borinquen, el país*, in the nimbus of utopia, went out to play the numbers, resigned themselves to a down/town *slave*, or gambled on the promise of salvation, that last hustle, or *the cure*: holy rollers, turf wars, drugs, or drink. It was decidedly the fifties.

In that setting, between the dark and some glimpse of a still hazy hope of daylight, James Baldwin's *Notes* arrived on the scene with an irruptive unobtrusiveness, like the muffled but distinctively audible seismic rumble of an imminent and long-awaited geological shift. Its impact on a *down títere*—or streetwise Puerto Rican—of looming intellectual ambition and very doubtful prospects can easily be imagined. It went well beyond any simple ratification of the most notorious, already clichéd truths of my own immediate environment. The Harlem of *Notes*, recognizable and familiar enough, was not, in any case, entirely identical to my own. There were evidently very few, if any, Puerto Ricans in it or, so far as one could straightaway tell, any other identifiably Caribbean folk. Nor, it seemed to me, were hard drugs yet as pandemically central or pervasively, inescapably corrosive. For all its similarities, points of general coincidence, and continuities, the atmospheric details and points of unspoken reference were anchored in the experience of another, earlier, perhaps more wily decorous, and deferential time fundamentally shaped, and still to a significant degree located, in the ambience of the thirties and forties.

Its spiritual coordinates, however attenuated, remained the historical move north from field to factory, an implacable Depression, a more lethally unpretentious—callous and overt—national experience of segregation, and the bitter social and ethical contradictions of World War II and the half-decade or so immediately after. It was, to that extent, informed by a subtly different—necessarily more forbearing, if equally shrewd, resilient, and resourceful—sensibility. It was the mood and climate of that epoch, its deadlocks and casual cruelties that ultimately gave Baldwin's prose its deeper structure of feeling. Beneath the surface of its smooth elocutions and cadence; calculated detachment; astute religious imagery; and eschatological, movingly poetic energy, there was always an undertone—a sometimes only barely detectable blue note—of poignant, imploringly plaintive, confessional *angst.* That note, sign of its distinct personality and authenticity as the product of that earlier time, would ever remain a vital element of Baldwin's writing, particularly his essays.[4]

Baldwin's Harlem had all the painful pedigree of "Fifth Avenue Uptown," Lenox and Seventh Avenues, the world surrounding the Apollo, Small's Paradise, the Red Rooster, the Abyssinian Baptist Church, the 116th Street Regun movie house, or any number of our endlessly proliferating, tumbledown backyards and ramshackle storefronts. Its boundaries blending easily and unnoticeably into his and, in many respects, hardly changed at all, my Harlem was, nonetheless, more thoroughly the product of a postwar—and postcolonial—world. It was already something of another country. It was—and Baldwin clearly adumbrated and indistinctly sensed this even then—considerably less inclined to forbearance. Exploited and smolderingly violent, it was more volatile, impatient, restive, and unforgiving. In this at least, Eldridge Cleaver was absolutely right: Harlem would have found Baldwin's equanimity and charitably *loving* compassion for those responsible curious, if not uncomely. Its style had grown more curt, abrupt, and confrontational; its edge, always keenly honed, was sharper, cut deeper, more swiftly and unpredictably.

Growing still more self-consciously "black," it was undoubtedly more brown. More racially textured, my Harlem was also more linguistically varied, polynational, and culturally syncretic. Its distinctively inflected Spanish—Spanglish—was, as much as its "Black English," our local Creole. Yams and collard greens mingled casually with its daily rice and beans, holiday *pernil,* and *cuchifritos.* When it looked south

and remembered—and, equally touched by the waves of a great migration north of surplus labor, it could hardly do otherwise—it looked
clear past the Florida Straits to the far side of the Mona Passage and
the anguish and ambiguity of an island colony still desperately immured
in the eclipsing shadow of the empire's *Pax Americana*. Its ideas of nationhood and nationality, despite a legally shared American citizenship,
were transparently extraterritorial, insistently, inescapably *Antillean*.
Our relation to the American Republic was, in consequence, all the more
antonymic, ambivalent, and, especially for the darker-skinned among
us, doubly tension-fraught, anomalous, manifoldly complex: like the
peculiar commonwealth status of our ancestral island sometimes all the
more elusively indefinite and paradoxical: *ni chicha ni limoná*.[5]

For all the differences, Baldwin's probing examination of race relations in the United States—and by extension, of the protean ubiquity of
racism in the "Free World"—made his *Notes* unwontedly, refreshingly,
irrefutably current. Its excavation, layer by layer, of essential motive,
elemental response, and larger historical consequence gave *Notes* an
incisive and powerful immediacy. With equal lack of sentimentality, its
vigilant general skepticism mooted the unctuous hypocrisy and long-
hallowed casuistry of foe and would-be friend alike. The particulars of
its generational coordinates seemed, in the event, so much secondary
trivia, minor matters of detail, relative circumstance, or emphasis. Reading sentences like the one on which the book admonishingly and so
splendidly concludes—"this world is white no longer and it will never
be white again"[6]—it was impossible not to celebrate as one experienced
the shock of recognition.

Catching just the right *mode, gestural voice,* and *inflection,* one
tasted in those sentences the salt of "dezombification" after which all of
us hungered and hunger yet today. Language, cultural idiom, and *style*
were crucially important—and Baldwin had, surely, found a *language*
that was at once beyond ignoring and distinctively, organically Afro
and American: this, by itself, was sufficient cause for celebration. The
cagey detachment of its ire and carefully modulated fury—which, in my
naiveté, I then took to be no more than the literary equivalent of any
young *títere*'s studied poise and ready cool—seemed as deceptive and as
dangerous to misconstrue as the smile of a tiger.

Still, it was the oftentimes incredible acuteness of Baldwin's deeper
perception that made *Notes* so irresistibly compelling: his sagacious
grasp of the patterns and secret contours of white hatred, liberal guilt,

and fear; his then atypical acknowledgment of the defiant stamina and enduring, creative ingenuity of the oppressed; his careful delineation of the form and unfolding dynamic of a profound social and cultural predicament of still uncertain outcome. *Notes'* breakdown of "the formula created by the [American] necessity to find a lie more palatable than the truth [which] has been handed down and memorized and persists yet with a terrible power"[7] became itself catalytic. Baldwin's capacity to synthesize and put into illuminating and provocatively new perspective what, in some visceral sense, one already knew allowed him effectively to tap into that ripeness and that readiness which, in the end, is all. Seeming to transcend the contingent profile of its own actual moment, *Notes* spoke directly to the substance of our common condition: one read it with a rapt, exhilarated attention.

To those of us then daily grappling with the knotty complexities of our own myriad identity as New-York-born-and-raised Puerto Ricans of rainbow "colored" working-class families (black *and* brown *and* white *and mestizo*) and—multiply Creole—utterly determined to deny not one iota of our rich—if, under the circumstances, not unburdensomely various and eclectic—inheritance, Baldwin's sustained essaying of the question of identity and the terms of its legitimate articulation proved especially pertinent and suggestive. Like the most moving pages of Marx, of Edmund Wilson's initial trip *To the Finland Station,* Isaac Deutscher's biographical histories, and Frantz Fanon's humane intransigence, it put the heat of real flesh on the bones of history. Like the *Prison Notebooks* of Antonio Gramsci, Paul Nizan's *Antoine Bloyé;* the lyrical insights of Aimé Césaire, César Vallejo, and Nicolás Guillén; or the novels of George Lamming, Chinua Achebe, and others whom I would later come upon, *Notes* unceremoniously tore away the enveloping veil of cobweb and hazardously cloudy self-delusion as it traced the intricate precisions of the link between private life and public expression and conduct. With encouraging exigency and exemplary self-critical assurance, in the irreverent tradition of Du Bois's *Dusk of Dawn: An Essay toward an Autobiography of a Race Concept,* and in advance of Amiri Baraka's articles in *Home,* Alice Walker's *The Color Purple,* or Derrick Bell's more recent *And We Are Not Saved,* Baldwin simply peeped everybody's hole card. Calling for its own new deal, *Notes* made it clear he would accept neither perpetual second-class citizenship nor, as writer and intellectual, shoddy goods.

In this respect, and with characteristic panache, "Many Thousand Gone" and "Encounter on the Seine: Black Meets Brown" were pivotally affecting. The first pointed to the self-betrayal resulting from a failure to see beyond an abstract image to the living souls of black folk. In doing so, it accentuated the gravity of the black writer's responsibility as emissary of a maligned and already misrepresented community. "The privacy or obscurity of Negro life," it surmised, "makes that life capable, in our imaginations, of producing anything at all . . . without fear of contradiction, since no American has the knowledge or authority to contest it and no Negro has the voice."[8] It was important, then, to open a way and work to achieve that more authentic voice, to speak frankly and without mediation for one's self.

Two related observations in Baldwin's penetrating, if otherwise excessively dismissive, critique of Richard Wright's *Native Son* struck me with particular force. The first asserted that "Bigger has no discernable relationship to himself, to his own life, to his own people, nor to any other people . . . [and that] his force comes, not from his significance as a social (or anti-social) unit, but from his significance as the incarnation of a myth."[9] With insightfully commanding bluntness, the second insisted "not that the Negro has no tradition but that there has as yet arrived no sensibility sufficiently profound and tough to make this tradition articulate."[10] Now, one instantaneously reinflected, *that* was *bad, together, . . . tough.*

Richard Wright's work still lay somewhere in my future. *Native Son* and *Black Boy* had yet to be incorporated into the established curricular canon of "English and American Literature"; Black—and Puerto Rican—Studies as well lay in that not too far off eventuality. Wright's *American Hunger,* appearing in only widely scattered segments, was, for the most part, virtually unknown. I certainly did not know it. Wright, at the time, was only vaguely and distantly familiar to me as the name of "some famous writer" Luis or Ralphie might, passingly have mentioned. Beyond stimulating my immediate interest in the texts that were the object of Baldwin's polemic spleen, the incidental references of his sporadically oracular essay naturally went rather past me. But the larger burden and wider implications of his argument did not; and I understood with an understanding beyond my ability then wholly to articulate, what was essentially at issue and at stake: the pressing necessity of a denser, more disalienating imagining and critical reappropriation of our deliberately marginalized experience and tradition(s), the perils of being reduced to—while at the same time appearing to be nobly elevated beyond—the status of a dominant, self-estranging fable. One, obviously, had to take great care, to be on guard and constantly on the lookout. This was hardly something difficult to comprehend for an already temperamentally suspicious spik and spade intelligent enough to feel insulted by the gossamer counterfeit of *West Side Story,* or, closer to home, contending then with the dishearteningly pernicious racial conceit of Antonio Pedreira's *Insularismo,*[11] as well as the evasive, patrician sentimentality of our own *jibarismo;*[12] and becoming, too, more conscious by the hour of the scarcity of genuinely useful literary or intellectual models. It was, on the contrary, a valuable reconfirming alert.

Opening on the subject of his experience as an émigré in Europe, Baldwin's encounter on the Seine dramatized the specifically national perimeters of his *Afroamericanity.* Its on occasion elusively formless— oblique, incorporeal—depiction of the non-American black presence might strike a denizen from one of *America's* colonies with an obscure, fugitive sense of self-absorbed—characteristically *American?*— insufficiency. It was plain, however, that as a more treacherously seductive and self-revealing city than those precincts in Spain in which the sun also rises, Baldwin's Paris had none of the hobnobbing, gossiping infantilism of Hemingway's movable feast. It was further apparent that, like the most nameless *trigueño* or *cocolo* back in New York City, Baldwin had found himself suddenly and unavoidably "involved in another language [in the case of the 'Nuyorican,' now also *his* language] in the same old battle: the battle for his own identity." Even more to the point, Baldwin had a strategic procedure for any effective engagement in that battle: one had to begin with an acceptance of "the reality of his being American . . . [as] a matter involving his integrity and his greatest hopes, for only by accepting this reality [could] he hope to articulate to himself or to others the uniqueness of his experience, and to set free the spirit so long anonymous and caged."[13] Transposed to the circumstances of one's own situation, this was a proposal with which one could easily identify. Puerto Rican writers of the sixties and seventies as various and distinct as Victor Hernández Cruz, Pedro Pietri, and Luis Rafael Sánchez would, each in his own way, acknowledge being directly encouraged by it.

Notes of a Native Son, not unexpectedly, made James Baldwin henceforth obligatory reading. In avid anticipation, I looked forward to everything he wrote. It was not always, to be sure, as invariably riveting. With the exception of *Go Tell It on the Mountain* and the odd short story I must confess, for example, that I found his fiction, generally speaking, no more than unevenly engaging. Though skillfully crafted and exceedingly well written, his fiction seemed to me to lack the igniting force of his essays. The publication of his "Letter from a Region of My Mind" in the *New Yorker* in the early sixties and the appearance of the collections of articles that followed his original *Notes* generally confirmed my earlier admiration of Baldwin's absolute mastery of the expressive power of the essay.

When in the late fall of 1962 I actually met James Baldwin for the first time, he was already enjoying some of the eminence and acclaim, to which he was fully entitled, in recognition of his achievement as a writer and social critic. Invited by the local intelligentsia, he came to give a series of talks, over a period of three days, at the liberal New England college to which I had been admitted only a couple of months before. In the short interval preceding his first formal presentation, I went up and introduced myself with the temerity of a homeboy catching the glimpse of a familiar face in a strange town. Coming to the stage-edge of a packed house to acknowledge this audacity, Baldwin heard me out and, leaning over with co-conspiratorial warmth, promised, "We'll talk later." And, so we did, however briefly.

I was, almost instantly, surprised at what seemed to me the incongruity between the man and his writing. A suave and angular elegance appeared to be all they had in common. Where the writing was august, muscular, and imposing, the man was physically slight, lean, lanky, and except when he took the podium to *preach,* soft-spokenly gentle and, by the standards of my street at least, almost fragile. Only a ceaseless darting of the eyes and an incessant chain-smoking gave any hint of a man hypersensitively alert to his surroundings or accustomed to protecting his every flank. His series of speeches and workshops completed, almost exactly two decades would pass before Baldwin and I would meet and speak again.

Already an active spokesman and something of a celebrity, Baldwin would go on to add to the already substantial corpus of his work and to his fame. Embarking on the first stages of a journey which—from student and acolyte to professional teacher, writer, scholar—was eventually to include our unanticipated reunion as faculty colleagues in Amherst, I had my own more modest itinerary that nonetheless would take me to the farther venues of my wider world: to Franco's Spain in the year of its first anti-government student strikes; home to Puerto Rico after long absence; to the truck farms and tobacco fields of Massachusetts as an organizer of migrant labor; to South America during a period of passionate political debate and intense revolutionary ferment; to a Cuba unconscionably blockaded and a Nicaragua under siege; to a Jamaica in dramatic transition and a fractured, disenchanted Guyana; and to a still wider Caribbean passing then, with equal uncertainty, through the crisis of old-guard populism, ferociously pressed by an implacably imperial American foreign policy moving with importunate paternalism and fearful alacrity toward the demagogic, demon-seeking right.

In the heretical, charged atmosphere of the mid-sixties and seventies, Baldwin's essays appeared in new perspective. The distinct glint of their subtler facets shone with still greater clarity. Against that backdrop—the international movement in opposition to a genocidal war in Vietnam; the insurgent mood, growing political impact and influence of a New Left both at home and abroad; and the insurrectionary temper of a "new" black militancy that would test to the point of breaking the traditional Negro-Jewish-and-White-Liberal alliance—Baldwin's pioneering defiance and nonconformity had, to no little extent, become a tolerable constituent of the left liberal mainstream consensus. Comparatively temperate, insistently dialogic, and even to a surprising and paradoxical extent fundamentally apolitical, Baldwin's chiding rebuke of his countrymen looked—by contrast with the mutinous incivility of the emergent radicals—relatively reasonable, prudently moderate. It was clear that, though more sympathetically appreciative of its sources and *raison d'être,* Baldwin was also uneasy with the most uncompromisingly militant variants of Black Nationalism and the more extravagant postures of every other radical persuasion.

This, too, gave him the appearance of "someone we can still talk to." Assuming, thus, the role of doubly loyal opposition and critically interpretive mediator, more and more, it seemed, Baldwin struggled with the difficulties of being a man in the middle. The curiously elusive quality he sometimes gave to his notion of *witness*—moving, as it did, with exquisite ease between the image of a traditional, religious practice of fraternal solidarity and that word's several passive and active meanings—sometimes acquired the vague aura of evasive artifice. To what degree, one occasionally was tempted to ask, was it Baldwin's way of dealing, symbolically if in no other way, with the circumstantial pressures and possibly untenable strain of his dilemma and with the demands of this new context?

The sometimes too deliberately detached cast of his witness, in any event, earned him the not entirely unmerited criticism of the more radical wing of younger black activists who, while conscious of their debt to him, were often baffled by what they regarded as his inner political diffidence and equivocation. Increasingly, Baldwin emerged as a moderate literary Martin Luther King, Jr., to the "by any means necessary" Malcolm Xs of, successively, Frantz Fanon, Eldridge Cleaver, and George Jackson. Though wholly consistent with his original premises and outlook, this position's essential idealism and congregational optimism, especially given the negative force of Baldwin's own critique of "white liberalism," sometimes appeared shaky and oddly contradictory. In the "moment of gentle apocalypse"[14] that was the peak of the black power movement, and save as his own apocalyptic tone had about it a not entirely unwelcome edge of *epáter les bourgeois,* Baldwin thus cut an orthodoxly heretical, incongruously maverick, and independent figure. The idea of the maverick stood at the heart of his conception of being a writer. That his writings had, ironically, helped to midwife black power into being while Baldwin himself still continued to lend it his not uncritical support, added to the poignancy and drama of his situation and to the disenchantment of his more radical critics.

My own reading of Baldwin gradually became more nuanced and analytically textured. Those features of his generational experience, which in my first reading of *Notes* impressed me as having only secondary or passing importance, progressively emerged as both salient and crucially decisive. The deficiencies in his treatment of the wider dimensions of the *colonial* black experience—which I had sensed only vaguely and vagrantly in "Encounter on the Seine"—began to emerge, in his later essays, in increasingly sharper relief. It proved, typically, to be intimately related to his overarching, unwavering belief in the exceptional, "profoundly and stubbornly unique"[15] experience of blacks in the United States. This belief was the Ptolemaic first principle at the base of his worldview. It would, on more than one occasion, obscure or impede the acuity of his perception of every *other* "black" experience.

Rather unexpectedly, the defining force of that conviction emerged as the sign of an extraordinary cosmopolitan writer's amaurotic provincialism. Indeed, Baldwin's subscription to the narcissistic idea of North American exceptionalism seemed at times effectively to isolate him within the margins of a thoroughly conventional national conceit. Its genealogy could easily be traced back to a time before St. Jean de Crevecoeur's *Letters from an American Farmer,* in a long unbroken line of thought whose various ideological offspring included the twin notions of an exemplary Arcadian democracy and the more transparently ominous doctrine of a Manifest Destiny.

Except for Baldwin's conspicuously insistent emphasis on his blackness, the overweening stress of that conceit could be accommodated, with identical facility, by the traditional platforms of both American liberal dissent and conservative reaction. Nowhere was the imperious isolation resulting from that conceit more apparent than in Baldwin's haughty interpretation of the 1956 Paris Conference of Black Writers and Artists which he set down in his essay "Princes and Powers," in *Nobody Knows My Name.* Baldwin's appraisal of that gathering of black intellectuals— one of the twentieth century's most impressive, with a predominant representation of writers from the colonies—provided Eldridge Cleaver with "shockingly clear" evidence of the "hatred for blacks permeating [Baldwin's] writing."[16] To me it seemed, on the contrary, a dramatic, if regrettably disappointing example of something else altogether: the reporter's almost boosterish American parochialism. For, Baldwin wrote, "what, at bottom, distinguished the Americans from the Negroes who surrounded us, men from Nigeria, Senegal, Barbados, Martinique . . . [Puerto Rico?] was the banal and abruptly quite overwhelming fact that we had been born in a society which . . . was open and, in a sense which had nothing to do with justice or injustice, was free."[17]

Compared to the pointed penetration of Baldwin's critique of the domestic American scene, this came uncomfortably near the self-servingly superficial half-truths of official cold war mythology. Baldwin's privileging of the American experience came perilously close to a kind of quiet vanity that, apart from a perfectly justifiable pride in his own cultural distinctiveness, could well strike one as the tacit expression of a sense of relief at his being born an American, tied to the destiny of American power in the world and *not,* like the majority of those present, a black from the colonies "whose distrust of the West, however richly justified, also tends to make them dangerously blind and hasty."[18] It was not, however, any hatred of black people that lay behind Baldwin's antipathy to the fiercely anticolonial tone of that conference. It was rather the distinctively *national* partiality of a vision that, in a context in which Baldwin's blackness conferred by itself no special particularity, revealed the extent of its deeper affiliation with one of the powers and, at the same time, its equally profound unease with the revolutionary politics of the newly ascendant princes. That this was so became all the more clear to me when, in the course of my ongoing reading, I stumbled on the transcripts of the conference debates later published in *Présence Africaine*.[19]

The extraordinary rhetorical vitality and continuing relevance of Baldwin's essays remained as admirably compelling as they ever were. But it was increasingly obvious that, apart from their rigorously *diagnostic* penetration, Baldwin had, in the final analysis, no effective program for directly counteracting the harsher realities associated with the arrogance and naked power of white supremacy—at home or abroad. What program there was was, in effect, limited to the enunciation of its moral illegitimacy, a portentous warning of the looming, long-term dangers inherent in its presumption, and an intrepid reliance on the power of moral suasion. Thus his essays were characteristically sparse on tactical specifics and notably opaque on the clashing actualities of class conflict, in general, and intraracial class confrontation, in particular. It would be one of the major, remarkably influential contributions of *The Wretched of the Earth*, and Frantz Fanon's other writings, that they faced the complexities of these issues frankly, unambiguously, and with a more genuinely political grasp of the dynamics of race and power in an international context, against the panorama of a positively untidy global process of cultural and political decolonization.

Echoing a sentiment at the core of much of Baldwin's later writing, Fanon noted that "the end of race prejudice begins with a sudden incomprehension"[20] on the part of those who most benefited from it. As careful as he was to avoid what he called "the pitfalls of national consciousness," Fanon refused still to restrict himself to the ethical idealism of predominantly middle-class strategies of nonviolence. Involved in what he regarded as a revolution "on the immense scale of humanity" for the "soul of man,"[21] he was indeed quite emphatic that "neither stubborn courage nor fine slogans are enough."[22]

Baldwin's vocabulary, on the other hand, was, and would remain, quintessentially and conscientiously moral. Baldwin spoke of and about power, of course. Power was at the decisive heart of any discussion of racism and so, unavoidably, could not but be at the center of his concern. His essays revealed both its corruptions and its self-deceptive allure. He could describe with stunning effect and an incisive accuracy the entire range of its appalling and lingering consequences, but Baldwin ultimately had no genuinely programmatic way of actually confronting power. His focus was invariably on a more abstractly *spiritual* and almost theological notion of redemption. Baldwin was himself sensitive to the demurs and criticism to which this emphasis made him vulnerable. "It can be objected that I am speaking of political freedom in spiritual terms, but," he would counter in *The Fire Next Time,* "the political institutions of any nation are always menaced and are ultimately controlled by the spiritual state of the nation."[23] It was, for all one's admiration of the man, a wobbly and not terribly persuasive defense. It only confirmed the force of the objection it was meant to allay.

One, after all, did not have to deny the validity of Baldwin's observation to indicate that it failed to address the truth and implications of the precisely reverse formulation: that the spiritual condition of any state is governed by the quite tangible facts of the actual interests and power which may be embodied in the political institutions that theoretically are supposed to epitomize the nation. Baldwin's defense was, finally, the defense of a moralist, an individualist, and a political skeptic. In a crucially determining way that had much to do with the legacy of his early evangelical training and a definition of himself as, above all else, a writer, Baldwin seemed almost to eschew *politics* altogether. Certainly he was cautious of the sometimes unsavory business of circumstantial politics or a too compromisingly *engaged* partisan obligation. When Elijah Mohammed, trying to draw him out and *in* during the course of his visit to the Muslim leader's Chicago home, coyly asked Baldwin, "and what are you now?," Baldwin, after some significant hesitation, responded, "I am a writer. I like doing things alone."[24] It was, in one way or another, the answer he would always give.

In the pitched climate of the late sixties and seventies, it was a response which did not always entirely satisfy. Nonetheless, one had to admire the constancy of his ethical commitments and the consistently high caliber and singularity of the work that emerged out of his devotion to them. By the eighties, when the majority of his generational cohorts and so many "radicals" and "revolutionaries" had already beaten a hasty retreat to neoconservativatism in yuppie- or buppieville, or labored to avoid so much as mention of the "L" word, the moral stamina and inner coherence of Baldwin's consistency would be even more admirably apparent. *The Devil Finds Work* and *The Evidence of Things Not Seen* confirmed that, with considerably more grace than they, he had kept his hand stubbornly on the plow, held on. It was a real measure of his stature.

What Baldwin finally wanted more than anything else, and to his everlasting credit, was to contribute to the achievement of an authentic "transcendence of the realities of color, of nations, and of altars."[25] No one was more painfully aware of the degree to which, under present circumstances, this was simply not yet possible. It was his certainty in that knowledge, joined to his outrage at the utter waste of human possibility that is the evil of racism, which gave every essay he wrote so powerfully anguished and tragic a sense of our collective travail. It is that sense of universal tragedy which, to the last, gave them their edge of pathos and singularly stirring poignancy. But tragedy, alas, is tragedy; it is easier to understand and to record than to transcend. And so, Baldwin offered us what he could: the unrelenting integrity of the chronicler, his passionate outrage and distress, the solidarity of his compassion, his seer's—and often searing—prophesy, and the candid prodigality of his love.

Baldwin's arrival in Amherst, in the fall of 1984, was greeted with great excitement and general celebration. His appointment as Distinguished Five College Professor of Afro-American Studies had been the result of sometimes tedious transatlantic negotiation, and, in an area already famous as a haven for writers, poets, and nonconformists of every description, it graced the community with the vital presence of one of the most eminent and influential American intellectuals of the last half of the twentieth century. Despite his many writer's obligations and the daunting press of invitations to speak throughout the country, his presence was immediately and palpably felt. It almost instantly further coalesced and continually served to bring together the community of distinguished black and Third World intellectuals that, among several others, included John Bracey, Mavis Campbell, Andrew Salkey, Archie Shepp, William Strickland, and Michael Thelwell. A constant round of talks, lectures, and private meetings—before the general public; at local colleges and high schools, with church, faculty, or more informally organized groups—made him a periodically goading locus of valuable dialogue and vernacular local awareness.

The exchanges which were an invariable staple of these gatherings were typically lively; occasionally spirited; and, by the particular blend of the intimate, the personal, and the public they could from time to time elicit, sometimes even unexpectedly touching. The lectures were, in content and style, vintage Baldwin. There were moments when, remembering other times and other places, one even had an obscure, quickening, evanescent sense of *déjà vu*. Certainly, each lecture I went to, like the distant one at which Baldwin and I originally met, was exceptionally well attended. In the level of energy and emotion they could sometimes generate, they were also fleetingly evocative of the eager hopes and ardent dramas of the two previous decades.

Baldwin himself seemed at once comfortable with, unperturbed, flattered, and bemused by the attention and solicitude which accompanied him everywhere. He was also excited and, initially at least, full of apprehension about his new incarnation as college and university professor. He worried aloud that, unfamiliar as he was with the terrain, he well might prove unequal to its demands. With sly modesty and gentle self-deprecation, he joked anxiously that "you professors are the really smart ones," that, very possibly, he might not do well with the students. But his writing workshops at Hampshire College were almost instantly over-enrolled, and his courses on the Civil Rights Movement, *radio bemba* reported, had become something of a campus event throughout his tenure at the University of Massachusetts. To students who were too young to remember Medgar Evers, Andrew Goodman, Michael Schwerner, James Chaney, Malcolm X, Martin Luther King, Fred Hampton, and so many others martyred, Baldwin's presence among them represented a rare opportunity. He was, beyond the fact of his celebrity, a living link to a still unsettled history. He could put them directly in touch with the emotional texture—and legacy—of their parents' time. At a time when, with Ronald Reagan in the White House, the radical *white-wing* was menacingly feeling its oats, Baldwin offered an intimate and privileged, firsthand appreciation for what, morally speaking, had gone with the passing of "the possibility of a certain kind of dialogue in America"[26] which the death of those men and women epitomized. They were evidently going to take full advantage of the opportunity.

I saw Baldwin several times in the two years after his arrival. In the more than twenty years since our last meeting, he seemed to have aged remarkably little. There was the more-salt-than-pepper grey of his hair. The lines in his face, around his forehead and eyes, were more visibly etched in and sculpted. There was, I suppose, some air of aging dependence in the careful guardianship and affable omnipresence of his factotum. At times, regarded from slight distance and standing atypically alone, he could give you the abrupt feeling, for all the attention and very real affection of which he was the object, of being canopied by an awesome loneliness, an ache and weariness of veritably millennial proportions. He was a veteran with a veteran's wounds and, at such times, one almost could see just how personally expensive the price of the ticket had been. Yet, Baldwin had lost none of his animation, warmth, or gentleness; and his expansive smile, cheerful laughter, and tactful prodding were all still there. He even had the mildly rakish habit, which I did not immediately remember seeing back then, of wearing jackets and coats draped across his shoulders, transforming them into rather stylish capes. The private Baldwin, though, I caught in snatches, if at all; and inevitably it was the public Baldwin I knew best.

One of my last memories of Baldwin is of a party at the house in Pelham that was his Amherst area home. It was, I think, something on the order of a housewarming. *The Evidence of Things Not Seen* had only recently been published. Not long before, we had been seated next to one another on a panel on race and racism at the regional junior high school. Having read the book in one sitting a few nights before, I leaned over as we were about to be introduced, congratulated him on its completion, and asked if I could trouble him to autograph my copy sometime. He readily agreed.

So, planning on getting there a little earlier than usual, I brought the book with me to the party. More or less at the appointed hour, I was, as I recall, the first to arrive: for some minutes at least there would be no interruptions. We had been chatting in the kitchen for a while when, rather awkwardly taking the book out of my pocket, banteringly I reminded him of his earlier promise to sign it for me. Delighted and smiling, he immediately sat down in a low wooden chair that struck me as too small even for him and proceeded to write something on the dedication page. When he had finished, I thanked him and, not wanting to add one gaucherie to another, slipped the book back into my jacket with the inscription unread. In the less than half an hour we still had more or less to ourselves, we went on to talk about the new book, the critical reception his novel, *Just Above My Head,* had received, of people and politics, Harlem and New York, and the changes they had undergone since his time and since mine. As more people began to arrive, it wasn't long before he was, first by one, then another, then generally and almost indistinctly, drawn away. He was, once more, the public person who belonged to us all.

I undoubtedly saw him at least a couple of times again before we left for Virginia the following summer. I simply don't remember those times with anything near the same clarity. It was not until I got home that I finally read Baldwin's inscription. The one he had scribbled in my tattered, discolored copy of *Notes* so many years ago—and which I have still—had simply read "James Baldwin." This time, he had written "For Roberto: with respect. God bless" above that signature. I was touched. When the news reached me of his death, I thought again of that evening and considered what, given the opportunity, I might have written in a book for him. It would have gone, I think, something like this:

> For James Baldwin, in gratitude and *fraternalmente,* with respect for his long and faithful struggle on behalf of us all; and, in the words of the poet,[27] because he did not sleep to dream but dreamed to change the world. *Que te proteja Changó.*

It is a tribute his generosity of spirit and the moral stature of his work wholeheartedly deserve and one, I would like to think, that would have touched him.

Notes

1. At his most Unamunesque, in *The Fire Next Time,* Baldwin writes: "Life is tragic simply because the earth turns and the sun inexorably rises and sets, and one day, for each of us, the sun will go down for the last, last time. Perhaps the whole root of our trouble, the human trouble, is that we will sacrifice all the beauty of our lives, will imprison ourselves in totems, taboos, crosses, blood sacrifices . . . in order to deny the fact of death, which is the only fact we have." *The Fire Next Time* (New York, 1963), 105.

2. Hugh Thomas, *The Spanish Civil War* (New York, 1961), 354.

3. James Baldwin, *Notes of a Native Son* (Boston, 1955), 175.

4. It was, to some extent at least, the failure of a Cleaver, who today seems hardly to have existed at all, to appreciate or wholly credit that subsoil of historical experience that allowed him, in *Soul on Ice,* to be so acidly dismissive of the man he otherwise acknowledges as having "placed so much of my own experience . . . into new perspective." Even as it marked Baldwin off, historically and temperamentally, from writers such as Cleaver or George Jackson, that undertone of plaintive angst and exasperation was, paradoxically perhaps, an inextricable element of what gave his writing its unique identity and edge, the wider resonance which helped prepare the ground for their later generation's impact and more acerbic tone.

5. Literally, "Neither Lemon nor Lemonade," that is, "neither this nor that."

6. Baldwin, *Notes,* 175.

7. Ibid., 16.

8. Ibid., 41.

9. Ibid., 35.

10. Ibid., 36.

11. Antonio, S. Pedreira, *Insularismo: Ensayos de interpretación puertorriqueña* (San Juan, 1957).

12. As romantic image of an idealized national pastoral, the *Jíbaro,* or rural mestizo peasant of the Puerto Rican highlands, became the symbol of a past, still longed-for way of life. After the ruin of the seignorial agricultural economy that once sustained them, this figure—and its dominant image was an invariable "he"—was invoked by disillusioned hacendados and aristocrats, a national elite struggling to maintain its domestic hegemony against an emergent, restive working class and politically frustrated in its historical project by U.S. intervention. It became a favorite trope of *hommes de lettres* and politicos descendent from or ideologically allied to them. Luis Muñoz Marín's Popular Democratic Party, which dominated local politics from the 1940s through 1968 and beyond, successfully transformed the Jíbaro into a popular synonym for "archetypical Puerto Rican," hence Jibarismo.

13. Baldwin, *Notes,* 121.

14. The phrase is suggested by a reading of H. Stuart Hughes's *Sophisticated Rebels: The Political Culture of European Dissent, 1968–1987* (Cambridge, Mass., 1988), particularly its discussion of Michel Tournier (22–29, 32–33) and of the German Greens' tactic of "gentle provocation" (138 ff.).

15. James Baldwin, *Nobody Knows My Name* (New York, 1965), 3. There is, of course, a sense in which everyone and everything is "unique." But to use the word in this way—and Baldwin does not—is, by tautology, to rob it of any meaning at all.

16. Eldridge Cleaver, *Soul on Ice* (New York, 1968), 99.

17. Baldwin, *Nobody Knows My Name,* 20.

18. Ibid., 18.

19. *Présence Africaine: Cultural Journal of the Negro World,* new bimonthly series, no. 8–10 (June–Nov. 1956) offered a selection, in English, of the proceedings. The original transcripts are reproduced in the French edition of the same special issue of the journal. The proceedings of the follow-up Second Congress, in Rome, were published in *Présence Africaine,* número special, no. 27–28 (août–nov. 1959).

20. Frantz Fanon, "Racism and Culture," in *Toward the African Revolution* (New York, 1967), 44.

21. Frantz Fanon, *The Wretched of the Earth,* (New York, 1963), 255.

22. Ibid., 108.

23. Baldwin, *The Fire Next Time,* 102–3.

24. Ibid., 84.

25. Ibid., 96.

26. "Why I Left America. Conversation: Ida Lewis and James Baldwin," in *New Black Voices: An Anthology of Contemporary Afro-American Literature*, ed. *Abraham Chapman* (New York, 1972), 412.

27. Martin Carter, *Poems of Succession* (London and Port of Spain, 1977), 14.

Boricuas, Jíbaras, and Jibaristas

Of Memory, Memoir, and Mimicry

APPEARING ONLY a year after its English-language original and in the author's own Boricua "translation," the Spanish-language version of Esmeralda Santiago's *When I Was Puerto Rican* includes a brief foreword, absent from the American first edition. The new preface explicitly articulates the specific cultural context, process of genesis, and narrative intent of her elegant autobiographical memoir. It specifically situates this chronicle of a child's uprooting from her rural Puerto Rican beginnings, the adaptations, "seasonings," and maturation in relatively more urban insular settings that end with eventual (im)migration to the United States; and the subsequent Creolization, ultimate success, and hunger of memory there which are at the heart of her not-so-unusual story.

Ms. Santiago's Spanish-language preface candidly acknowledges a permanent nostalgia, an abiding inner ache of irretrievable loss that rationalizes her title's conscientious use of the preterit and the pervading aura of romantic yearning which hovers over her suasive prose. It is part of the price of those seasonings and that success. It also adds a distinct present-tense immediacy, gives larger historical dimension, a certain generational resonance, and some clarity of authorial outlook to a personal narrative whose sometimes too sharp stress on the decisive pastness of the past can seem unduly absolute; and which, for all its authentic novelty and autobiographical and lyrical authority, can still on occasion also appear as conventionally exotic, as oddly equivocal and inconclusive as it is seductively appealing.

Like Antoinette Cosby's otherwise melancholy passage across the *Wide Sargasso Sea*, *La mulâtresse Solitude*'s analogous gropings, or *Annie John*'s darkly haunting journey from the sometimes dubious certainties of a colonial Antiguan adolescence to North America's own contradictory pleasures of exile, and Magali García Ramis's delicately nuanced fictional account of a more middle-class Puerto Rican coming of age in *Happy Days, Uncle Sergio,* Ms. Santiago's introduction to her Spanish text insists on the unbroken continuities, multivalent layerings, and textured complexities of her Boricua experience. Its intimate commingling of past and present and personal dramatization of the resourcefulness and variable dynamism of an unpredictably evolving Puerto Rican culture are finally more thoroughly compelling and persuasive than the triumphal conceits of closure of a Horatio(a) Alger, the static consolations and spurious pastoral of Luis Lloréns Torres's *jibarismo,* or the *costumbrista* tropes and anachronisms of a latter-day Manuel(a) Alonso which the narrative itself, formally and thematically, also deliberately evokes.

The story's opening chapter, originally intended to serve an identical introductory purpose for the English-language edition and more plainly a structural part of its overall literary integrity is, by comparison, oblique and incomplete. It can consequently, at least partially, misfire. Its contemporary autumn in New York reflections on "How to Eat a Guava," aroused by examination of unripe samples taken from a display of tropical fruit at a local Stop & Save, have a rather more cryptic, if not unregretful, metaphorical finality. Returning a dark green Guava to its stack, our narrator significantly concludes by pushing her cart "away, towards the apples and pears of my adulthood, their nearly seedless ripeness predictable and bittersweet." Far from intimating any still unfolding protean shifts, syncretic inventiveness, or the fraught innovating continuities of experience, this preamble's symbolic *putting down* and *turning away* seems substantively to confirm, however unwittingly, the implications of that decisive curtain and dissociative closure the book's provocatively categorical title almost immediately suggests.

The absence of any more contextualizing preface from the American first edition is all the more unfortunate. This single difference may, I suspect, account for both the book's evidently more cordial and sympathetic insular reception and the critically mixed, oftentimes even indignantly censorious, reaction its connotative ambiguity almost instantly gave rise to among sectors of its Latino readership in the United States.

As if in direct response to some of the latter's reproachful accusations of an abjuring or repudiating assimilationism, Ms. Santiago's later prologue tersely asserts:

> The title of this book is in the past tense . . .
> This does not mean that I am no longer Puerto Rican, but that the book

describes that stage of my life defined by the culture of the Puerto Rican countryside. When we "jumped across the puddle" and arrived in the United States, I changed. Superficially, I stopped being a Puerto Rican *jíbara* to become a hybrid between one world and another: a Puerto Rican who lives in the United States, speaks English nearly all day, and day and night lives within North American culture.

Thus allaying the anxieties of any erstwhile or would-be critics, she goes on to eschew the ingenuous dichotomies and essentialist polarities of both nationalist border guards and cultural purists. A more eclectically manifold view of a disparate Puerto Rican experience emerges, one whose reach and scope stretch properly beyond strictly proprietal notions of national "authenticity" and the restrictive or genteel boundaries defended by the ubiquitous guardians of our ethnic chastity and virtue on either side of the water. Affirming the crucial role of historical contingency, a mercurial social process and its revelatory potentialities, Ms. Santiago's own view is unapologetically synergist and symphystic. Accenting the crucial realities of cultural miscegenation, it also appears firmly to disavow the tenacious *pureza de sangre* prejudices which tacitly postulate that any such cross-fertilizations necessarily verge on national infidelity and renunciation or the equally "shameful" cultural degeneration of native castaways, putatively hapless or pathetic victims. Her own appreciation for the tangled sinuousities, mutable conditions, and contradictions of identity is here more frankly ample, positively inflected, and incisively expressed. "I do know what, for me, it means to be Puerto Rican," she pointedly, refreshingly declares. "My Puerto Ricanness includes my life in North America, my Spanglish, the sofrito that seasons my rice and gandules, the tomato sauce and salsa of the Gran Combo. One culture has enriched the other, and both have enriched me."

So forthright and frankly impenitent an affirmation of this dialectically composite, multiply Creole Boricua sense of self is both admirable and welcome. It further confirms the contemporary self-assurance and maverick vigor of an increasingly myriad (im)migrant community whose demographic heft is no longer ignorable and whose heterogeneous modalities, unorthodox *mestizajes,* and reciprocally heretical cultural force continue to defy our conventional complacencies and most cherished myths. The supple "impuries" and canny amalgamations of its "new Creole" fusions and syncretic literary explorations have, for some time now, been among the most significant and creatively original of its many *señas de identidad*. Comfortably bicultural twin to the aerial suspension, forever hydroponic commuting, and bipolar oscillation of any regular rider of our *guagua aérea,* the author's affiliative emphasis on this holistic doubleness of identity and sense of place is also recognizable kin to the "nuyorican's" *Am e Rícan,* or *DiaspoRican's* lithe and passionate ambidexterities. Its identical *Puertorriqueñidad,* in any event, provides the broader private backdrop and wider communal landscape to her narrative.

Between its preface(s) and a final epilogue, the primary core of the story focuses on the nine years from 1953 to 1962. Negri's—the young Ms. Santiago's—fateful, gypsy passage from her fourth to thirteenth season is thus, not unexpectedly, concurrent with a series of major insular transitions. The national impact and colloquial local effects of a formally ratified (1952) Commonwealth status, the "modernizing" reorientations of Luis Muñoz Marín's Free Associated State, the critical cresting of The Great Migration, and the polemic apogee and incipient decline from its halcyon days of his Popular Democratic Party's (PPD) New Deal populism are all allusively mooted elements of the tale.

It is, however, Negri's emotional itinerary and often lonely epiphanies as the eldest sibling in a family which rapidly grows to eleven children that are the story's immediate center. It is Negri's loss of innocence and maturing intelligence as forlorn witness to the anguish caused by her father's culturally sanctioned philandering and as privileged observer of her mother's quietly unyielding powers of recovery, hard-won self-reliance, and determined ambition for herself and her children that give it its dramatically reverberating poignancy. Written "For Mami" it is, in some measure, a grateful daughter's tribute to the signal touchstone of her mother's feminine pluck, resiliency, and dedicated maternal constancy.

The slow, spasmodically turbulent breakup of her parents' common-law marriage is catalyst for the first of Negri's epiphanies. Finding in her own secret distress and fear of parental abandonment the gloomy echo of her mother's repeated hurts and increasingly lonesome disenchantment, Negri was learning that men "were *sinverguenzas* . . . indulged in behavior that never failed to surprise women but caused them much suffering. . . ." The capricious inconstancy of an otherwise sympathetic—loving and affectionate—father reveals, too, the contradictory impulses of a society whose mores and traditions are at once earnestly familial and incorrigibly *machista*. The disruptive fallout takes mother and children away from Negri's rustic and idyllic Macun to the fetid Santurce shantytown of El Mangle, where "the air smelled like the brewery, and the water like human waste." When they move to a cramped apartment behind a more centrally located bar shortly thereafter, their nights, she notes, "were punctuated by the deafening percussion of drunken ballads, clashing billiards, clinking glasses, and nightly brawls." The change of landscapes confirms Negri's perplexed earlier intuition that popular national celebration of the rural peasantry as representative cultural icon is not incompatible with the realities of regional snobbery and middle-class prejudice. She is able palpably to corroborate that in the city, however endlessly and positively invoked, "*jíbaros* were mocked for their unsophisticated customs and peculiar dialect" and presumed ignorance.

Negri's experience of being ridiculed as a provincial "hick" by teachers and students in her new city school encourages a retreat of her "well-guarded soul" to the refuge of memory and imagination. From Santurce her determined mother moves the children to a succession of decaying tenements in Brooklyn, where she supports them making bras in a factory and where Negri, transporting the family beyond its drab surroundings, enchants it with comforting fantasies of "distant lands where palaces shimmered against desert sand and paupers became princes with the whoosh of a magic wand."

Wishing to give up neither parent, Negri is constantly torn between her father's unwavering attachment to the island he absolutely refuses to leave, whose provincial culture he embodies, and her mother's logical wish for a change in the status quo and vaguely more cosmopolitan dreams of a better life. On the eve of their departure for the States, Negri finds herself feeling that she may, in fact, be losing them both. It is, perhaps, her most ruefully prophetic epiphany.

The break that gives Negri her chance genuinely to escape the Brooklyn ghetto comes, barely a year after her arrival in New York, at an audition for entrance into the High School of Performing Arts. Her delivery of a dramatic monologue of which neither Negri nor the judges can understand a word is, indeed, the fateful event on which the main body of her story, perhaps a bit too abruptly, ends. A scant page and a half epilogue, set in 1976, too quickly tells us Negri was successfully graduated from Performing Arts a decade earlier. She is now a scholarship student at Harvard, living in Boston. It concludes, in the writer's present, remembering a retrospective visit to her alma mater, during which Negri resolved one day to be recognized among her high school's distinguished alumni, with the pride and tacit triumph of a pledge fulfilled which the book itself, to some extent, represents. Dropping suddenly away from its larger familial setting, the narrative's focus abruptly narrows to a finish which fixes exclusively on Esmeralda's achievement. Her individual success, actual and proposed, is the only source of catharsis. Readers curious to know something about those ten in-between years, the effect on the family of her extraordinary accomplishments, or the, no doubt, arresting dramas of a scion of the working poor at post-sixties Harvard are left to wonder. The overall effect is, in any case, of an important story too quickly ended and only half told.

Ms. Santiago's recreation of the psychic atmosphere, varying moods, and emotional tone of a precociously alert child's consciousness and her struggle to cope with an elusive, changing reality is especially artful: convincing and deft as the best fiction. Her partial inversion of our literature's more characteristically middle-class, urban or, in the States, "proletarian" bias, in addition, brings new dimension to an almost daily expanding canon. In the first strictly nonfictional personal memoir of its kind written originally in English by a woman, her unique point of view brings the (im)migrant experience of the rural working poor into more distinctive focus. It also confirms the decisive centrality of contemporary Puerto Rican women writers and the general trend toward the kind of literary craftsmanship and formal polish Ed Vega, among others, especially applauds.

Rich in elements and the ambience of local color, *When I Was Puerto Rican* brings an almost anthropological attention to the details of popular custom and ritual. Like the pithy *refranes* of folk wisdom which set the temper and introduce each chapter, tableaux of communal rite, belief, and convention, occasionally reminiscent of Manuel Alonso's *costumbrista* vignettes of a bygone era, have a formal pride of place in this remembrance. With a warmly attentive precision, as if the author were willfully cleaving to and precisely savoring the landscape and pleasures of memory, those not already familiar with Puerto Rico's cultural traditions are brought into contact with, among others, the conventions of Christmas season, varying religious protocols, indigenous burial rites, and sundry other examples of native mores ranging from culinary habits to *velorios* and *vaguadas*.

But the author's vital perception, the text's overarching aura, is, for all that, ultimately exotic, archaic, typically utopian: the defining vision

is more sentimentally "literary" than rigorously documentary. The wistful rendering of a magical countryside and nostalgic image of the *jíbaro*
has, in particular, all the Arcadian and imaginary texture of a "Valle
de Collores'" melodic and noble tropic pastels. The poet Luis Lloréns
Torres is, not surprisingly, the book's reigning deity and guiding spirit.
It is the author's literary endorsement and adroit echo of his sanguine
national pastoral, simple binary oppositions, and noble-primitive tropes
of "*aquella apacible calma*" that, ironically, leave us with a narrative
in which the *jíbara*'s very real poverty and experience yield in the end
to the *jibarista*'s patrician and colorful view of the poor. Simultaneously reactivating and remapping the exact coordinates of her inherited
turn-of-the-century tropes, a single epigraph perhaps best captures, in
sum, the overall prevailing air and peregrine climate of Ms. Santiago's
assorted mosaic of memoir, mimicry, picturesque fantasy, and rumbling
intertextualities. It, longingly, reads: "no siento lo que me llevo / sino lo
que voy dejando" (I feel not that I take with me / so much as all that I
am leaving behind).

III

OCCASIONS, VIEWS, AND REVIEWS

Mankind is like a closed fist pushing
from the depths of the earth to break free

JOSÉ MARTÍ

The past hissed in a cinder.
They heard the century breaking in half

DEREK WALCOTT

"Soul of a Continent"

WRITING IN 1888 from his exile of more than seven years in New York, the intellectual architect and political organizer of Cuban independence, José Martí, then only thirty-five years old, privately disclosed the broad outlines of an enterprise to which his omnivorous attention was consistently and ineluctably drawn. "Do you know that, after eighteen years of thinking about it," he confided to his friend and colleague, the Uruguayan diplomat Enrique Estrázulas:

> I have lately been turning over the idea of publishing here a journal, *El mes,* or some such, entirely written by me with each issue so complete in itself as to be something like the running history and synthesis, at once clear and critical, of everything of outstanding and essential interest—in high politics, theater, the movements of nations, contemporary science, books— that occurs here [in the United States] and there [in Latin America], and in any other place where the world truly lives.[1]

The sheer audacity and sweep of this project must seem nothing short of foolhardy hubris to an intelligentsia gone hoary with disciplinary specialization and cliquish parochialism. Advanced by an intelligence less vigorously polymath or productive, a proposal so intimidating and encyclopedic in its aspiration might even have been casually dismissed with patronizing indulgence by Martí's correspondent as the pardonable sign of an outsized ambition in an otherwise fetching naiveté.

But Martí was neither presumptuous, naïve, nor easily dismissed. One of the most remarkable figures to have come out of either America in the second half of the nineteenth century, he had, in the years since 1870, given dramatic evidence of a precocious, polygeneric talent, amply cosmopolitan interests, and revolutionary initiative and convictions.

The publication of *El presidio político en Cuba* in 1871, on the eve of Martí's eighteenth birthday, revealed a liberal Creole patriot of powerful moral sensibility and a literary personality of impressive force and resources.[2] His moving denunciation of the horrors of prison life under

Spanish colonialism and the failure of metropolitan policy which he saw embodied in the "hell of stones and groans" (*OA*, 184) that he himself had only recently experienced had the compelling ethical authority and importunate fury of a Bartolomé de Las Casas or of Émile Zola's *J'accuse* and an intellectual and political sophistication unusual in one so young. Its author, who had paid for the *independentista* sympathies of his earliest poetry with six months at hard labor and immediate deportation to Spain, had at the time already published the first of his dramatic pieces. The eloquence and acuity of the commentaries on art, literature, current affairs, and civil society which Martí subsequently published with daunting regularity throughout the hemisphere as pamphlets, and in books, magazines, newspapers, and journals that he was often instrumental in establishing or editing, earned him a reputation as a keen observer of the contemporary scene and as a thinker, polemicist, and prose stylist of the first rank. The verse of the mature poet would come to be regarded as an exemplary precursor of the formal originality and innovative spirit of the seminal *modernista* movement. A gifted orator, he was also to acquire an increasing celebrity as a powerful and effective public speaker.

At the peak of his powers and entering upon the most decisive period of his intellectual and political life when writing to Estrázulas, Martí was particularly well positioned to carry off the project he proposed. An anticolonialist in the breach between the final collapse of one empire and the formidable emergence of another, he was pivotally situated (by his talents, romantic temperament, liberal outlook, Creole middle-class affiliations, and strategic location) effectively to engage the drift and import of an entire panoply of emerging cultural and political forces. A radical nationalist from a distinctively agricultural Hispanic-American country who resided in an industrial, presumptively Anglo-Saxon metropolis, Martí acquired an uncommon perspective from which to view an epoch marked by critical historical realignments and accelerated social transformations. It sharpened his ability to intuit and to draw out the implications of the shift of axis represented by an emerging working class and an increasingly heterogeneous community of old veterans from the protracted First War of Independence (1868–1878; 1879–1880), and a new generation of rebels, economic exiles, and émigrés. And successfully to give to that intuition an ideologically cohesive institutional form—El Partido Revolucionario Cubano (PRC)—which transformed that community into a consequential revolutionary force.

It gave to his sustained assault on the sophistry and pseudoscience of racist ideology—"the bookshelf races" (*OA*, 94) of craniologists, physiognomists, and phrenologists—a wider comparative range and authority. Circumstances also gave strategic point, mediating urgency, and hegemonic efficacy to the all-inclusive formula—"Cuban is more than white, more than black, more than mulatto" (*OA*, 313)—that Martí invoked in defense of his syncretic definition of the nation, in defiance of the insular sugarocracy's racial conceit, against Spanish attempts to capitalize on the fear of "Africanization," and as one element contributing to his growing wariness of Cuba's northern neighbor. He was among the first to presage the dangers to Spanish America posed by an expansionist American Republic and to see in a unified, independent alliance of Latin American nations a means of avoiding those dangers. In the years immediately before and after 1888, Martí was particularly instrumental in bringing an end to Spanish America's long flirtation with the benign mythic image of the United States, which, admired as a model of development, earlier had the very influential Argentine educator and statesman Domingo Faustino Sarmiento exclaiming "Let us become the United States." No Spanish-American before Martí, certainly, had ever presented so widely informed and textured a panorama of life in the United States or so sobering an analysis of its internal dynamic.

Martí's death, in an unexpected skirmish with Spanish troops in 1895, added the aura of romantic myth to the truth of his patriotic devotion. The posthumous (ongoing) publication of his collected works, which in one edition runs to as many as seventy volumes, ratified his stature as the most persuasively articulate of Cuba's national spokesmen, symbol of its emergence into self-reliant nationhood, and the most eminent and capacious chronicler of his era among Latin Americans of his generation. It confirmed too that, in a body of work of exceptional breadth, lucidity, and prescience, he had splendidly achieved the kind of running history and synthesis he had earlier envisioned as *El mes*.

It is one of the great merits of Philip S. Foner's four-volume anthology that it offers the American public the first broadly representative collection of Martí's prose writings yet available in English. Only two now out-of-print single-volume editions had even appeared before: Juan de Onís's *The America of José Martí* (1945) and Luis A. Baralt's *Martí on the U.S.A.* (1966). In conception, focus, and tone these editions compressed Martí's multiplicity to the more manageable dimensions of an admirably responsive sojourner and uncommonly capable *homme de lettres.* More conventional examples of a still powerful tradition of hagiography—to which Foner is himself not always immune—they also inclined to a sometimes ingenuous and ritual iconolatry. With the exception of the canon-legitimized "Our America" and one or another isolated document, they largely ignored their author's anti-imperialist and political writings. The result was a congenial, if truncated, and rather domesticated Martí who, in addition, showed no immediately apparent stages of development and was otherwise generally unproblematic.

Foner's compilation, which includes some of the essays made available earlier by his predecessors, slights neither the acumen of the émigré nor the polyglot and urbane cultivation of the man of letters. His volumes, though, offer the reader a more thoroughly layered perception of Martí's activity as the moving force behind the Second Cuban War of Independence (1895–1898) as well as material evidence of the distinct phases and overall vital coherence of his evolving view of the world.

Foner also brings a historian's appreciation of context, competing social agendas, and ideologies to his task as compiler. The editor's introductions to each volume place his choices more properly in the biographical setting and against the historical conditions which informed them. The annotations to individual essays and the inclusion of a "Chronology of the Life of José Martí" demonstrate the latter's vast range of general reference, and experience, giving added depth to those introductions. With only occasional lapses and procedural inconsistencies, each volume generally permits us direct access to Martí's contradictory impulses, his simultaneously moderating and radical, alternately pragmatic and utopian, rich, varied, and not infrequently ambiguous universe of meaning. Taken together, they echo and underscore the ideological convergence of his distinct thematic foci. That "the problem of independence did not lie in a change of forms, but in a change of spirit" (*OA*, 90) and, whether in politics, esthetics, or pedagogy, that "permanent strength comes from a just balance" (*OA*, 249) were the underlying premises of that symbiosis. "That all the elements of nature have a moral character" (*AL*, 160); that "to suffer is . . . to be born to the life of the good, the only true life" (*OA*, 163); that "men who concentrate everything in themselves suffer greatly" (*IM*, 95); and that nonetheless "apostleship is a constant daily duty" (*IM*, 218)—these are the propositions at its ethical and philosophical idealist core. Cuba, Martí became convinced, was a crucial historical linchpin. That "the free Antilles will preserve the independence of Our America, and the dubious and tar-

nished honor of English America, and perhaps may hasten and stabi-
lize the equilibrium of the world" (*OA*, 403) was, therefore, the central
raison d'être of his political vision.

Foner's preferential emphasis throughout is on the maturer thought
of Martí's transitional (1881–1887) and later years: his arrival and settlement in New York, his founding of the PRC, and the clandestine work
as a Delegate that, near the century's end, culminated in the *Grito de
Baire* and what eventually became the Spanish-Cuban-American War.
Our America, however, and to a fuller extent *On Education*, give the
reader a glimpse into the formative period (1871–1882) which includes
Martí's *El presidio político en Cuba*, included in its entirety in the first
mentioned volume, and the important impact of his post-Spain exiles in
Mexico (1875–1875), Guatemala (1877–1878), and Venezuela (1881).
Martí's impressions of the United States (1881–1895), Coney Island,
and individuals like Longfellow, Emerson, Pushkin, Oscar Wilde, Dar-
win, Goya, Fortuny, Fromentin, Detaille, "the French Water-Colorists,"
our "Aboriginal American Authors," Flaubert, and the "Modern French
Novelists" that are also part of this period are included in *Inside the
Monster* and *On Art and Literature*.

Martí's early experience in each of these countries is an important
source of his ideas about the process of state formation and cultural
articulation. Mexico confirmed both his radical anticlericalism and
his ripening conviction that Latin America must turn to the challenge
of more authentically reflecting "the light upon Ximantecatl and the
pain in Cuauhtemotzin's face . . ." (*AL*, 53, *OE*, 93), a major emphasis
of his later ideas on its art and literature, and an anticipation of the
characteristic observation that "There can be no literature, which is expression, unless there is some substance to express in it. And there will
be no Spanish-American literature unless there is a Spanish America"
(*AL*, 306).

The legacy of Martí's experience in Mexico, Guatemala, and Venezuela
informed his congregational concept of a society "with all, and for the
good of all" (*OA*, 249), his theories about popular education, social
policy,[3] and the imperative of a moral republic. Most notably, it contributed to the mature writer's view of the continental wars of independence
(1810–1824)—and the governments that came in their wake—as decisively foundational and yet socially and politically inconclusive. The intensity of Martí's ideological campaign against *caudillismo* in the Cuban
revolutionary ranks, admirably and meticulously documented in *Our*

America, owed much to his experience with the governments of Porfirio Díaz, Justo Rufino Barrios, and Guzmán Blanco. It gave critical nuance to the larger strategic vision Martí brought to the tactical battles out of which the PRC emerged in the decade after 1882 and, still later, to his determination that the epigenetic war he was preparing for "should at once encompass the spirit of redemption and decency" (*OA*, 402).

Autocracy, personal egotism, and the lack of responsiveness to civilian rule or a popular base are the fatal flaws to which Martí repeatedly points. These are the recurring themes of his tributes to Bolívar (1893), San Martín (1891), and José Antonio Páez (1888) that (with "Hidalgo" [n.d.] "Mother America," [1889] "Our America," [1891] "Guatemala" [1878], and Martí's famous Venezuelan letter of farewell "To Fausto Teodoro de Aldrey" [1881]) make up the continental Latin American section of *Our America.* Men of genuinely epic proportion, they "made the mistake of confusing the glory of having served, which grows and is a crown that no hands can take from [their] brow, with the mere accident of power that was [theirs] to wield" (*OA,*101). What coalitions they were able to build, in consequence, eventually collapsed. The building of a lasting coalition is as central to Martí's concept of the Party as is his notion that good government strives to reconcile constituent contradiction and is no more than the equilibrium of all elements which define a country. A different conception of the source of legitimacy and authority, if not of sovereignty, is the essence of Martí's dispute with elder, more prominent, combat-tested warriors like Máximo Gómez and Antonio Maceo. He shared their belief in the unavoidable civic duty of a Cuban revolutionary war against Spain. But, in helping to organize and carry it out, Martí rejected their tendency to *caudillismo,* an inheritance from an earlier war, and their confidence in the military necessity and immediate efficacy of a revolutionary dictatorship. He firmly insisted that "A nation is not founded, General, the way one commands a military camp" (*OA,* 211) and that "From its beginnings, the country must be built with viable forms originating in its own needs and character, so that an unsanctioned and unrealistic government will not lead it to partiality [that is, racial division, class war, or internecine strife] or to tyranny [that is, *caudillismo*]" (*OA,* 397–98).

These are the assumptions at the heart of Martí's estimate of Cuba's Carlos Manuel de Céspedes, echoed again in his stunning essay on Grant, his sketches of Tammany Hall's Boss Kelly and James G. Blaine, and any number of Martí's portraits of similar North American public personalities, who often add the imperialist vice of wanting to "go through this world digging their fingers into other people's flesh to see if it is soft or resistant" (*OA*, 358).

It is the absence of the autocrat and the egoist that Martí finds compelling in men like Henry Highland Garnet, Peter Cooper, and the abolitionist Wendell Philips, of whom he writes: "He bartered the ambition of shining by his own natural gifts for the humble glory of sacrificing them for the benefit of others" (*IM*, 60). The strong utopian strain in Martí's conception of state and society also draws him to the social outlook of individuals of equally utopian inclination: to Henry George, John Swinton, Terrence Powderly and to the moderate, conciliatory politics of the Knights of Labor.

Martí's years in the United States coincide with the conclusion of the Indian Wars, the dominance and corruption of the Robber Barons and Trusts, the aggravation of the struggle between capital and labor, the general acceptance of lynch law among whites, and the political awakening of some of its new immigrant populations. It is Martí's perception of these developments that *Inside the Monster* especially highlights, whose assessments *Our America* confirms. Initially taken by the productive capacity and the democratic character of the American polity, Martí eventually regards the United States as, first, two countries, each with a distinct and contrasting moral personality. "The good country regards them [corrupt politicians] with rancor, but sometimes, enmeshed in their snares or dazzled by their projects, it trudges after them" (*IM*, 204). By the 1890s, he sees it as a place in which "democracy is being corrupted and diminished, not strengthened and saved from the hatred and wretchedness of [the] monarchies" of a rigidly class-defined Europe (*IM*, 51). Martí gradually despairs of the ability of the United States to ensure itself a permanent state of national consolidation, lasting racial harmony, or equitable condition of economic and social security for all of its citizens. Its ethnic and class confrontations become evidence of the tendency toward internal fracture which he is struggling mightily to avoid in a future Cuban republic. They also suggest "an incredible reign of terror, unfortunately latent in the heart of this country" (*OA*, 356). Given that country's greater economic advantage and imperialist plans, acceptance by Latin America of any of its proposals for a Pan-American union is all the more inadvisable.

Martí is, not unexpectedly, especially uneasy with the concept of class warfare and with those, like Karl Marx, who sanction working-class violence. Perhaps the most enlightened representative of the radically progressive wing of a core of middle-class Creole liberals poised to assume the reins of state, Martí did not believe that any intrinsic or essential conflict of interest divided classes. His views reveal the ambiguity typical of the most far-reaching members of that class. His response to confrontational working-class sentiment (socialists, Marxists, and anarchists; of Germans, Italians, and Russian Jews), while expressing genuine solidarity with its sense of justice, is quite ambiguous. Anarchism's conception of the State was wholly antithetical to Martí's own. Its Cuban variant, of Spanish origin and initially cool to independence, was an ideological competitor for the political loyalty of the island's working classes. American anarchism, whose tactics Martí rejected but whose motivations he understood and could, to some extent, even sympathize with, he ultimately regarded as well meaning but strategically misguided. It is only after the Haymarket Riots, in the last of his three dispatches on that event, that Martí grudgingly admits the possibility and moral legitimacy of working-class violence, but only *in extremis* and as an instrument of last resort made inevitable by the stupidity of the upper classes and bosses. Martí's passages on race, women, Native Americans, and other "minorities" are similarly ambivalent. By current standards problematically or naively assimilationist and male chauvinist, Martí was at once antiracist and a white Creole liberal characteristic of his time. Foner's volumes fully register all of these tensions and complexities.

Readers will, for all that, be struck by Martí's pointed penetration, the blend of analytical realism and idealism, his renunciation of materialistic values, lack of soul, and the implacable brutality of American capitalism which emerges in essays like "Crisis and the Cuban Revolutionary Party," "To the Root," "The World's Poor," "Indians in the United States," "Political Corruption," "The First Voting Women in Kansas," "Mob Violence in New Orleans," "The Schism of the Catholics in New York," "The Washington Pan-American Congress," and "The Labor Problem in the United States."

The tension between the realist and the romantic in Martí's temperament is thrown into particular relief in *On Art and Literature*. At least eight of the essays included, it is worth noting, were originally written in English, and at least one appeared in French. The commentaries it brings together demonstrate Martí's knowledge of a dazzling array of national schools, general trends, emerging fashions, and individuals. He is ever alert to the telling details of concept, composition, style, and execution. Keen and exact, he seldom fails to register his sensitivity to the material and practical socioeconomic context. "No private person," he speculates about one painting, "could have paid for a composition which must have taken the painter some years to paint" (*AL,* 93.) The essays on Emerson and Whitman included here were Latin America's first substantive introduction to these writers. The excesses of their exuberance notwithstanding, they are solidly insightful readings of the formal and conceptual departures their work represents. Martí knows— and considers it part of his duty as critic to examine—the derivation, cohort, and unique distinction of each artist; the strengths of talent, schooling, or individual personality; as well as the weaknesses of insufficiency, lack of daring, underutilized potential, or undue discipleship. Among the more interesting details, typical only of his art reviews of the early eighties, is Martí's use of the pronouns "we" and "our" even when directly addressing the work or institutions of North Americans. It suggests a global "Americanness" and the establishment of a primary line of demarcation between an authentic *American* art and the art of Old Europe. "American art," he writes, "is in its cradle. It must be improved, but in an original direction; the old methods must be imported, but not the old ideas" (*AL,* 75). He is, therefore, constantly looking for some sign of native genius and originality.

His critique of the esthetic premises of outdated Spanish romantics, of the Parnassians, Symbolists, and their early *modernista* Spanish-American imitators, adumbrated in the essays "Heredía," "Francisco Sellen," "Julían Del Casal," and more obliquely, in "Modern Spanish Poets," is predicated on his rejection of the tyranny of the inappropriate model. He also condemns any proclivity among writers to assume an aristocratic perch in the rarified air above the multitudes. "Poetry is durable when it is the work of all . . ." (*AL,* 261) and, he avers, "must have its roots in the earth and a basis in reality" (*AL,* 238). Still, even as he rejects their mimicry and warmed-over Platonism, Martí's esthetic ideas reflect the irrationalist essentialism of a few late-romantic tropes. In poetry, he insists, "emotion is the main thing, as a sign of the passion that moves it . . . It is a certain state of spiritual confusion and tempestuousness, in which the mind functions merely as an aid, putting and taking away, until the music is able to contain what comes from outside of it." Poetry, in fine, "is an aerial art . . ." (*AL,* 238–39). Sincerity and passion, pure and transcendent, are its two cardinal virtues. This dialectic of contrary elements and ideas is synthesized in a notion of the beautiful in which balance, again, is central. Thus, Martí approvingly tells us of the painter Fromentin: he "had the instincts of an adventurer, restrained by the habits of a born cavalier. He had the boldness of genius, without the turbulence and disorder. Ardent, as an innovator, he was precise as an academician. He improved the rules of art without breaking them" (*AL,* 84). It is as if, but for the singular inaptness of the word "academician" Martí was describing himself. His ideas *On Education* are of a piece with this emphasis on balance and the requirement that education equip Latin Americans—at home or abroad—to respond to the real needs of and effectively contribute to life in their native countries.

Among the more annoying of Foner's procedural quirks is a tendency to give us, in several instances, only partial commentaries or short texts excerpted from more extensive essays. "Passages on the Racial Question" in *Our America,* for example, includes capsule observations from essays covering the period 1880–1894 taken from various sources, but only two complete articles—"My Race" and "The Dish of Lentils"—from the last two of these years. These are a fair representation of Martí's views (which the reader will also find embedded in various other texts throughout the four volumes), but the procedure decontextualizes and gives those texts an air of thematic axioms with a hint of the iconographic about them. Foner's emphasis on the later Martí compounds our sense of dissatisfaction. The absence of, say, "The Charlestown Earthquake" (1886) from these four volumes is thus all the more lamentable. This critical transitional piece, perhaps more than any other, vividly dramatizes that an unimpeachable solidarity was not always incompatible with a whiff of philanthropic paternalism and an exotic picture of African Americans, in whose "fright and joy there is some of the marvelous and supernatural that does not exist in the other primitive races."[4] It would have, I think, added to a subtler appreciation of the literary dimensions of those conceptual blemishes which are inseparable from the dynamic complexity of Martí's human individuality. The selections on Guatemala and Venezuela, strong on Martí's positive responses to these countries, might have pointed less obliquely to the motivations and causes of his departures which the general introduction notes. The editor's choice of what and how much to annotate can, from time to time, appear oddly inconsistent: Figures generally accessible or more or less familiar—Luther, Lincoln—are occasionally given the kind of attention usually justified by obscurity of reference, while some genuinely obscure figures merit no more than the dates of their existence. One misses Martí's commentary on Edward Bellamy, the utopian author of *Looking Backward, 2000–1887*, whose critique of capitalism in many respects dovetailed with his own, and which would have nicely complemented some of the essays included in *On Art and Literature* and *Inside the Monster*. But this is, all in all, quibbling about details. Foner's four volumes are still an excellent introduction to a man of whom it might well be said, as he said of Bolívar: "The soul of a continent never entered so fully into that of one man" (*OA*, 104).

Notes

1. Ezequiel Martínez Estrada, *Martí: El héroe y su acción revolucionaria* (México-España, 1969), 6.

2. My quotations from Martí in English rely on the four-volume anthology of his work edited with introductions and notes by Philip S. Foner: José Martí, *Inside the Monster: Writings on the United States and American Imperialism* (New York: Monthly Review Press, 1975), abbreviated hereafter *IM*; *Our America: Writings on Latin America and the Struggle for Cuban Independence* (New York: Monthly Review Press, 1977), abbreviated *OA*; *On Education: Articles on Educational Theory and Pedagogy, and Writings for Children from The Age of Gold* (New York: Monthly Review Press, 1979), abbreviated *OE*; and *On Art and Literature: Critical Writings* (New York: Monthly Review Press, 1982), abbreviated *AL*.

3. Thus this early version of a yeomenry which anticipates Martí's more fully developed critique of the monopolist thrust and materialism of American capitalism in "Crisis and the Cuban Revolutionary Party" (1893) as well as his later sympathy for the ideas of Henry George: "A nation having many small landowners is rich. A nation having a few wealthy men is not rich, only the one where each of its inhabitants shares a little of the common wealth. In political economy and in good government, distribution is the key to prosperity" (*OA*, 140).

4. José Martí, *Páginas Selectas* (Buenos Aires, 1939).

A Poet's Century

THE YEAR 2002 marks the centennial anniversary of the birth of Cuba's internationally acclaimed national poet Nicolás Guillén. Born in the provincial city of Camaguey on July 10, 1902, Guillén was the son of a silversmith turned journalist and newspaper editor who, as a member of the island's black middle class, became a leader in the local branch of the National Liberal Party. His father's assassination by conservative government troops during the 1917 uprising against the presidency of Mario García Menocal, popularly known as "La Chambelona," deprived the son "of his friend and teacher, of his firmest spiritual support." With his father's death came a period of severe economic hardship for the family. The young Nicolás, now a major source of its economic support, went to work as a typesetter in a local publisher's printshop. Completing his high school studies at night, he also later sought to further his education at the University of Havana. After only a year, however, he gave up the study of law that he started there. Instead, he turned to a career as a journalist, writer, and poet, to which he was more compellingly drawn and in which he would rise to become his country's most important twentieth-century poet, one of the Caribbean's most seminally original voices, one of Latin America's most distinguished literary figures, and one of the contemporary world's lyric giants.

On his return to Camaguey from Havana, Guillén co-edited the literary page of *Las Dos Repúblicas,* his father's former newspaper. He also saw his first verses published in *Camaguey Gráfico.* By the summer of 1922, indeed, he had collected forty-six of his poems into a first book. That book, *Cerebro y corazón* (Head and Heart), would nonetheless remain unpublished for more than four decades.[1] Paying due homage to the influence of Rubén Darío and his followers, it revealed the lingering, still powerful effect of their *modernista* esthetic. But it was "the worst Darío," Guillén would later aver, perhaps too dismissively, "the Darío of tintypes and enamels, with swans, fountains, abbots, pages, counts, marchionesses, and all those other knick-knacks." *Cerebro y corazón*, for all that, argued the young poet's excellent ear and technical prowess. The poet's rhythmic skill and casual, conversational command of lyric forms as time-honored as the madrigal and ballad, as culturally authoritative and demanding as the sonnet, were plainly apparent. A mood of somber melancholy—"Lord, Lord, . . . why is humanity so evil"—, at the same time, hinted vaguely at that elegiac, less misanthropic mood which would later become one of the distinctive features of the mature writer's verse. There were also flashing glimpses of that determination to "flap the wings of your audacity / in the face of any obstacle's impertinence" and of a desire to see lit "in the rebellious shadows / of my soul / the love of him who suffers" which would also soon emerge as more characteristic of his poetic temper and positive lyric purpose. In its concise *agonic* synthesis of the calculated dialectic between tears and laughter and its intimation of the tone and themes of "sad, subtle complaint," of love, of struggle, that would also be key elements of the later poet's "verso doloroso" the collection's final poem, "Rhythm," in particular, is evocative of things that were yet to come. Its resemblance to the "Riddles" that appeared in *West Indies Ltd* more than a decade later is particularly striking.

The years between 1922 and 1927 mark a period during which Guillén wrote no poetry but worked almost exclusively as a journalist and literary magazine editor. He founded and edited *Lis,* a literary biweekly. He also wrote for the newspaper *El Camagueyano*, and, for a brief time, even served as a typist for the Government Secretariat in Havana.

Finally breaking his silence, in 1927 Guillén began once again to write poems. The journal *Orto* in which these new poems appeared was one of the island's provincial participants in the burgeoning *vanguardista* movement. The movement's promotion of an *avant garde* esthetics found some resonance in occasional elements of the surreal and, especially, in the echoes of futurism's accent on the ordinary machinery, new technologies, and urban detritus of modern life and experience suggested by the imagery, rhetoric, and strategies of some of these more clearly transitional poems. "They spoke," Guillén himself tells us, "of airplanes discovered in some future world and mistaken for the skeleton of unidentified monsters; or of the sun, drunk and staggering on a street corner; or, finally, of clock hands crucified at a quarter to three. It was . . ." he concludes, "the language of the time." Long preoccupied and growing increasingly concerned with "the great problem of the relations between whites and blacks in Cuba" and the urgency to avoid what a year later he would critically refer to as the (racially segregated) "Road to Harlem," in 1928 Guillén, a mulatto, became a contributor to *Ideales de una raza,* the Sunday literary supplement devoted to Afro-Cuban culture and affairs of the *Diario de la Marina,* an otherwise conservative Havana newspaper. It was in this Sunday supplement that the eight poems of his epoch-making *Motivos de son* were first published on April 20, 1930.

The appearance of the eight poetic monologues that, later that year, would become Guillén's first published book of verse, proved a sensational turning point and something of a national epiphany. Allowing its various black and mulatto protagonists an unprecedented independence of voice and their own very distinctive "street savvy" point of view and proletarian comportment, *Motivos* gave readers a more boldly immediate and unmediated glimpse into the assorted socioeconomic and racial realities daily faced by the "colored" inhabitants of Havana's slums than any poet had ever previously dared. Its critically penetrating realism, social and psychological density, and intraracial complexities brought, too, a new, comparatively less exoticized and more layered texture to the *poesía negrista* then coming into vogue in Cuba and, as early as 1926, throughout the wider Hispanic Caribbean. Guillén's calculated invocation of and reliance on the vernacular musical form that emerged from the Creolization of African and European traditions on Cuban soil, in addition, were as broadly strategic as they were deliberate. Regarding the *son* as "perhaps the form most appropriate" to his culturally representative purpose, Guillén declared that he aimed to "incorporate into Cuban literature—not simply as a musical motif but rather as an element of true poetry—what might be called the poem-*son*." Presenting readers with "ordinary people just as they move around us. Just as they speak, just as they think," *Motivos* thus also strove for a culturally apt modality, a uniquely *Cuban* lyric inflection and focus. The poet's compatriot and biographer Angel Augier vividly recalls the extraordinary impact the signal debut of the *son*-poems had at the time. "We all suddenly felt," he observes, "as though we were being offered elements for the resolution of an artistic and patriotic problem which we had more than once posed to ourselves, . . . [we were] at the same time surprised to find that those elements were in fact so very close to hand . . ." A year later, in 1931, the poet's *son*-motifs were once again published, with a series of eight new "mulatto" poems, under the title

Sóngoro cosongo. Guillén's long and outstanding career as the herald and envoy of a nationally representative and distinctively Cuban verse, Antillean sensibility, and integratively Creole perspective had now been launched in earnest.

In the years after the publication of *Motivos de son* and *Sóngoro cosongo,* Guillén went on to become, in more than fourteen subsequent books of poetry and the nearly three decades of literary activity that preceded his death in 1989, the most capacious lyric observer and visionary poetic chronicler of the evolving national experience, cultural and ethnohistorical dramas and social-political aspirations of his people, his region, and his time. Beyond the incisive ironies, instructive wit, and revelations of its regular deflation of any hint or tenacious deposits of pigmentocratic snobbery or (even tacit) white supremacist racial conceit—addressed variously, for example, in poems as diverse and widely separated in time as "High Brown" (1930), "West Indies Ltd (1934), "Son Number 6" (1943), "My Last Name" (1953), "Maus-Maus" (1953), "Little Rock" (1958), "Governor" (1963), "KKK" (1967), "What Color?" (1968), "European Slaves," (1972), and number "XXIII" of his "Epigrams" (1972)—Guillén's poetry unwaveringly embodied the view that "the spirit of Cuba is *mestizo.* And [that] from the spirit through the skin our true [Cuban] color will emerge." It was to the national project of the emergence, articulation, candid recognition, and steadfast defense of the historic unfolding, cultural distinctiveness, and current condition of that more encompassing *Cuban color* that he would henceforth devote his life and his art. Thenceforward his poetry would also bear resolute testimony to the vicissitudes, noxious consequences, and persistent urgencies to sovereignty of Cuba's—the Caribbean's and Latin America's—colonial or neocolonial dependency on the United States and to the imperatives of an equally urgent need to transform a manifestly unjust social system. Like his own *son*-singer José Ramón Cantaliso, he too always sang plain that system's failings "so everyone would well understand."

Informed by his congregationally integrative vision of Cuban national identity and by the drive to secure its cultural independence and its ambitions to a genuine political autonomy and freedom, from *West Indies Ltd* (1934) through *La paloma de vuelo popular* (1958), the poet's work would register a progressive expansion of the scope of his geographic and thematic horizons, an increasing internationalization of perspective, as well as a deepening of his commitment to the necessity for fundamental change in a world where "to get enough to eat / you work 'til you're almost dead" and "it's not just bending your back, but also bowing your head." But, as in the poems he devoted to the Republican struggle during the Spanish Civil War, Guillén's elegiac testimony to the satrapic corruptions and general suffering an unjust society casually inflicts, mournfully unflinching as it invariably is, never succumbs to despair. He always confidently notes the approach of "A Joyful Song in the Distance." Inextricable from the aura of dirge-like lament is an unshakable historical optimism and hope whose overarching historical perspective and sense of gradual unfolding, as in the "Four Agonies" of *España: Poema en cuatro angustias y una esperanza* (1937) and the extraordinary *Elegies* that later followed, ultimately allow the poet always encouragingly to conclude with a vision of how "John People speaks . . . / . . . his brilliance armed and crowned / . . . / . . . tak[ing] up the ancient cry" to "greet a future drenched in blood, / red as the sheets, as the thighs / as the bed / of a woman who's just given birth." It is his verse's intimate, dialectic linkage of the reality of "a torn and blinded countryside, vomiting its shadows on the road beneath the lash of a field boss" with the vision of this future which, as the critic Alfred Melon aptly points out, intimates and evokes the stubborn resilience "in the peoples thought of as passive, the strength and immense revolutionary potential that lay behind that exterior patience, that serene smile, beneath which there seethes a subterranean fury."

In the years after 1959, collections like *Tengo, El gran zoo, La rueda dentada,* and *El diario que a diario* would go on to register the singular sense of exhilarating triumph, of quotidian historic changes, and of new challenge, ushered in by the unprecedented success of the reality-transforming Revolution Guillén's previous verse obviously looked forward to and appeared even to prophesy. A perceptible change of emotional tone and general mood, occasioned by the achievement and promise of the Cuban Revolution and the New Era it inaugurated, is certainly one of the distinctive features of Guillén's writing after 1959. A clear shift of stress, from the anguished and elegiac to the buoyant and celebratory is as evident in *Tengo*'s title poem, "I Have," in "Whatever Time Is Past Was Worse" and "I Came on a Slave Ship" as in the later books' "The Bourgeoisie," "Batistaph," and, however more implicitly, "Problems of Underdevelopment." If the elegiac note is palpable still in "Tell Me," "The Inheritance," "Sunday Reading," and "Guitar in Mourning Major," poems like "The Flowers Grow High," at the same time, give some indication of the sudden surge of militant hope, eager optimism, and radical conviction and action the revolution then encouraged not only on the island but across the Americas.

The publication, in 1967, of Guillén's shrewdly emblematic bestiary, *The Great Zoo*, brought yet another dimension of formal novelty to this fresh air of joyfully triumphant zest. Its figurative tour through a microcosmic menagerie of "animals"—human, mineral, vegetable, and emblematic —put on striking display the poet's creative and meta-phorical audacity, even as it once more confirmed the astute elegance and cunning subtlety of his already long-recognized satirical wit and humor.

El diario que a diario (*The Daily Daily*) still more dramatically ex-hibited its author's gift for playfully inventive renewal and seriously thought-provoking flair for probing literary experimentation and novel explorations in structure and form. Offering a synthesizing panorama and critical reconfiguring of Cuban history from early colonial times to the *barbudos'* victorious descent from the eastern Sierra Maestra moun-tains in 1959, *The Daily Daily* compels the reader to gauge the charac-ter, deeper salients, gathering import, and enduring momentum of the island's unfolding odyssey as much, indeed much more, from the rhe-torical, cultural, and ideological signature(s) each of its periods leaves behind in its assorted *papers*. The abbreviated chronology of decisive pinnacle moments and *events* it also points to serves both as confirming general epochal frame and as the intermittently punctuating circum-stantial climatic peaks of those signatures. A category of allegorical saga in the form of an ordinary newspaper, the poem presents us with a log or register in which "extraordinary things can be found" and of which Guillén is "the notary" and "inventor of the inventory." This *Daily's* pages are full of the "announcements, messages, warnings" that emerge from the textual debris and production of everyday life: the state or-dinances, public notices, classified ads, product commercials, jingles, linguistic fads, prosodic and poetic fashions, social notices, ephemeral fragments of newsflash, and the anonymous public gossip "official his-tory" rarely privileges, though these can give, as they do here, an eclectic energy, a specific *human feel,* and intangible, transient rationality to the myriad *activity* of the past and its lingering, if often unnoticed *present-ness.* A sustained collage of texts of all kinds— bureaucratic, mercantile, historic, literary, bibliographic; at once "factual" and invented or, as with the "Classified Ads" offering "European Slaves" for sale, with but slight, telling modifications of authentic historic originals—*The Daily Daily* ingeniously gives new, still more complex dimensions to the epic contours of Guillén's historical outlook. Its insistence on the dialectic of ineluctable confrontation and exchange, on an active cultural-historical unfolding, and on the enduring legacies of the past and the present to the future further corroborate those central elements which, from the first, have always informed his vision. The book's canny juxtaposition of the most heterogeneous texts—of both verse and prose—brings to new heights that inclination to the inspired combination and collage-like fusion of varied forms which is, in fact, one of the compositional hallmarks of "West Indies Ltd" and his several pre-revolution *Elegies*. The aura of pedagogical frolic and whimsy of *Por el mar de las antillas anda un barco de papel* (On the Sea of the Antilles Sails a Little Paper Ship), by the same token, attests at once to the poet's new exuberance and to his long-standing commitment to the exigent art of writing for the very young. Its title is a line from his earlier (1943) "Song for Antillean Children." "The Flight of Big Frog and Frog Tot" is an especially compelling example of his felicitous command of a genre that Guillén, unlike most, plainly does not regard as dismissively "minor."

Originally written in the mid-sixties, though appearing posthumously, *In Some Springtime Place* likewise brought continuing resonance and novel reverberations to the confidential intimacy and passionate intensities of an abundant repertoire of excellent love poems to be found across the length and breath of Guillén's oeuvre. Distantly reminiscent of the avid stirrings, voluptuous expectancies, and hushed poignancies of secret erotic encounter and the "courteous, cordial, fortunate, fatal" romantic nostalgias of "A Poem of Love" (its perhaps most comparable predecessor), and of the "broken sighs, / chimeras burned to ashes" that "Ovenstone" recollects, this affectionate elegy, too, as its translator Keith Ellis notes, "explores . . . the idea of lost love and exhibits a void that comes to be inhabited by [the poet's] perplexity and vivid memories." Moving testimony to an affair that has ended and a love, now unrequited, that still vitally endures, a finely shaded *tendresse* shimmers from all the facets of its yearning melancholy. More textured by the maturer man's keener consciousness of our mortalities, as lovers and human beings, death and bereavement, indeed, become its virtually interchangeable central metaphors. Not knowing "if I should say goodbye, or what I'll do / when I no longer see you," the possibility of ultimately attaining "in some springtime place / humid with the new

moon's kiss" "your resplendent return" is all of immortality the poet
seeks and all the epiphany of transcendence abiding love can imagine.
A requiem as compelling in its sustained emotional force and power
as any of Guillén's better-known elegies, this one brings a more soul-
saddening timbre, depth, and nuance to "Nocturne"'s previous sound-
ings of erotic ache and to the desolate incredulities of "If Anyone Had
Told Me."

In a language and region known for the exceptional caliber of its
poets, Guillén, as Henry James might have said, is master in a whole
class and in a class all his own. He stands alongside César Vallejo and
Pablo Neruda as one of the three most original and influential voices of
his generation. Incomparable chronicler and defender of Cuba's— and
the Caribbean's—legacy of national experience and sense of identity, he
gives his verse the ecumenical reach and communicative efficacy that
have, at the same time, everywhere struck chords of sympathetic response and recognition of our common humanity. Unambiguously engaging with the most pressing and volatile issues of our time, "all of
his work," the Argentine writer Ezequiel Martínez Estrada has rightly
observed, "is a battle against oppression, against the privileges and
rivalries that separate human beings of whatever condition." Eschew-
ing the insular comforts of the merely parochial, its unique blend of the
popular and of the partisan and political with the most demanding exigencies of literary excellence equally avoids the tacit condescensions of
confusing the progressive with the pedestrian and banal. A Marxist for
fifty-two of the eighty-seven years that he lived, Guillén would also remain consistently active in the civic struggles definitive of his era and, in
the period before 1959, suffered persecution, imprisonment, and exile
for the firmly held radical convictions which informed his literary, jour-
nalistic, and political activities.

Universally acknowledged as a "classic" in his own time, Guillén was
the object of numerous accolades and honors over the years. Recipient
of the Lenin International Peace Prize in 1954, he was in 1961 formally
awarded the title "National Poet of Cuba." Elected first president of
the Union of Cuban Artists and Writers (UNEAC) in that same year,
he served in that capacity for all the years that still remained to him.
Earlier elected to membership on the National Council on Education,
he would, in addition, later be entrusted with duties and offices of similar import and distinction. Already widely traveled abroad at the time
of the Revolution's triumph, Guillén oftentimes led or participated in

Cuba's cultural and diplomatic delegations to countries throughout Latin America, Europe, Africa, and Asia. In the later years of his life, more critically celebrated than ever, he could look back with increasing satisfaction upon a career which had attained the kind of emblematic and iconographic status a literary and political life devoted to the collectivity, to the welfare and spiritual integrity of the ordinary citizen, had earned and was earning still. The more mysterious and still more enviable consecration which only that anonymous mass of undistinguished commoners can ultimately confer by their ongoing popular appropriation of his poems, lines, and phrases in song, in speech, in the critically uninscribed praise of fragmentary reference and unacknowledged but universally familiar recital had already, long before, begun. Its more enduring tribute of oral absorption into itself with which a community rewards its Cervanteses, Shakespeares, Hugos, Zolas, Daríos, Whitmans—and Gulléns—continues to go on as actively and unabatedly as ever. The most casual reading of his verse immediately gives its reader palpable evidence to appreciate the substantive why and wherefore of this rare privilege and double accomplishment.

Notes

1. It was not made public until Angel Augier included the book in the first volume of Guillén's *Obra poética 1920–1958*, published in 1972.

The Stoic and the Sisyphean
John Hearne and the Angel of History

For Franklin Knight and J. J. Arrom

History dig a gulf between us, boy,
An' it don't fill in yet. Not yet.
Land of the Living

UNDOUBTEDLY ONE of the most accomplished, articulate, and distinguished of contemporary writers from the Caribbean, John Hearne is
also, after V. S. Naipaul, quite possibly the most controversial and enigmatic. Though he is less internationally celebrated than his Trinidadian
colleague, Hearne's fiction has, nonetheless, been an object of the most
intense and diverse commentary. Critical response to his several novels,
unanimous in its recognition of his superb craftsmanship and the artistic effectiveness of his gift for description, is dramatically divided in its
appraisal of their final implications, the worldview they bear witness to,
and, inevitably, the place they ultimately occupy in the larger context of
an enduring Caribbean canon. Here, like Naipaul's, Hearne's work has
provoked everything from an impassioned, dismissive ire to acclama-
tory encomium. Considered, rather approvingly one suspects, "the most
classic of British Caribbean novelists" by the Guyanese poet and critic
A. J. Seymour,[1] he has, at the same time, been accused of being conscientiously outside the mainstream of the most genuinely representative
creators of the contemporary Caribbean novel.

> What he puts into his books [George Lamming argues] is always less inter-
> esting than the *omissions* which a careful reader will notice he has forced
> himself to make. He is not an example of that instinct and root impulse
> which returns the better West Indian writers back to the soil. For soil is

a large part of what the West Indian novel has brought back to reading; lumps of earth, unrefined, perhaps, but good, warm, fertile, earth.[2]

The more recent assessments of Frank Birbalsingh, Barrie Davis, Sylvia Wynter, Mervyn Morris and John Figueroa continue, from their different perspectives, to dispute the issue. For Birbalsingh nearly all of Hearne's fiction is so much escapist evasion.[3] At once less biting and more circumspect, Davis laments that "his eye has not more variation in [social] focus," acknowledges that a certain authorial ambiguity "unbalances" his work, but is finally impressed with "Hearne's sincere attempt [...] to appreciate an institution [the world of the rural squirearchy] that has caused so much bitterness in the West Indies" and with the way in which he has "broaden[ed] the scope of the Caribbean novel, particularly in the area of sex."[4] Among the more perceptive and incisive and certainly one of the severest of Hearne's critics, Sylvia Wynter concedes the originality of his contribution to a general experiential awareness which "extends to all the areas of the senses"[5] but, witheringly, concludes that he "is still imprisoned in a European scale of reference, a very arrogant Eurocentric view"[6] of the Caribbean.

More strictly formalist in their assumptions Mervyn Morris and John Figueroa would seem intent on rescuing Hearne from his more hostile detractors. Rejecting the disdainful sweep of their interpretations, Morris is particularly sympathetic to the structural complexity that gives pattern and meaning to the artist's work. The reader is "encouraged to return to the text instead of replacing it with the more impressive ideas of the free-wheeling critic."[7] Figueroa is similarly skeptical of too premature or categorical a judgment. In consequence, he emphasizes the virtue in what others see as a crucial shortcoming. It is precisely Hearne's ambivalence, "the predicament of being caught 'between'"[8] which, he affirms, makes him "both *more* and less radical than [his radical West Indian critics] and than most West Indian novelists."[9] The barely concealed irony in Morris's "more impressive," and the equivocal *hauteur* of his reference to the "the free-wheeling critic," like Figueroa's striving "to achieve a certain coolness,"[10] are all symptomatic of a controversy showing no signs of immediately abating.

Something more is at stake, of course, than minor differences of emphasis or literary opinion. Personal idiosyncrasy contributes, to be sure, its own spice to the discussion. It cannot, however, be by any means reduced to a simple matter of individual taste and preference. Inextricably bound up with any consideration of the esthetic and formal merits of Hearne's work are important, still incandescent, historical, ideological, and political questions. These include: the nature of class and racial conflict in Antillean—in this case, Jamaican—society; the source and rightful repository of whatever claims might be made to an indwelling authenticity; the particular content of any felt relationship to the past; the prospects that lie ahead; and, crucially, the scope of the novelist's compass—no less than his *attitude*—in coming to terms with these several fraught and crucial issues. In the Anglophone Antilles, no single group, certainly, has yet managed to achieve an undisputed hegemonic consensus about them.

All vividly felt daily realities, the aftermath of slavery, the legacy of post-emancipation immigration patterns, the immediate memory of a still powerful colonial past, and the impact of neocolonialism provide the context for a spate of as yet unresolved contradictions. Notions of "national" representation, communal authority, and cultural definition become, under the circumstances, critically significant, a vital element in the continuing bid for hegemony among contending groups and interests, issues of paramount importance implicit in the work of the critics and writers of the region.

For Naipaul (who, almost alone among the major writers from the area, has assumed the role of perpetually displaced, wandering commentator on societies he repeatedly concludes are bereft of possibilities) the source of any cultural authority or authenticity must forever lie beyond the archipelago. For the great majority it is, on the contrary, properly domestic. Increasingly, it resides in acknowledging the centrality of the primarily black—rural and urban—underclass in the historical formation of a genuinely Caribbean culture and in the identification of the fortunes of this underclass with the health and fate of the polity as a whole. It is here that one is struck by the larger significance of the work of, among others, George Lamming, Samuel Selvon, Vic Reid, Earl Lovelace, and, more recently, N. D. Williams, Michael Thelwell, and Harry Narain. The attentive reader will notice how the classic version of the epic, concerned with the noble and the great, has been transformed in the fiction of such writers. One sees an inversion of perspective and the mindfully deliberate articulation of a new epic: an epic of the wretched, the anonymous, the obscure and neglected—of those hitherto absent from History. The careful reader will be equally impressed by a peculiar departure from the conventional bourgeois novel. The claim to a uniquely individual experience, typical of novels in the European and self-consciously modernist tradition, is impossible to sustain in even the most studiously autobiographical of this fiction. It collapses under the weight of its subject: a society in which literacy cannot be taken for granted, in which, a measure of social privilege, reading is far from being a merely leisure activity; and in which, on assuming his vocation, the writer can hardly avoid being conscious of the masses of those who are unable to read him but for whom it is invariably assumed he, in one way or another, speaks.[11] The burden of responsibility is both palpably felt and, more often than not, transparent. In the most insistently personal voice there is always, if only in the tone, an implied "we" lurking just under the surface. We are thus made aware that the focus of the work, the real subject, is not merely a circumscribed private *experience* but, above all, the contours of a collective *condition*. It is to the actual structure and content of that "we" that one must be alert. More and more, the distinctive characteristics, the press and urgency of the world of the folk become, in one way or another, emblematic of its condition.

Against the backdrop of this panorama, Hearne's fiction is at once wholly orthodox and, as his critics suggest, oddly anomalous. It seems to me clearly to concede, however obliquely, the decisive emergence—the primacy even—of the presence and priorities of the dispossessed. It is, though, a reluctant, equivocal concession. Hearne's penchant is patrician. His recognition is qualified and the scope of his vision restricted. In the age of the socialist revolution, he is "at home in the big plantation house."[12] Sensitive, at times acutely so, to the drift and import of contemporary social trends, he appears to be, at the same time, curiously out of synch with the time. His work is an almost Faulknerian eulogy to a class, the rural mulatto squirearchy, which history appears to have "suddenly" gone beyond.

Between the damning ironies and overtly colonial sympathies of Naipaul and the Black Nationalist, populist, or frankly proletarian sentiments of his other *confrères,* John Hearne stands rather heretically alone. He eschews as equally inapt the generic metaphors of Prospero and Caliban. His own symbol is the isolate Crusoe. His plots oscillate, in a kind of permanent stasis, between an irrepressible longing for the security of an idealized rural arcadia of gentlemen farmers and the "dangerous" allure, perilous and seductively compelling, of an all-inclusive radical engagement. The tension is fragile and unstable, and fraught with an inescapable existential angst. Hearne's is a poignant and, in the philosophical and ordinary sense of the term, an absurd predicament. It is the invariable lack of any satisfactory resolution that gives his novels their particular aura of stoic suffering and tormented resignation.

Hearne's novels are, as well, a response to—and part of the legacy of—the dissolution of the temporary alliance between the *avant garde* of the colored elite and black masses of Jamaica which emerged in the wake of the strikes and riots of 1938. It is this historical dimension of his work which has to date received the least critical attention. Sylvia Wynter perhaps comes closest to seriously engaging the issue when she writes: "Hearne's political philosophy [. . .] seems to me to be the [. . .] *'liberal'* politics of the present status quo." She does not, however, go on to examine the concrete historical roots of that politics. She even, surprisingly, finds it odd and particularly "disturbing" that "a man of his generation" should assume such a posture.[13] It is, on the contrary, just those facts of his distinct "generational" experience—most notably his loyalty to that class whose political reliability the disintegration of the coalition had dramatically called into question—which inform and largely help to explain it. The suggestion, mooted in more than one of his novels, that cross-class alliances are vulnerable to the volatility of the disinherited seems to me symptomatic. The similarly recurrent conceit that portrays any binding commitment, especially to the promise of a revolutionary transformation of society, as misguided or tragically Sisyphean is no less telling. The edge of shattered idealism and disillusionment one might expect in a disenchanted patrician is, in any event, unmistakable. The combination of these several dimensions imbues Hearne's fiction with its singular air of visceral skepticism and a vaguely Spenglerian historical outlook.

History is, predictably, one of Hearne's major preoccupations. "History," he writes, "is the angel with whom all we Caribbean Jacobs have to wrestle, sooner or later, if we hope for a blessing."[14] The conditions of his own encounter with that angel are ineluctably prescribed by the character of Jamaican society,[15] its crisis and transformations, and the rapidly shifting terrain of his peculiar place in it. A thorough appreciation of these is necessarily preliminary to any critical assessment of Hearne's struggle with his seraphic antagonist.

The most decisive fact about the Jamaica into which Hearne was born is its pyramidal social structure and, alongside a keen class consciousness, the existence of a multitiered pigmentocracy. Of the two decades after 1918, which include Hearne's childhood and adolescence, James Carnegie writes:

> Class, colour and income lines usually ran together. The upper class consisted of the white planters, professionals, merchants and administrators with a few coloured added. It was dominated by 1300 Jews and Lebanese. [. . .] Some Chinese, coloured and blacks qualified financially but not socially. [Lord] Olivier noted that these people gathered round the snobbish afternoon tea tables; they also had exclusive clubs like the Jamaica Club and the Manchester Club. [. . .] The younger set frolicked at Bournemouth Club and similar spots. [. . .] The middle class was mostly coloured with a few blacks. They were of the secondary echelons in administration and business, first class clerks and storewalkers, etc. [. . .] They shared upper-class "cultural" aspirations and [like a majority of the upper class] were usually resident in the Corporate Area. Their values were white-oriented. [. . .] An American student [of Jamaican affairs] described the lower class as the "great underlying proletariat of African descent mainly agricultural, propertyless, destitute, semi-literate, insecure, separated [. . .] from coloured and white by institutions of marriage and church, opportunities in education and business, and restrained by law, force, and custom from [. . .] protest or revolt." This description [Carnegie concludes] was generally accurate.[16]

By mid-century this wage-earning peasantry, displaced from its mostly rural element, would dramatically augment the population of the corporate areas and slums. The economic dominion of the planters, in addition, would be severely curtailed. For the rest, the pattern of hierarchy remains roughly the same.

Hearne's origins are with the privileged sector of coloured aristocrats. He traces his own roots back, partially, to refugee French journalists and encyclopedists. He is also directly related, on the maternal side, to H. G. de Lisser (1878–1944). Author of the now classic *Jane's Career* (1913) and one of the island's most prominent and influential citizens, De Lisser served as editor-in-chief of the pro-planter newspaper *The Gleaner* for some thirty years. One gets the impression Hearne's family had, too, the clannish extension, as well as atmosphere of sheltered intimacy and camaraderie of a late Victorian club. Hearne attributes his choice of profession, in part at least, to the nourishing environment with which it provided him. "It was," he recalls, "a bookish family [. . .] most of our entertainment was very wide reading. There was always something in the various households of my family [. . .] always something new to read. So my own childhood seems to have been spent going from book to book [. . .] one became a writer because he couldn't do anything else really."[17]

Hearne himself was to attend the prestigious and then exclusive Jamaica College. He also served a three-year enlistment, at seventeen, as an Air Gunner in the Royal Air Force and, immediately after, went on to the Universities of Edinburgh and London. His wartime stint in the Air Force appears to have been seminal. It opened him up to a practical knowledge of the wider world, to a broader perspective from which to view his own, sharpening, as it did so, his growing perception of the ubiquity of politics, of ideological nuance, and of the subtleties and complexities of cultural and class antagonisms. Perhaps more important, it brought into further relief the equivocal contours of his particular identity as a colonial and "coloured" Jamaican. The experience seems to have confirmed, even as it textured and seriously challenged the salients of that identity. The presumption of a certain social rank and the ambiguity and uneasy comfort of being "almost white" were, in any event, the prevailing convictions in the ambience of Hearne's youth and young manhood. The strain and increasing untenability of the coloured elite's midway position and caste assumptions would, in fact, become one of his central themes as a novelist. It is precisely this personal and social tension in which Mark Lattimore, the octoroon protagonist of *Voices Under the Window,* the most evidently autobiographical of Hearne's novels, is caught, with "The black people bellowing at me to get off their backs, and the whites, too, screaming nervously, not so often, more refined, when I come nearer than a certain limit."[18] It is from the pivot of this tension that Hearne, like his character, initiates his encounter with History.

Hearne's Jamaica was at the same time—then as now—a society in uncertain transition. He was twelve when the strikes and riots provoked by popular dissatisfaction with the existing economic and social order erupted in 1938.

That explosion of worker discontent proved to be a critical assault on the hegemony of the upper classes. It precipitated a decisive realignment of forces that, as the middle classes saw their opportunity and momentarily joined ranks against the common adversary, would effect the political demise of the old plantocracy. It marked the emergence of an organized labor movement and the formation of mass-oriented political parties. The People's National Party (1938) and the Jamaican Labour

Party (1942) both issued out of that crucible. Under the patrician guidance of Norman Washington Manley and the flamboyantly charismatic Alexander Bustamante, respectively, they became permanent fixtures of the national scene. The achievement, in 1944, of universal adult suffrage gave the middle class—for which their leadership came increasingly to speak—an important and decisive instrument for its own attack on the traditional distribution of power. By the nineteen fifties and sixties its policies and ideological assumptions had firmly established themselves as the new status quo. Its very success was, in large measure, to dramatize and exacerbate that antagonism which estranged it from the lower class of blacks.

The decline of British economic predominance and its substitution, in Jamaica and throughout the Caribbean, by North American corporate capitalism was further eroding the position of the traditional agricultural oligarchy. World War II, the discovery of bauxite (1942), and the postwar policy of industrialization by invitation which gave rise to the building boom of the fifties accelerated and completed the eclipse of the old regime. A "dominant power complex of [. . .] American and Canadian commercial and industrial companies, with their local Jamaican allies [. . .] [among the newly elevated professional groups] has [since] filled [. . .] the vacuum left by the stagnation of the sugar-citrus-banana-rum economy."[19] The era was similarly marked by a revitalized nationalist fervor. To secure and extend its political authority, to garner local support, and to retard American economic encroachment, the plantocracy relied, ideologically, on a classless notion of "The Great Jamaican Family." It naturally stressed the fact of its own Jamaican nationality and what it argued were its essential contributions to the economy and well-being of the clan. The proletariat responded to the prevalent premises of racial and cultural superiority with a retributive messianism and the progressive articulation of a radical negritude, typified by Marcus Garvey and, after 1930, by the expanding influence of the Rastafarians. At once more capacious and more cautious, the middle class was split and, to the degree that it could, strove to reconcile the contradiction. In contrast to what it perceived as the shortsighted proprietal nationalism of the more conservative planters and what it regarded as the "atavistic" or "escapist" illusions of the heightened African emphasis of Black Nationalism, it argued for what might well be described as a *civic nativism*. Blending the familial accent with a more positive recognition of the facts of cultural Creolization, it also combined affirmation of the syncretic singularity of Creole society with a somewhat more attentive, if guardedly paternal, receptivity to the elements of racial pride typical of working-class militancy. A tacit Anglophile bias nonetheless informed its cultural outlook. With the Westminster model and parliamentary consensus as its political ideal, it elevated the idea of class convergence to the status of a strategic principle. It proposed, by gradual amelioration, to avoid the dangers of a racial war, on the one hand, and, on the other, the equally fearful possibility of an uncompromising revolutionary upheaval. The achievement of self-government and independence, which its progressive wing promoted and spearheaded, was at the core of its historical project. To greater or less extent, an anticolonial sentiment was, however, an ingredient in each of these distinct positions.

It is in this atmosphere, and exactly at the juncture of coincidence, that the PNP emerged, took shape, and assumed its particular personality.

> In the beginning [Rex Nettleford writes] Manley saw the P.N.P. as a kind of Congress-type party [. . .] and actually struggled between 1938 and 1942 to bring all and sundry (including the powerful union leader Alexander Bustamante and his following) to the cause. In this sense the P.N.P. in these years was more of a "movement" than a party. This in turn determined the nature of the membership which ranged from planter and mercantile interests through the strong core of middle class professionals and intelligentsia to urban working class and rural dwellers. [. . .] the presence of a left-wing socialist group [he goes on] acted as a catalyst to the party and [was an] irritant to the moderates and liberal conservatives all co-existing under the same umbrella.[20]

A crisis was inevitable. It became apparent, first, in Bustamante's break with Manley.[21] It surfaced again, as the PNP succumbed to conservative apprehension at the growing influence of the left within the party and moved further away from even its muted form of socialism after 1948,[22] in the definitive internal split between "moderates" and Marxists which was settled, in 1952, by the expulsion of the latter. "In this 'purge' the PNP lost its most active organizers and political educators. Most important, working-class organizations fell into disarray and the dominance of middle-class positions in the councils of the party was firmly established."[23]

Despite a continuing rhetoric of convergence, this delivered the coupe de grace to the original idea of a broad-based coalition, intensifying, as it did so, the class-conscious suspicions of the masses of blacks. For its sponsors and for Manley himself of course, it represented the most pragmatic expedient by which to preserve the liberal integrity of the party in the pitched climate of the emerging Cold War.

Hearne's sympathies and background inclined him to the more moderate, Manleyite wing of the PNP. It was under the auspices of the National Movement that, like others of his contemporaries, he might even be said to have served his literary apprenticeship. His first stories, appearing in the early fifties, were published in Edna Manley's journal *Focus* and O. T. Fairclough's *Public Opinion*. He was a friend and intimate of Roger Mais (1905–1955), a writer of extraordinary force, of a precursory and emphatic social realism who, from early on, was closely identified with the National Movement and the PNP. It was with Mais that, in the year of the socialist purge from the party, he left for Europe in search of a more congenial and demanding literary environment. It was at Norman Manley's urging that a decade later, ending his alternation as teacher between Europe and Jamaica, Hearne returned definitively to participate in the cultural aspects of the preparations for independence and to assume posts as Information Officer for the Government, Resident Tutor at the University of the West Indies and, later, Director of its Creative Arts Center.[24]

The natural and understandable product of Jamaican history, politics, and his generation, Hearne is the authentic voice of a class for whom, as for the young PNP, the main problem was "quite simply one of making contact with the broad mass of workers and peasants, and more deeply whether the class forces for which Manley and his party were the spokesmen were really willing, let alone able, to mobilize such support."[25] It was a problem that neither ever satisfactorily resolved nor, despite their temporizations, that they could ever really elude. The impasse itself became, in the end, their theme and signature. It is the lingering subtext of all of Hearne's fiction.

The catalogue of his acknowledged literary ancestors has about it a generational familiarity: Dickens, De Maupassant, Eliot, Fitzgerald, Hemingway. Its conventional contours are, though, less compelling than the selections of affinity. Kipling, too, was an important influence. One is tempted to speculate about the degree to which Hearne might have recognized in Kipling's state and anxiety as a colonial and "half-caste" Englishman some identity of condition. Isaac Babel's regional and ethnic nationalism, particularly as reflected in "Pan Apolek," struck a similarly sympathetic chord. It was the encounter with Faulkner, though, which proved decisive. In Faulkner Hearne discovered, in addition to a writer of fertile imagination and an original repertoire of literary devices, a fundamental kinship of subject, attitude, and interests. His depiction of the decline—and fading "virtues"—of the antebellum south offered a historical analogue to and a stimulating confirmation of Hearne's own concerns. Here was an author profoundly conscious of the historical fallout of slavery who was, like him, caught in the maelstrom of what Hearne refers to as "a profound tribal clash."[26] The saga of Yoknapatawpha County would give him both the confidence and the conceptual means for engaging, in Hearne's own words, the "obligation to redress the injustice to which you are an heir as best you can by giving dimension, articulation, to the enormous endurance, and real creativity which must have sustained these [. . .] societies for three hundred, four hundred years."[27] His vision tinged with a patrician nostalgia, Faulkner naturally further corroborated the particular bias of Hearne's liberal nationalist loyalties. It was, in any case, to the Southerner's "Sense of place, [to] his obligation [. . .] his biological obligation to that corner where his ancestors were born, and [to] his duty to give those faces, those people, that race, a real importance"[28] that Hearne was especially receptive, a receptivity which responded to—as it was also nourished by—the forces of national awareness and sharpening class division that were the hallmark of the epoch in which he came to maturity and emerged as a writer. Whatever else they may be said to exclude, it is the essentials of its collisions, seen from the perspective of a "coloured" liberal skeptic, that give point to the drama in his novels.

Hearne is the author of six published novels. As a group, and with the possible exception of his last, they present the reader with a distinct chronological continuity. Though located in the present, *Voices Under the Window* (1955) flashes back crucially to the protagonist's, Mark Lattimore's, loss of class and racial "innocence," the source of his "psychic wound,"[29] in the late twenties and thirties. It is during this period that he comes suddenly to the realization that he is not white, to the knowledge and significance of his *mulatez,* and so "had sprung a trap on himself that would never quite let him go"; "more than anything else [we are told] he was astonished and a little angry at this uncalculated, definite intrusion into the comfortable pattern he had thought was his life."[30] The novel effectively charts the consequences and his responses—social, political, and personal—to the breakup of that pattern. *The Autumn Equinox* (1959) concludes on the eve of the Cuban

Revolution. Between them these two novels span nearly the whole of the period immediately before independence. The others, save again for *The Sure Salvation* (1981), are concentrated in the decade after 1947, in almost reverse order of their publication. Set against the chicanery and corruption of the development boom, *The Faces of Love* (1957) centers on the months from May 1953 to March 1954. *Land of the Living* (1961) opens just after the war and goes on to explore the political emergence of the Reverend Marcus Heneky's Pure Church of Africa Triumphant, a populist, messianic, quasi-Rastafarian protest movement. It comes to a close with Heneky's final defeat and death, circa 1956. The events depicted in *Stranger at the Gate* (1965) occur a year or so prior to those that are the subject of *The Autumn Equinox.*

The novels are also formally and organically interrelated. *Voices Under the Window* is explicitly located in Jamaica. The remaining novels nearly all take place in the fictional island of Cayuna. This invention, however, is no more than a metaphorical substitution. It offers the possibility of greater authorial distance and objectivity and, by abstraction, the suggestion of a composite—that is, Pan–West Indian—image and scope. But one quickly recognizes in Cayuna a minimally disguised surrogate for Jamaica. Queenshaven and Kingston, their respective capitals, are entirely interchangeable. Growing and developing, gaining or losing prominence, characters too can be followed from one novel to another. Each work, consequently, represents a separate chapter, a distinct frame, in the same continuous story.

Only *The Sure Salvation* appears, on first glance, to reflect a radical departure from this unity of conception. It is located neither in the twentieth century nor in Cayuna. Tempting comparison with Melville's *Benito Cereno,* Conrad's *The Nigger of the "Narcissus,"* and Lamming's *Natives of My Person,* the tale focuses rather on the moral, social, and cultural drama aboard an illegal English slaver, bound for Brazil in the early summer of 1860, well after the official abolition of the trade. But the inconsistency is only apparent. Despite the break in chronological, geographic, and "biographical" sequence, the novel nonetheless reflects a certain formal and conceptual continuity with Hearne's earlier works. Caught in the doldrums, becalmed and adrift, the ship that serves as its narrative setting, significantly mired in its own muck and refuse, is a symbolic island. As the narrator notes, this "ship is a world."[31] The inhabitants of this island, its officers, crew, and "cargo," reveal again significantly, a hierarchy of social and ethnic divisions, conflicts of class and race, manifestly reminiscent of those characteristic of Cayuna-Jamaica. The tale itself borders on allegory. As a meditation on a portion of the history to which the archipelago is heir, the novel is, indeed, a commentary on the historical roots and sources of the persistence in the present of the social, racial, and class confrontations which form the substance of Hearne's previous works. In that sense, it is rather like a retrospective prologue to them, part of the "prehistory" of their present, and quite possibly the first installment of a never completed antecedent cycle. In any case, however transposed or transfigured, the "locale" remains the same: whether as ship or fictive landscape, it is Jamaica. The subject and focus is also unchanged: it is the ambiguous, often ironic predicament of men who, like Captain Hogarth and Reynolds, the second officer, suddenly displaced from an inherited prominence, are denied both the privileged stability of a former time and the evasive comfort of "the sentimental falsehoods [they] learned so early to swallow . . ."[32]

Hearne's novels are all in this double sense, and in the precisely Lukacsian definition of the term, historical novels: they strive to give fictional reality to epochal encounters and, if sometimes unwittingly, reveal how "certain crises in the personal destinies of a number of human beings coincide and interweave with the determining context of an historical crisis."[33]

Hearne's islands are, like Jamaica, riven by caste and class suspicion. The remembrance of things past, unpropitiated, remains obdurately omnipresent. The emergence of a consentient "selective tradition,"[34] inchoate and as yet uncongealed into any definitive hegemony, continues to elude them. No one is unaffected. As a consequence:

> There is no history in Cayuna: only politics. There is no established trust fund from which all the heirs are allotted, impartially, their respective incomes. Everyone is engaged in an immediate competition for rightful inheritance [. . .] Jealous siblings who wait for their unreconciled ancestors to lie down and die.[35]

At the apex of this society are the distinguished, now fading families of light-skinned planters, planters-turned-merchant, and rural squires. They invariably date their ancestry back to the English settlement of the colony in the seventeenth century. Their names—Brandt, Fabricus, Stacey—, engraved on the landscape, are a familiar part of the scenery. They thus appropriate to themselves the power of a heraldic and historical legitimacy. The establishment of a pedigree seems to be one of

Hearne's more anachronistic obsessions. The members of these several families are, moreover, related intimately to each other by an almost claustrophobically incestuous bond of blood, class, and fellow-feeling. They frequent the same clubs and saloons, intermarry, and, in general, form a network of shared assumptions and mutual self-reliance. Carl Brandt, the preeminent exemplar of this class, is the last of a distinguished line of planters, president of the All Island Polo Association, and present owner of Brandt's Pen Estate. He is a man of solid integrity and abiding personal loyalties. A competent administrator of his inheritance, honest and hardworking, he is the scion of a class that, without its former economic power or self-assurance, is in retreat and stands on the verge of collapse.[36]

By contrast with other comparatively less appealing members of that class, he has shown an exceptional ability to fend off that eventuality. A resolute holdout, he continues to resist the seductive offers of overseas capitalists to buy him out or enter into a profit-sharing partnership with him. Most of his peers have already succumbed to the big sugar or bauxite companies. Some having done so, like Ambrose Fabricus, a vagrant vestige of "the real old plantocracy"[37] and once eminent master of Fabricus Head, cling pathetically to the hollow remnant of their former selves. Others, like Lloyd Pearce, beneficiary of the once great Tolliver estate, neglect and dissipate their holdings, hobnob among "that set of luxury class tourist and winter residents [. . .] who liked him for his fantastic good looks, his money, and his amiable servility," all because of "snobbishness, the most casual, understandable lust and a need to convince himself that he, a highly colored Cayuna boy, had really made the top."[38] Unable to live up to the obligations of their position, they have all fallen from grace into the urban middle class. By force of will and the strength of his personal integrity, Carl Brandt has managed to avoid either fate. He has had the stamina, resources, and self-confidence to retain both his estate and his sense of wholeness. He is the only one of Hearne's major figures who appears as a sort of sympathetic prototype in each installment of the Cayuna cycle. The evocation of his world is, similarly, uniform and consistent. Brandt's Pen is a manifest reincarnation of the Edenic estate of Mark Lattimore's early childhood. It is to the world of Brandt's Pen that Hearne's middle-class characters, many of them direct descendants of the island's diminished elite, are invariably drawn. The attention of Andrew Fabricus, the narrator of *The Faces of Love,* is almost entirely fixed on regaining title to the land sold by his father and so reconstructing his past as a man of property; and he is perhaps the most eloquent in describing the importance they ascribe to it. To enter the world of Brandt's Pen, he tells us,

> was to pass from a world where people did things more or less well, but untidily, and to enter a place that had moved for a long time with a secure, confident rhythm, like the beating of a powerful heart. All sorts of people [he significantly adds] had told me that places like this were bad. And I had read one or two books which said the same thing. But for me it was one of the places where the life of my country had been cast and carefully nourished. *Whatever people had done since then, nobody had been able to make anything so efficient, so beautiful, and so enduring.*[39]

The passage highlights a characteristic tension. There is, on the one hand, the appreciation, in the minor key, of the cruel legacy, criticism, and historical rejection associated with the plantation system. There simultaneously emerges, more compellingly, a lyrical homage to its presumptive achievements, the vaguely apologetic confession of the powerful attraction its ambiance exercises on the character's—and his author's—imagination. There is, finally, the assertion that, its vices and flaws notwithstanding, its *beau monde* virtues are not without some claim upon our gratitude. Reiterated in *Land of the Living,* the idea is brought, through contrast, to a succinct point by Stefan Mahler, the Jewish European émigré who narrates the story. Asked by one of the descended gentry with whom he has chosen to identify, in whose company he is most at home, what his black lower-class mistress is like, he answers: "She's like what Sybil [a Black *evolué* married to one of their circle] would have been if she hadn't found out she could paint and hadn't acquired all the tricks and graces of our sort of life." Interpreting the remark as a muted critique, his inquisitor presses: "You think those tricks and graces are bad?" To which Stefan, predictably, appeasingly, responds: "No, they're necessary. They're what helped turn a dirty little village on the Seine into Paris. And they're what made Shakespeare claim a coat of arms."[40] Andrew Fabricus's tribute, quoted above, culminates here in praise of the plantocracy's contributions to "cultural progress," "civil development," and the invocation of historical necessity.

Critical perception of its contradictions gives way, in either case, to the sentimental, though entirely genuine attachment to a world in large part already lost. Hearne, it becomes apparent, is not merely "at home in the big plantation house"; a part of him at least finds itself adrift and ill at ease in the world beyond its orbit. Brandt's Pen is, at one and the same time, his paean to the remembered certainties of an aristocratic past and the representation of a sanctuary from the assault and travail of the unavoidable present. It is above all a refuge in an otherwise divided, chaotic, and decidedly uncivil society, increasingly dominated by crass, grasping, and resentful *arrivistes*. Of these, Rachel Ascom, the cunning and calculating editor of the Cayuna *Newsletter,* is perhaps the best example. One of the newly emergent black middle class, she is fully aware that her recent distinction as one the island's elite is "a conquest held by chance: on approval."[41] She therefore wages a fierce, uncompromising struggle to hold on to and consolidate her gains against the disdain of ex-plantocrats and the visionary idealism of those of her own class and color. This involves her in opportunistic speculation, political corruption, the betrayal of her erstwhile consort, and, in an effort to achieve the social legitimacy which no amount of economic prominence can give her, a partnership with the decadent plantocrat Ambrose Fabricus. Its sociocultural prestige is the one element of power remaining to the latter's class. Decorum in the event assumes the symbolic importance of a coat of arms; pointing to *faux pas* and breaches of good taste, a part of the ideological arsenal brought to bear in its defense.

As lacking in illusions as she is cynical and insecure, Rachel understands the full dimensions of these subtleties. "I am nothing, you see," she says to the priggish Andrew Fabricus when he mentions her "instinct" for a very expensive poor taste; "I came from nothing and none of you people will ever forget that when I make a mistake. Everything I become, I've got to show. That's why I buy such good clothes. Every time I spend ten times what I should on clothes it's like a standard I've set myself."[42] The alliance with Andrew's father, the terms of which she sets, is equally a part of that standard which she has established for herself.

To the overreaching of the new black middle class has to be added the restiveness of the black population in general. Its even more indecorous behavior further aggravates the volatile unpredictability of the present. Brandt's Pen, under the circumstances, borders on a nostalgic vision of an irretrievable utopia. Even Roy McKenzie, the revolutionary communist lawyer and protagonist of *Stranger at the Gate,* is not immune to its seductive appeal:

> . . . this is the thing that could really corrupt me [he muses while on a visit to the estate]. Not the wealth of it, he thought, feeling the solidity of old polished wood beneath his feet, looking at the spacious bright interior [. . .]

regarding the strong, nourished, confident face of his friend [Carl Brandt] opposite. No, wealth and luxury I can handle, he said to himself, rubbing the unbelievably sensuous smoothness of the old linen between his fingertips. But it's the closeness of it that could change me. This incestuous, happy, kindly, closeness where everyone fits into his place like a cork into a bottle.[43]

Whatever their reservations Hearne's brown middle-class characters are all drawn to the safety and familiarity of this world, to its self-assured "naturalness," its casual refinement, its durability, and aura of social cohesion. They crave its atmosphere of protective self-sufficiency and belonging, its air of apparent serenity: its quiescence and historical stasis, in sum.

For all the celebration of its virtues, Hearne's fiction is not without criticism of this squirearchy. Its content is reminiscent of the convergence of pragmatism and moral idealism typical of the moderate wing of the PNP. The practical, utilitarian critique, personified in the "modernizing" individualism of his black middle class, is most cogently articulated by Jojo Rygin. Risen from the black "big" peasantry, Jojo is an energetic and enterprising builder with his eye on the future. Seduced by the promise of American capitalism, he pins his hopes on a secret oil land scheme, the U.S. investors he expects to interest in it, and his confidence in his own ability to achieve a spectacular success and, because of it, to secure the love and shaky loyalty of Rachel Ascom. Though he is not unappreciative of the better qualities of Brandt's Pen, his admiration, unaffected by any romantic longing, is tempered by realistic appraisal of its stagnation and unfulfilled potential. "This is a damned fine place," he says to the younger Fabricus during his first visit. "It's been worked well, even if it's dead." Caught by surprise, Andrew is quick to the defense: "*Dead?* What the hell d'you mean it's dead?" Dramatizing the contrast between seigniorial capitalism and its more aggressive, expansionist successor, the discussion continues:

> Just what I say, man. You don't feel it?
> No.
> Well, it is. You can't take this place any further. Not the way it's run. It's old and dead. It's still nice though, and that Brandt is a big fellow.
> What, d'you mean it's dead, Jojo? Go on, show me how it's dead. Don't just leave it like that.
> Look at it. It's organized round one man. It's too small. That little dam up there, for instance. You know how much power I could get out of that river if I was to build a real dam?"[44]

Jojo concludes the argument by pointing out that

> . . . This place is stuck where it was a hundred years ago. If you made it part
> of a big thing then it would start doing something again.

The profound difference of outlook between the speakers, between
the historical alternatives each represents, is further emphasized when
Jojo, taking oblique aim at the aristocracy's complacent and self-serving
reverence for a frozen tradition, reasserts the imperatives of his own
initiative and enterprise.

> I don't like to live in something that somebody else built. I like to make my
> own place. I like to trouble things.[45]

The ethical critique, evident in Hearne's treatment of the less than successful group of ex-planters like Ambrose Fabricus and Lloyd Pearce,
is in effect a case for *noblesse oblige*. Individually and as a class, they
failed to see and comply with the duties—social and moral—that were
concomitant with their station and its privileges. That they have lost
the vantage of their original historical initiative and earned instead the
passionate resentment of the newly emergent classes is their punishment
for that failure. Carl Brandt, whose dealings with his retainers are typified by a benevolent authority, is the vindication of the best that was in
them. Taken together these landed families, their various and extended
branches, represent distinct facets of an identical class experience which
the reader is asked to judge in terms of the morality of its own seigniorial ideal. Hearne has himself said as much. "I am trying," he observed
in one interview,

> to establish the reality of people whose privilege has made their lives con-
> sciously more difficult because with every privilege a dozen duties attend.
> [These people, he goes on to generalize] are also symbolic of, I think, the
> dozen duties that attend every privilege that we, as Caribbean men who
> dispossessed indigenes, [. . .] who murdered, [. . .] inherited [in] a terri-
> tory of astonishing fertility and kindliness and beauty. We've knocked it
> up, sure, in a dozen different ways, but all of us—and maybe that's what
> I'm trying to get at in the Brandts, the Fabricuses, in the Staceys, in *The
> Autumn Equinox*—that every privilege that we've got, because of an ac-
> cident of history, has imposed these real obligations, this necessity that we
> must fulfill of making this place more than just a plantation.[46]

Hierarchy aboard *The Sure Salvation* is of course more sharply strait-
ened by the structure of command. Hogarth, as owner and Captain of

the vessel, his wife, Mr. Bollen, his barely competent first officer, and Reynolds, are at the apex of a pyramid that, flaring out and downward, includes Alex Delfosse, the African-American cook, the assorted congregation of Portuguese sailors, British old salts, and cunning, revengeful, or resigned escapees from the Bristol slums who make up the crew; and, below deck, the mixed grouping of African slaves who represent everyone else's "cargo of invested ambitions."[47] Official rank, the rigid conventions and conservative traditions of the sea, and the particular security requirements of their enterprise are the fixed cornerstones of this pecking order. They are the formal guarantors of this microcosmic society's otherwise tenuous political stability and social order.

The informal, symbolic, and ideological structure that emerges is, still, of a piece with Hearne's earlier fiction. The Victorian era, at the pinnacle of its imperial, post-industrial-revolution self-assurance and its Spencerian, Social-Darwinist certitudes, naturally provides a more credible backdrop for Hearne's patrician assumptions. Cleaving admirably to the particularities of yet another moment of transition (particularly and characteristically in its appreciation for the details of its material environment and atmosphere), the narrative gains thereby a more compelling fictional verisimilitude and historical consonance. Hearne's analysis of distinctively English class antagonisms and how, as replicated and realized on the slaveship, they constitute part of the legacy of Caribbean history, an old cynosure but novel emphasis in his writing, gives, too, fresh accent to his usual themes and concerns. The aroma of nostalgia to which he had accustomed his reader, though hardly absent, yields to a considerably more effective sense of the ironic: shrewd, self-conscious, and multivalent. The worldview, for all that, remains fundamentally unchanged. Attention is focused still on the trauma, ethical dilemmas, inconstancy, and deterioration attending aristocrats *manqué*.

Hogarth and Reynolds are both former *hijos de algo*, "gentlemen spoiled" as the latter puts it,[48] whose personality and experience, like those of the Fabricuses, et al., represent the extremes of response to a similar condition. "There's been a Reynolds at Style two hundred years almost to the day, and money to go with it."[49] Deprived of his proper inheritance by the greed of an elder sister, Reynolds chooses the Trade's promise of a new fortune and the "purifying terror of the sea's indifference" over "the cloying hypocrisies" of the world that formed and so abandoned him.[50] The implacable, cynical efficiency he brings to his job, born of his abhorrence for the pieties of his own community of peers and an avenger's passion to expose the realities hidden behind its civilized façade, is, as with Conrad's Kurtz, the expression of the malignant underside, the inexorable erosion of rationality, corruption of ideals, and negative realizations of the culture he represents. Reynolds's encounter with the young African slave he makes his mistress gives the reader a powerful, synoptic image of his character and the scorn with which he views conventional society. As his unwilling concubine, she confirms the absolute power of the slave trader and the prerogatives of Reynolds's rank and station; as slave and sex object, she serves simultaneously as vehicle for the acerbic demolition of the haughty, dignified pretensions to superiority of the women of his own class and race. He follows the assuagement of his lust by teaching her to pronounce her first words of English with the misanthropic impiety of one who sees in a catalogue of the grossest obscenities the epitomized wisdom and achievement of his kind. "Absolutely splendid," Reynolds cheers when she completes this introduction to Anglophone culture and, with pointed irony and a bitingly laconic calculation, he concludes:

> And yet there are the bigots among my race who maintain that your kind is ineducable. I'd like to see some of them master the essentials of your language as quickly as you have ours [. . .] it's a pity we're selling you in Brazil. It would be pretty to think of you adventuring your English among those dainty simpering misses in Virginia or the Carolinas.[51]

The resonance of "essentials" extends beyond mere grammar or the lexicon. Reynolds, however, is neither reformer nor revolutionary.

Even as he vilifies them, he is merely a renegade who caricatures, without fundamentally rejecting, the premises of the society he spurns. His peculiar form of redemptive retribution is to return to England, embodying in his person "the purifying terror" of his amorality and brandishing a wealth gained at the cost of human degradation, to reestablish his claim to a place among the nobility of his former milieu. His corrosive perversity is no more than the bleak tribute disenchantment pays to lost illusions.

Hogarth is an aristocrat of even more distinguished ancestry. "He's old breeding"[52] and, as Reynolds's more fastidious complement, a man of conscience and considerable moral scruple. It is his ethical sensibility and sense of rectitude that, paradoxically, deny him access to the full benefits of his pedigree, the prestige of a potentially brilliant career, and leads finally to his involvement in a business he acknowledges to be reprehensible. A sense of obligation and loyalty to the memory of his deceased mother, his hostility to the moneyed arrogance of the man who disowned her after her marriage to a poor, untitled curate, compel him to refuse the offer of a Royal Commission from his influential grandfather. Later he assumes public responsibility for the pregnancy and illegitimate still-born child resulting from his affair with the daughter of a suburban tenant landholder with insufficient social credentials. The decision to marry Eliza Madden, against the advice of his associates among the mercantile elite, costs him the directorship of one of England's most successful commercial partnerships, to which he became entitled by virtue of his many contributions to its profitability. It also burdens him with the Calvinist frigidity and guilt of a woman who sees in the infant's death a sign of divine punishment for their libidinous transgressions. As her penance and his purgatory, she determines to isolate herself with him aboard the ship, the *Sure Salvation,* with which his former employers and would-be colleagues dispose of him. Reduced to reliance on his comparatively meager resources and small gains as a newly independent ship-owner and merchant man, he is eventually seduced, by Alex Delfosse, into participation in the illegal commerce in slaves that is responsible for his current predicament. He does not easily succumb and, tormented by his regrets, is not unmindful of the

> irony and irrationality of it all [:] that my probity, my faithfulness to obligation, my subscription to the Christian usages which I imbibed as joyous habits from my mother and father, brought me no resolutions but only the final impatient dismissal by men who looked on me as a friend who would enhance their fortunes, the refused flesh of a woman who had once offered herself to me as she would have turned her face to the sun, and now a cargo that I would have repudiated ten years ago had I been offered the opportunity to convey it from the uttermost darkness to the Gates of Paradise[53]

His willingness, indeed his agonized need to atone in the face of the defining paradox of his life, heightens our appreciation of his essential decency. Hogarth is, however, virtually impotent against the force of circumstance and the pull of his own entelechy: His pain and protestations culminate, consequently, in no concrete mitigation of the suffering of his victims. They therefore amount to little more then the necessary proof and reaffirmation of his dilemma and moral crisis. Hogarth thus becomes the dramatic personification of the existential difficulties of an adherence to principle among the privileged with which Hearne expects us to sympathize. For, despite his choices, his class consciousness and assumption of noble prerogatives remain wholly intact. It is the threat to the foundations of these that, on their first meeting, Alex Delfosse presages with his take-charge manner, his cavalier lack of deference, and the manumitted slave's easy manipulation of his familiarity with the refined usages of upper-class culture. It is a threat that, fascinated as he is with the cook's mysterious authority, Hogarth does not take lightly. It fills him "with a *physical* revulsion as inaccessible to [. . .] a cool and even [. . .] analysis of his behavior as indigestion or a toothache."[54]

He goes on to articulate the source and basis of this reaction.

> My rank and class [he says] will condone—or at least treat with a near-affectionate rough justice—minor offences such as theft, deceit, immorality, even murder, on the part of our inferiors. *By such acts they assure us our appointed rights and duties and obligations—even if we have to hang or flog or imprison them. But assumption of equality attempts to usurp our behavior and earned attitudes, constitutes the challenge we must meet with implacable harshness: with cruelty if harshness proves insufficient a lesson.* There is [Hogarth concludes] a frailer safeguard between the chaos of the mob and the order we maintain [in society at large] than there is between this cabin and the savage creatures below whose children [the anonymous crowd of *Voices Under the Window*] may someday learn of the salvation which their parents can no more imagine than an ape can understand the sempiternal laws of the universe.[55]

The allusion to an imminent collapse of the established social order is far from gratuitous. It anticipates the subversive, catalytic role Alex will in fact assume as a harbinger of radical change aboard the *Sure Salvation*. It is this ex-slave who, taking advantage of the confidence invested in his mysterious authority, lures the Captain into the Trade and then, by an equally skillful cultivation of his access to the captive Africans, secretly arranges and checks to his purpose an uprising of slaves that, in the end, gives him control of the ship. It is a fact that proves doubly ironic. It provides the measure of Hogarth's actual helplessness, his initially unperceived enslavement to another's design. As the moral equivalent of a betrayal and an empirical demonstration of his original foreboding, it ironically justifies and confirms the otherwise contemnable premises of Hogarth's sense of *noblesse oblige*. It is, in any event, his class situation as a man of good will that, in the final analysis, is the novel's definitive protagonist. It is the sun around which all other dramas cluster, from whose intensity and opposition they draw their heat. It is the specific gravity of his class predicament which, akin to that of a star expiring from the force of its own generation of light, compels our primary sympathies. Mr. Bollen, whose presence on board is attributed to a lapse in the Captain's judgment, is, in his own way, as unattractive a figure as Reynolds. He is a gullible buffoon who fails to win the respect of either colleagues or crew. He intervenes very little in the plot and, it is interesting to note, his background, unexplored and practically unexamined, remains murky and obscure. It is clear, however, that he has neither Reynolds's impressive antecedents nor the Captain's susceptibility to questions of morality. His lack of authority, given his rank, is the correlative of his lack of "class." The reader is allowed to dismiss him as a figure of, at best, secondary importance. This underscores the symbolic importance and specifically class character of the contrast between the other two men. Hogarth emerges, then, as the ideological and social parallel of individuals like Carl Brandt.

Like his counterparts in Cayuna, Captain Hogarth is also a man at odds with the emergent spirit of his time, engaged unfruitfully in an outmoded enterprise on an obsolete ship. He had won his once fine reputation for seamanship and success in the days when "there were few rules and little interference from jacks-in-office," as a pioneer of the colonial Asian trade. As part of the advancing edge of imperial expansion, his pluck and skill under sail, his shrewd intimation of its future importance, and acumen in seeing to the interests of his employers, helped to open up "this new area of venture for our race many years before the [Indian] Mutiny [of 1857] was even dreamed of, and the dull, predictable career of the John Company had become, with its fine salaries and its safe returns, regular as excise, for its directors."[56]

The notoriety and respect it brought him have faded with the halcyon days of sail. The lethal immobility of the *Sure Salvation* puts this in stark relief. Hogarth mourns this passing as much as he regrets his involvement in slavery and his impotence before an absence of wind. A twinge of pained chagrin at the ingratitude that has been the reward of his contribution is intrinsic to his mood of wistful melancholy. The flutter of breeze that—after a month of calm and an increasingly volatile general frustration—releases the ship, becomes the opportunity Alex has been waiting for to assume command and proves, finally, insufficient to the task of outrunning the partially steam-powered naval frigate which, concluding their venture, enforces Her Majesty's laws. The man who commands her, a passionate advocate of the new technology, is the herald of "a new species."[57] His capture of the *Sure Salvation* is a testimonial to England's industrial development, the reorientation of imperial priorities in the wake of Emancipation, and the end of the predominance of the ship under canvas. Realizing its inchoate potentialities, it also marks the end of the mercantile colonialism of Hogarth's heyday and the speculative adventurism of his current command. The Captain of H.M.S. *Beaver* thus both ends and inaugurates an era:

> Lieutenant Honeyball did not despise sail [. . .] he knew that no man could ever understand the sea who had not to learn how to live with the sea under sail alone. But the power he now had to command from his bridge [. . .] made him a dedicated, almost obsessed man. (When he made his last speech in the House of Lords, half a century after he boarded the *Sure Salvation*, it was on the greatness that more steam in ever-larger ships could bring to England). And men listened with respect and attention to this old Admiral who had never fought a battle, but who had quartered down on the last of the slavers fifty years before and taken it as casually as a child might have lifted a toy boat from a bath . . .[58]

Captain Hogarth, like Carl Brandt, is Hearne's appreciative obituary to a vanishing epoch and a dying class.

A transfiguration and historical projection of Hearne's vision of the black middle class, Alex Delfosse is literally and figuratively poised between the extremes of class and culture. He is master of the midshiphouse, from which he oversees the handling of the ship's stores and plots his takeover, and his berth connects the eminence of the poop and relative freedom of the forecastle to the hopeless constrictions of the hole. As a manumitted slave, fully conscious of the vulnerable ambiguity of his status, he stands at the strategic axis of the conflictive encounter between Africa, Europe, and the New World: between the Captain, his crew, and slaves they carry. His impressive accomplishments—his wide experience, his force of presence, his knowledge of "all the blues of the white man's eye"[59]—are one salient of the dual inheritance of his Machiavellian personality. He harbors the plutocratic ambition of his former masters, whose disdain for those below their station he imitates, as well as the seditious aspirations of the ex-slave in a racist society. He has the pragmatic ruthlessness, all the toxic narcissism, of a Rachel Ascom.

Alex has a rogue's easy familiarity with the dockside demi-monde and, in a way that reminds one of Jojo Rygin's assessment of Brandt's Pen, his knowledge exposes the economic excesses of Hogarth's operation. The cost effectiveness he introduces, indeed, wins the latter over, gains his confidence, and secures Alex's place aboard the *Sure Salvation*. The short-lived success of his coup is directly attributed to the advantages of his intermediary position and, as if to confirm this, reflects a merger of the contradictory goals of opposing social forces: the slave's wish to be free and the slaver's concern to safeguard his "cargo of invested ambitions." Alex allies himself with both. The coup itself is a revolutionary act tied to an ultimately conservative purpose: for Alex the release of the slaves is but the necessary preliminary in a scheme to found his own dominion and establish a commercial colony in the far reaches of the Amazon. Only the intervention of Lieutenant Honeyball prevents this from happening.

Honeyball's intrusion, however, proves only a partial—and perhaps even temporary—achievement. The formal attributes of his power as a guardian of the Empire's interests, his ability to conduct his investigation aboard the commandeered ship, are subject to the limits imposed by an unavoidable need for a go-between and buffer: "he needed the black cook, Alex, to act [. . .] as a translator between him [, the Africans,] and the Portuguese. Besides, there should always be a distance between the examined and the examiner: a space which the examiner [as a representative of the Empire] could fill with righteous anger, or could imply was necessary to protect him from possible contamination."[60] Turning setback into opportunity, Alex, by once more manipulating the poles of his equivocal position, continues to exercise an invisible but palpable control and sinister authority over events, "as though it was he, not Honeyball, who must decide how much of the inquiry's time should be spent on each witness."[61] The inquiry itself is conducted on Alex's turf, under his constant presence. Lieutenant Honeyball's choice of the Midshiphouse, over Captain Hogarth's cabin or the officers' quarters, to avoid invasion of a woman's privacy, a breach of intraclass courtesy, or the constrictions of insufficient space, further accentuates the definitive eclipse of the old regime. It also identifies the new social locus of the power restively and rather more consciously, if not equally, shared by the cook and the crown's interrogator aboard the *Sure Salvation*. It is Alex, however, who, by virtue of his ambidextrous cunning, appears finally to gain a certain pre-eminence. The damage inflicted upon his own ship by a steel connecting rod—an industrial innovation that, as the consequence of the still timid reformism of his superiors, opens a hole in his wooden stern—ultimately compels Lieutenant Honeyball to release his prize to secure his own safety. Entrusting the black slaves and his white prisoners to the care of a very reluctant minor official on an obscure British possession on the Guiana coast, he makes a final reference to Alex Delfosse, the only one of the slavers not in handcuffs or under guard.

> "You'll need that chap," Lieutenant Honeyball had advised the mulatto Barbadian Clerk of the Courts who was the only officer of the judiciary left in Abari while the Governor and the real people of the colony were on a picnic, two days up-river . . . "You'll need him, by God, until your Governor and all the *sahibs* return. He'll have to stand trial, of course, but he don't have any place to run off to, and if I were in your place I'd let him roam free—under your eye, naturally—until you've got enough help to keep this lot in order."
>
> He gestured with great satisfaction at the five hundred black people dancing on the *stelling*—and at the fifteen thousand black people in white people's clothing and white people's expression who were watching them with incomprehension, resentment, and mounting interest from the green at the *stelling*'s edge [. . .] "If I were you, I would use this man as your *aide* until your . . . your . . . your real people come back from their holiday, what! He'll be invaluable."[62]

The almost allegorical symmetry of the parallels tempts one to see in the scene, indeed in the entire sequence of events following upon the capture of the *Sure Salvation,* the fictionally transposed and concentrated analogue of the period that, after emancipation and the events of 1938 in Jamaica, culminates in what Trevor Munroe refers to as the process of constitutional decolonization which presages the hegemony of the colored middle classes.[63] The period, that is, out of which Hearne himself comes, that is at the core of his political and social experiences, and whose contradictions are the burden of his Cayuna cycle.

It is Alex, in any case, who has the last word:

> "Don't fret yourself, Mr. Waddington," Alex said from where he sat on the bollard (watching Lieutenant Honeywell's ship pull away). "It's only five hundred niggers you got to worry 'bout . . . I'll help you settle 'em in . . . An' they sure as hell don't have no place else to go."[64]

The comfort he offers the clerk is guilefully ironic. It is also edged with the portentous imminence of a danger the latter only vaguely intimates. Though Hearne comprehends and points to the force of circumstance— to the psychological effects and illegitimacy of the social constraints originally imposed by a class-conscious, slave-holding, and racist society—and to the consciousness of deprivation that, in part at least, sanction his actions, Alex's lack of loyalty to anyone but himself, his utter lack of a morality beyond expedience, ultimately condemn him. It is the ominous menace of the black ex-slave, not the radical possibilities inherent in the uniqueness of his position, which the novel emphasizes and on which it dramatically closes. It is, once again, Captain Hogarth to whom the author, now obliquely, draws our sympathy: a good man in a criminal trade undone by his own best intentions; his anguish and defeat are, finally, the compelling measure of his higher moral—no less than social—stature.

Hearne's characterization of the lower class—those anonymous, mostly black voices under the window—emerges as confirming counterpoint to his treatment of the black middle and upper classes. Tinged with a patrician estrangement, it is informed by a certain apprehensive dread and foreboding. It argues, with a vaguely self-reproachful remorse and irresolutely, an ambivalent tension between Hearne's perception of the need for a change in the social order, which the lives of the disenfranchised make manifest, and his fear of the consequences of their historic distrust, accumulated bitterness, and resentments. His prognosis is, on balance, pessimistic.

Separated from their antagonists by a gulf of values, class, social experience, cultural outlook, and the cumulative effect of their historic victimization, Hearne's lower class is an inevitable, almost incomprehensible disappointment to even its most radical supporters—white or colored—among the more favored classes. Hearne's work suggests that, for the moment at least, the breach between them may be beyond healing. "History dig a gulf between us, boy," Marcus Heneky warns the otherwise empathetic Stefan Mahler, "an' it don't fill in yet. Not yet."[65] The observation is an important leitmotif of the Hearne canon. His characters, like the people aboard the *Sure Salvation*, "all are caught in the painful rigidity of position held in a century's sleep."[66] The cruel apprenticeship of the proletariat's poverty, an improbity nourished on deprivation, and the enduring reality of racial and class privilege and confrontation are at the root of the impasse. Interclass alliances are, consequently, tenuous, temporary, doomed to be perpetually undone. As with Sisyphus pushing his stone up the mountain, a commitment to the underclass by those outside it implies a kind of martyrdom, the eventual admission of an almost certain defeat; the retreat into a "stoic acceptance [. . .] that the moment of justice for which [Hearne's real and fictional] society is still waiting is not yet."[67] Emblem of the liberal elite's frustrated good-will and disappointed hopes, this "stoic acceptance" is most often inspired by the undirected actions of the lower class. Thus Mark Lattimore stoically accepts and, albeit regretfully, surrenders to the irony inherent in his approaching death: he is mortally wounded in a labor riot, at the very moment he prevents a black child from being trampled in the rush, by a faceless unemployed worker to whom he, a liberal defender of "the people," was equally without identity except as a "white bitch."[68] It is, clearly, the larger significance of Roy McKenzie's inability to lastingly penetrate, despite his dedicated attempts at a class alliance and the respect he has earned among the Jungle's proletariat, the wall of custom and habit of suspicion of any lower-class black characters in *Stranger at the Gate*. The support for a protest march against the government and governing class he is able to elicit from Tiger Johnson, the leader of an organized slum gang, evaporates when the latter interprets its unexplained, tactical postponement as a breach of faith. It is the depth of the unbridgeable division between the classes that, almost instantly, then results in the collapse of their uneasy coalition:

> To Tiger the march itself had meant nothing, or very little. As a gesture, though, and a gesture against the class and colour he hated, and as a display of his own strength it had meant a great deal. When Roy and Bob Daniel had come to him to call it off, they had only confirmed his instinctive, customary belief in himself and the unrelaxed mistrust of others [especially those of their class] which were the things he moved by and used to protect his integrity. The sense of betrayal had come . . . [of a] savagely wary intuition . . .[69]

It is the action of a member of the black masses that, again ironically, also leads, indirectly, to Roy's death.

His chagrined resignation to the frustration of his social organizing is evident in Roy's reaction to the abandonment of his pregnant, common-law wife by his protégé Campbell,

> the ex-sugar worker, ex-garden boy, ex-portman, ex-wharf labourer, who had been a good worker for the party . . . and who with this sudden, frightened denial of all the people who had needed him and trusted him was now an ex-everything.

Made up primarily of the marginal unemployed, petty thieves, messianic followers, and the anonymous, amorphously hovering mass of the derelict and desperate, Hearne's proletariat is perpetually on the verge of an identical recidivism. It is the lingering anxiety it produces, in them and among their more aristocratic friends and adversaries, that makes his black *arrivistes* so opportunistically cunning, so perfidiously equivocal, and, in the last analysis, so fearfully objectionable. The more apparent their roots in the black underclass, the less altruistic their motives, the more suspect their only recently acquired, still questionable respectability, the thinner the veneer of civilized gentility. Among the proletariat, this relapsing has its source in the lack of cultivation that separates it from the elite and the brutalization of sensibility Hearne considers incident to the facts of its existence: it is, therefore, the "primitive," atavistic quality of its responses his novels emphasize.

The members of Hearne's marginalized black and working classes—Tiger Johnson, Scissors Clark, Ralston Edwards, the unidentified striker of *Voices* . . .—invariably have no time for (or comprehension of) motivations or emotions more complex than an efficiently animal hunger and an impatient, remorseless instinct for survival. Though this is especially characteristic of his black proletariat, Hearne's portrayal of the refugees from England's slums aboard the *Sure Salvation* suggests it is as inextricably related to class, if not more so, as it is to race. Thus Joshua, the cabin boy rescued from the harshness of the Bristol streets, remains incapable "of imagining any human exchanges other than those based on immediate hunger, lust, and the ruthless preservation of the self."[70] Numbed by the experiences of his Coketown youth, Ned Dunn is similarly defined by "the brimming charge of vigilant hatred he carried within him like his blood . . . ,"[71] an attribute that, race notwithstanding, he shares with Tiger Johnson. Like the barmaid Bernice Heneky, Stefan Mahler's lover and his link to her father's movement for social redemption of the masses in *Land of the Living*, they are still all "irremediably anarchic."[72]

Assuming the qualities of a "natural propensity" and the aura of an intractable flaw of character, this recidivist tendency, this anarchism of response, reduces these usually secondary proletarian figures to a composite of essential appetites and inchoate angers. The conversion of a class confrontation to the terms of a contrast among personal moralities, further, imbues the struggles of the upper-class protagonists with the tragic nobility and dimension of an eschatological drama. It also suggests that, in Hearne's work, impoverishment is an ingredient—possibly the critical catalyst—in the alchemy of evil, against which his liberal elite, despite its best efforts, is impotent. "All that [. . .] characters (like Roy McKenzie, Mark Lattimore, and the rest, including Captain Hogarth) can do," Hearne argues, "is to explore the possibilities [. . .] establish, as it were, a beachhead."[73]

Invariably they fail: the effort proves fruitless: their alliances across class and caste cannot be sustained; and more significant still, those attempting them are usually sacrificed. It is one of the paradoxes of a Hearne novel that the responsibility for that failure is, largely, the burden of the black and lower classes. The individual who precipitates the tragic denouement is, more often than not, a member of the marginal proletariat. As earlier indicated, that is the case in *Voices Under the Window* and *Stranger at the Gate*. It is also true of *Land of the Living*. There it is Ralston Edwards, one of the Sons of Sheba (read Rastas) with whom he has allied himself, who, machete in hand, puts an end to Marcus Henekey's revolutionary apostolate in favor of Cayuna's underclass: "tired an' sufferin" [had] turn[ed] his brain to madness . . ."[74] In *The Faces of Love*, which focuses almost exclusively on the strains between the aristocracy and the new black middle class, it is the latter to whom that burden shifts. An identical shift is evident in the determinism, disguised as disappointment, into which Captain Hogarth retreats following Alex's coup. The black man's betrayal of his trust only confirms the impossibility of a bond beyond caste, class, and race in which he had begun to believe.

> I was coming to an understanding . . . of brotherhood with all men, despite this trade, because of you [he tells Alex]. I was beginning to realize that men like you and I, despite our differences in appearance, truly belonged to a greater purpose than we could prove in an argument . . . And now you have betrayed me in a fashion for which I could never have forgiven one of my own class . . . *In your betrayal, Alex, I discern an inevitability, a fixity of* future if you like against which I had begun to hope, foolishly, for equality and fraternity . . .[75]

That "inevitability," that "fixity of future" is one of the principles of composition of Hearne's novels. In this, as in so much else, *The Sure Salvation* is both the culmination and synthesis of his previous work. The action of Hearne's underclass is just as consistently unpremeditatedly vengeful, irrational, and spontaneous. He finds this unharnessed violence particularly disquieting. It is its unsettling portent, conveyed in its title, that hangs in the atmosphere of his first novel and that, like the augury of some menacing peril, looms over the whole of Hearne's work. It is the image of a passion that, in its instinctual ferocity, borders on pure malevolence: "a purposeless and indescribable spirit of destruction: something at once cruel, greedy and insignificant, outside the explained conflicts of race, class, or commerce, and far older and more obstinate than these."[76]

Abstracted beyond mere circumstance, it becomes the image of "a wickedness, a greed, a callousness older than time itself and as natural to man as his hands or eyes . . . [the reflection of] an illness, perhaps incurable"[77] and intrinsic to our "human nature." It is this malignity beyond fealty or the hope of conciliation, embodied in the visceral violence and opportunistic nihilism of his black and proletarian characters that, for Hearne, constitutes the ultimate threat to civil order, an authentic social discourse, the premises and possibilities of a civilized society. It reveals, past any retrieval of innocence, the fragility of its stability and "polite contrivances."[78] Like the Sheba man Stefan Mahler one day unexpectedly encounters, it exposes his liberal protagonists to "the haggard countenance of an antique, irremediable terror: something of itself, desolate and inaccessible, rising from the chaos that lurks at the centre of our small, decent achievements and from which we turn avidly into the factitious warmth of illusion, betrayal and sordid, desperate alliances of cruelty."[79]

The brooding, indecorous inaccessibility of the proletariat, sign of an essential and vagrant perversity, unappeasable, mercurial, incorrigible, and contumacious, is Hearne's *bête noire*. Despite a very real, if shadowy, recognition of the masses' social condition, claims on society, historical urgency, and realistic skepticism of white and brown liberal leadership, the reader is, in the end, presented with a curious inversion in the identity of the victim: it is the latter that, once again, individually and as a class, are given that role. In that he is ultimately unreconciled to the unpredictability, the alienated *disorder*, of his underclass, the nuances of Hearne's fear of chaos are reminiscent of the disillusioned Fabian's peculiar combination of social conscience and aristocratic presumption.

There is, though, a perhaps unintended irony obliquely palpable in his corpus of fiction. The attentive reader notes that, despite a generally negative characterization[80] and their apparent relegation to the background as secondary characters, it is in fact and rather paradoxically the black masses that insinuate themselves as the unarticulated and unavoidable protagonist. It is with the black's emergence as historical subject that, however grudgingly, Hearne's more favored characters—white and brown—must contend. It is the author's resignation to that obscure centrality that, one suspects, gives his novels their tone of defeat, that Spenglerian historical outlook earlier referred to. The historical ascendancy of a class unmindful of its debt of honor to the liberal elite and no longer willing to accept its patrician leadership, calling into question both its historical and moral authority, constitutes a challenge to the legitimacy of its most cherished traditions and assumptions. To the degree that these traditions and assumptions are synonymous with the accumulation of "our small, decent achievements," Hearne appears implicitly to argue, its ascendancy and lack of proper decorum verge on the end not merely of *a* history but of history itself. Hearne's expectation of recidivist slippage, acquiring the status of a universal, is unamenable to strictly political solutions. His work therefore amounts to a virtual rejection of the political. Conventional politics is nothing short of a cynical charade. It is the inherited attitudes of caste and class, not any fundamental dissimilarity of outlook, that distinguish Cayuna's two official parties from each other.

> Between Barnet for the Radicals and Purfrock for the Democrats, there was no more difference than the fact that the first belonged to the party formed by men like Eugene Davis, staffed by men like Andrew Fabricus [who, since *Faces of Love,* has managed to become a "planter and politician"], supported by men like Oliver Hyde [the son of an old planter turned journalist and culture-critic-intellectual] and that the second was the hired hand of a predator like Thomas Littleford [a venal black politician of the new middle class]. Into the prescribed rituals of this [electoral] tournament now stepped Marcus Heneky: a cuckoo in the nest of hereditary legislators.[81]

The comment reflects, more or less accurately, the nature of the confrontation between Norman Washington Manley and Alexander Bustamante. It also conveys the conservative ideological convergence and political paralysis of their respective parties in the post-purge years to which, as an element in the increasingly pervasive disenchantment of the masses, the radical black nationalist disengagement of the Rastafarians—dramatized here in Heneky's representation of the Sons of Sheba—was a symptomatic reply. In the context of the novel, however, the particulars of its probable points of reference have the allusive scope of the allegorical.

Hearne is equally skeptical of revolution and the revolutionary impulse. Beginning in idealism, they must inevitably end in either shattered hopes or tragedy. Wholehearted commitment to such a course, though it may indicate extraordinary, even awe-inspiring qualities of personality, as a consequence of the abstract, impersonal character of the conviction, necessarily results in the sacrifice of some aspect of our humanity. "To do it you have to give up everything that makes you a separate person. [. . .] to do the work faithfully you have to kill a little of yourself everyday, till it's only the work and your faith that's left."[82] Thus "the only part of himself that Etienne [a Haitian revolutionary, the *Stranger at the Gate* Roy McKenzie must smuggle out of Cayuna,] had permitted to remain—the only selfish part . . . [was an] appreciation of good food and drink. All the rest he had abandoned . . . Even the interest he showed for everything around him was a little inhuman . . ."[83]

This surrender of their individuality is incomprehensible to men like Carl Brandt, who sense in it a vague but powerful threat. When they are caught between the pressures of contradictory claims, it is the moment of decision between them that often proves fatal to Hearne's reformers. The futility of their sacrifice tends only to heighten the pessimism of the assumption on which they are all drawn. At their best they epitomize, like the Reverend Marcus Heneky, the "incorruptible obstinacy of an ideal as meaningful in essence as it was mistaken for the time and place." It is the conclusion to which Hearne's reader is unerringly led.

But it is perhaps Nick Stacey, an older, more jaded version of Mark Lattimore and himself once a revolutionary, who best synthesizes the author's view of revolution, black nationalist or otherwise. On hearing of an old Venezuelan comrade's involvement in the anti-Batista underground, he reflects:

> Surely he must have learnt by now how ephemeral is the life of what passes for justice which such revolutions achieve . . . A brief, intoxicating weekend in which those who fought for truth and liberal catchwords use up their honesty, and then the takeover bid by the realist. The reign of those who are not so much corrupted by power but corrupt in their very nature, as is every man who feels that he is competent to govern and speak for others.[84]

Hearne himself has confessed that

> the explicit and political resolutions [. . .] that Roy McKenzie [et al.] think [they provide] to the chaos of our relationships in the Caribbean, [. . .] those explicit, consoling political [resolutions] are not enough. [. . .] a more important area of experience [. . .] will have to be lived through, suffered through, and understood with something else, something else than the mind.[85]

For Hearne, that something else lies in the region of the heart. "Love" is his ultimate refuge and what little remains of hope for some way out of the endemic impasses typical of his fiction. A concept as protean and elusive as it is lacking in specificity, it is akin to an "innate, undefended compassion."[86] It encompasses the elemental intimacy and reverence of sexual passion and a *tendresse* and pity beyond class and race, as well as the empathetic knowledge of a common pain, the implicit acceptance of an abiding affection, and the fidelity born of a sense of honor or a purely personal loyalty. It represents, at best, a leap of faith, the desperate, rather abstract solution of the cornered idealist. There is about it, too, the reminiscence—and "generationally" authentic evocation—of the civic nativist idea of the Jamaican family, in which the grim confrontation among opposed interests, castes, and classes is reduced to the more manageable terms of a lamentable domestic misunderstanding. In his novels, social, political, and ideological questions are, in consequence, couched in the idealist and individualistic vocabulary of the moralist. The only viable solutions are personal and individual. Only an identifiably personal relation of loyalty and love is capable of *transcending*, however briefly, the limitations of circumstantial politics and the inherited divisions of race, caste, and class. It is as a testimony to their affection for him that, in spite of their conservatism and disapproval of it, Carl Brandt and Sheila Pearce get involved in Roy's scheme to help Etienne escape to continue his revolutionary activity. Sheila, like Carl, makes this quite plain. "I want to help," she says, "because you— because Carl and you asked me to. Politics don't come into it."[87] It is with the disappointment of an invested confidence and the defeat of this ideal of sympathy, of a vulnerable but essentially Christian code of behavior, that Hearne's villains are rebuked. Not unlike the elder Manley's original conception of "Socialism as a Christian way of life," of which it is perhaps the lingering, nostalgic, now disabused echo, it is, consequently, not unrelated to the specifics of his class allegiance.

Like the transitional epoch in which he came to maturity, Hearne is a writer effectively astride two histories: one dead or dying, one emergent, yearning desperately to be born. Living inescapably in an increasingly agitated and disconcerting present of heightened racial, class, and political conflict, he is, at the same time, rooted himself in, clings to, and longs for the vanished serenity, consoling intimacies, and convivial security of a past nostalgically idealized, utopianly reimagined. Thus "sitting in limbo," he becomes that Crusoe he avers, effectively marooned and adrift, shipwrecked in a world no longer recognizable as wholly familiar or his own. Memory and the recollection of a childhood before history, before the awareness of an unexpected displacement or the unsuspected defeat of ancestral expectation were abruptly thrust upon him, are all the refuge and safe haven on which he can now rely.

It is, in the end, Hearne himself who, in the voice of Nick Stacey, provides us with the key to the peculiar blend of patrician Creole nationalism, critical wariness of the popular masses, and pessimistic determinism—all expressive of his thought, outlook, and predicament— that is the signal hallmark of Hearne's universe. "With what tenacity of purpose," Nick observes, "do we old men assail our past, trying to tickle it into life. Is it to feel ourselves once more part of all the active suffering and loving with which we are surrounded? Or do we pursue, undiscouraged . . . [an] illusionary freedom from circumstance?"[88] Like being a Fabricus or a Brandt, a Lattimore or a Hogarth, it is the central, circular dilemma that, like an unburied ghost, lingers in the atmosphere of everything Hearne writes. It is the unrelenting ubiquity and omni-presence of history from which he can find, in truth, no sure salvation.

Notes

1. A. J. Seymour, "The Novel in the British Caribbean (III)," *Bim* 11, no. 44 (Jan.–June 1967): 239.

2. George Lamming, *The Pleasure of Exile* (London: Michael Joseph, 1960), 46.

3. Frank Birbalsingh, "'Escapism' in the Novels of John Hearne," *Caribbean Quarterly* 16, no. 1 (March 1970): 28–38.

4. Barrie Davies, "The Seekers: The Novels of John Hearne," *Caribbean Quarterly* 16, no. 1 (March, 1970): 115.

5. Sylvia Wynter, "We Must Learn to Sit Down Together and Talk about a Little Culture: Reflections on West Indian Writing and Criticism, Part ii," *Jamaica Journal* 3, no. 1 (March 1969): 36.

6. Ibid., 37.

7. Mervyn Morris, "Pattern and Meaning in *Voices Under the Window*," *Jamaica Journal* 5, no. 1 (March, 1971): 55.

8. John Figueroa, "John Hearne, West Indian Writer," *Revista Interamericana* 2, no. 1 (1972): 72.

9. Ibid., 75.

10. Ibid., 72.

11. It is one of the ironies of Naipaul's predicament that, his own wish to be seen as an English writer notwithstanding, the metropolitan literary establishments can absorb him only as a self-flattering *native interpreter* of the ex-colonial societies that are, inescapably, his subject. See, for example, Ian Hamilton: "Without a Place," in Robert D. Hammer, ed., *Critical Perspectives on V. S. Naipaul* (Washington: Three Continents Press, 1977).

12. Seymour, "The Novel in the British Caribbean 239.

13. Wynter, "We Must Learn to Sit Down Together," 36.

14. John Hearne, *Caritesta Forum: An Anthology of Twenty Caribbean Voices* (Kingston: Institute of Jamaica, 1976), vii.

15. He was actually born in Montreal, of Jamaican parents who brought him home while still quite young: it is, clearly, his Jamaican experience and identification that inform his outlook and sense of "nationality."

16. James Carnegie, *Some Aspects of Jamaica's Politics, 1918–1938* (Kingston: Institute of Jamaica, 1973), 32–33.

17. Unpublished Interview recorded by R. Márquez, Mona, Jamaica, February 8, 1978. Hereafter cited as Unpublished Interview.

18. John Hearne, *Voices Under the Window* (London: Faber, and Faber, 1955), 27–28.

19. Gordon K. Lewis, *The Growth of the Modern West Indies* (New York: Monthly Review Press, 1968), 190.

20. Rex Nettleford, ed., *Manley and the New Jamaica: Selected Speeches and Writings, 1938–1968* (Trinidad and Jamaica: Longman Caribbean, 1971), xxix–xxx.

21. That was early in 1942. Bustamante left with his massive trade union following and, trading on his characteristic appeal, formed the JLP. Insisting it was tantamount to "Brown Man Rule," he declared against independence, emphasizing instead immediate betterment of economic conditions. After a couple of unspectacular terms in office, during which it failed entirely to "deliver the goods," the JLP took up the cause of independence. The two political parties then moved toward a virtual ideological consensus. By the fifties and early sixties, save for the personalities of their leaders, they had become almost indistinguishable. The masses of unemployed, increasingly disenchanted with both, turned to strikes, stoppages, Rastafarianism, and other forms of protest.

22. "The P.N.P. statements of policy between 1940 and 1955 moved from the rhetoric of public ownership through the notion of socialism as a Christian way of life in favor of private ownership to the inclusion of 'socialism' merely as a label." Nettleford, *Manley and the New Jamaica*, lviii. Michael Manley's reintroduction of the democratic socialist theme in the decade of the seventies, his assumption of certain elements of Rastafarian symbology, and increased emphasis on a politics of the grass roots is, in some sense, an updated version of the original notions of

the party, an attempt to revitalize its moral prestige among the masses and regain the ground lost in the wake of the purge without, at the same time, alienating its primarily middle-class constituency. It is interesting to note that as the younger Manley gave clearer articulation to his new radicalism, Hearne, a long-time party sympathizer, became disenchanted and broke with its new leader.

23. Trevor Munroe, *The Politics of Constitutional Decolonization: Jamaica, 1944–62* (Kingston: University of the West Indies, Institute of Social and Economic Research, 1972), 80.

24. Jamaica continues to be his permanent place of residence. "I am now centered here," he says, "politically caught, hooked here. And when I say politically, I don't mean in any private sense. There is (here) a sense of involvement, attachment, or at least of one's presence in an evolving society [. . .] where our contribution is not only necessary, or useful, but where I don't know where else in the world I could get the range of daily experience and encounter I do here. In London and New York one is a specialist [. . .] you tend to meet other specialists [. . .] before you know it [. . .] [you are] doing all your living, or almost all of your living with people in the same trade [. . .] The sort of diet of personal encounter that one gets here becomes [. . .] addictive [. . .] I find living abroad now a bit bland after about a year" (Unpublished Interview).

25. Ken Post, *"Strike the Iron": A Colony at War. Jamaica, 1939–1945* (Atlantic Heights, N.J.: Humanities Press and Institute of Social Studies, 1981), vol. 1, 46.

26. Unpublished Interview

27. Ibid.

28. Ibid.

29. Morris, "Pattern and Meaning in *Voices Under the Window*," 54.

30. Hearne, *Voices Under the Window*, 36–37.

31. J. Hearne, *The Sure Salvation* (London, Faber and Faber, 1981), 195.

32. Ibid., 82.

33. Georg Lukács, *The Historical Novel* (Harmondsworth, England: Penguin Books, 1962), 42.

34. Raymond Williams, *The Long Revolution* (New York: Harper and Row, 1965).

35. J. Hearne, *Land of the Living* (London: Faber and Faber, 1961), 89.

36. One is reminded of Giuseppe di Lampedusa's chronicling, in *The Leopard*, of the twilight of the Sardinian aristocracy during the Risorgimento. Brandt may lack the brooding self-consciousness and despairing self-dramatization of Prince Fabrizio—that will be reserved for Andrew Fabricus and, most especially, Captain Hogarth, about whom we will have something more to say—but the essence of the predicament, the general mood and attitude, is more than passingly similar. The Italian aristocrat's comment to Father Pirron, the parish priest, summarizes the tone, lack of innocence, historical condition, and vision of both: "We are not

blind, my dear Father, we're just human. We live in a changing reality to which we try to adapt ourselves like seaweed bending under the pressure of water. Holy Church has been granted an explicit promise of immortality; we, as a social class, have not. Any palliative which may give us another hundred years of life is like eternity to us." *The Leopard* (New York: Time-Life Books, 1960), 38.

37. J. Hearne, *The Faces of Love* (London: Faber and Faber, 1957), 71.

38. Hearne, *Land of the Living,* 67.

39. Hearne, *The Faces of Love,* 180. Emphasis added.

40. Hearne, *Land of the Living,* 174.

41. Hearne, *The Faces of Love,* 6.

42. Ibid., 67.

43. J. Hearne, *Stranger at the Gate* (London, Faber and Faber, 1956), 151.

44. Hearne, *The Faces of Love,* 201.

45. Ibid., 202–3.

46. Unpublished Interview.

47. Hearne, *The Sure Salvation,* 73.

48. Ibid., 73.

49. Ibid., 120.

50. Ibid., 81.

51. Ibid., 95.

52. Ibid., 121.

53. Ibid., 167.

54. Ibid., 154.

55. Ibid., 154. My emphasis.

56. Ibid., 166.

57. Ibid., 206.

58. Ibid., 205.

59. Ibid., 56.

60. Ibid., 207.

61. Ibid., 210.

62. Ibid., 222–23.

63. Munroe, *Politics of Constitutional Decolonization.*

64. Hearne, *The Sure Salvation,* 224.

65. Hearne, *Land of the Living,* 248.

66. Hearne, *The Sure Salvation,* 47.

67. Unpublished Interview.

68. Hearne, *Voices Under the Window,* 18.

69. Hearne, *Stranger at the Gate,* 237.

70. Hearne, *The Sure Salvation,* 63.

71. Ibid., 33.

72. Hearne, *Land of the Living,* 84.

73. Unpublished Interview.

74. Hearne, *Land of the Living,* 276.

75. Hearne, *The Sure Salvation,* 201. Emphasis added.

76. Hearne, *Land of the Living,* 57.

77. Hearne, *The Sure Salvation,* 211.

78. Hearne, *Land of the Living,* 57.

79. Ibid., 50.

80. The portraits of Tadene, the African slave, and her niece, Reynolds's mistress, show Hearne attempting an imaginative recreation of the clash of cosmologies which the Middle Passage represented for those forced to adapt their universe of meaning to the incomprehensible terms of their captivity. In their poignancy and the comparative empathy with the point of view, the perplexed musings of the niece are particularly arresting. It is, I think, rather unique in the Hearne oeuvre. See *The Sure Salvation,* 83–89.

81. Hearne, *Land of the Living,* 202.

82. Hearne, *Voices Under the Window,* 60.

83. Hearne, *The Faces of Love,* 189.

84. Hearne, *The Autumn Equinox* (London: Faber and Faber, 1959), 100–101.

85. Unpublished Interview.

86. Hearne, *Land of the Living,* 72.

87. Hearne, *Stranger at the Gate,* 178.

88. Hearne, The Autumn Equinox, 163.

Grenada

History, Neocolonialism, and Culture in the
Contemporary Caribbean

SEEN IN the context of a long progression of imperious intrusions into
the archipelago by external metropolitan powers and empire-builders,
the invasion of Grenada on October 25, 1983, by a final total of approximately 6,000 U.S. Marines, Rangers, and paratroopers supported
by heavy artillery, tanks, and the most sophisticated weaponry gives one
a rather bluntly palpable appreciation for the degree to which issues of
culture, cultural definition, and development can be intimately related
to the particulars of social and political history. Continuous with a virtual tradition of American interventions in the region, it at the same
time signaled something of a turning point and striking shift of accent.
To the extent that it added one more to the scores of direct U.S. military interventions in the Caribbean and Latin America over the last
century, it represented no more than "business as usual." That the occasion and pretext were, in this case, provided by the unconscionable
behavior of those responsible for the assassination of Prime Minister
Maurice Bishop and his colleagues in government and labor made it as
particularly distressing as it was ironic. Their actions brought to a tragic
end the achievements and continuing promise of a Grenadian revolution already under siege, and bear more than passing responsibility for
the consolidation of conservative power and opinion throughout the
region, as well as for the relative success of a jingoistic American campaign which rivals anything one can point to since the McCarthy era.

There was, nonetheless, something tellingly different about this particular intervention. The country being invaded with such heavy-handed,
disproportionate force seemed, at one level at least, hardly to justify the
expenditure of time, energy, money, and personnel. Smaller than the
state of Massachusetts, populated by barely 110,000 people (less than a

fifth of the current population of Washington, D.C.), and with an army totaling barely 2,000 men and women, Grenada was hardly a match for one of the world's military leviathans. Only by the widest stretch of the imagination could it be seriously considered "a military threat to U.S. national security." Its timing, though, argues that, in a very real sense, this invasion was actually an assault on the revolutionary and anticolonial temper of an entire epoch—in tactical terms, a genuine "holding action." Its intent, as one senior Reagan administration official put it just a few days into the operation, was "to keep the United States from being perceived as a 'paper tiger'"[1] in the wake of Iran, Lebanon, and the general collapse of American invincibility and prestige in the post-Vietnam era. The invasion of Grenada, in consequence, was as signally symbolic as it was real. As symbolic act, it was unwittingly instructive. It was, in the final analysis, a tacit negation of what it sought most forcefully to affirm: that the erosion of U.S. supremacy and power in the Caribbean region, and around the world, was illusionary. It was an implicit confession that exactly the opposite was the case. Like the earlier mining of Nicaragua's harbors, it revealed how dangerously desperate the United States had become in the face of its growing lack of moral authority and the increasing untenability of its imperious presumption.

The invasion of Grenada also further accentuated the significant linkage between "politics" and "culture." It was, after all, Admiral Wesley McDonald, Commander-in-Chief of the Atlantic Forces, who made plain that the imposition of a particular "culture" was, in fact, intrinsic to American designs in the Caribbean. The real purpose of the invasion, he averred, was to guarantee that Grenada would henceforth have a government "more sympathetic to the American way of life."[2] It was, indeed, the challenge that the Grenadian revolution posed, in the words of Aimé Césaire, to "this [interventionist] habit of making our arrangements, this [presumptuous] habit of thinking in our behalf, this [seigniorial] habit of contesting our right to initiative . . . which is ultimately the right to a personality of one's own"[3] which ultimately made it so critically portentous and forbidding. It was the auguries of that challenge which made Grenada's revolution, for all the island's Lilliputian size, an event of pan-Antillean, world-historical importance and impact. It brought into even starker relief the broader scope and comprehensive character of the clash between American empire-builders and the immediate priorities of an authentically Caribbean society and consciousness. The need to see that clash and its consequences in historical perspective becomes all the more compelling in the wake of the events of October.

The Cuban Revolution was undoubtedly the single most significant contemporary event to have taken place in the region's evolving perception of itself. It dramatically announced the passing of the mimetic, patrician paternalism of the Creole middle classes that, little more than two decades earlier, had effectively replaced traditional hacendados and plantocrats as local arbiters of the domestic Antillean scene. The limits of the solutions the former proposed to the most pressing of the area's many problems were increasingly revealed and became daily more apparent. Despite the unfavorable circumstances in which it was compelled to carry them out, Cuba's early successes in health, education, and welfare, its effective mobilization of the masses of its people behind the Revolution, made the failure of "the Puerto Rican Model of Development," so popular among that new Creole elite, all the more strikingly public. The latter's "modernizing" proponents and beneficiaries throughout the Caribbean—Muñoz-Marin, Norman Washington Manley, and Eric Williams are perhaps the most representative figures of its populist liberal wing—were suddenly put as much on the self-justifying defensive as the Trujillos, Duvaliers, Batistas, and Somozas of the region. The restive alliance they had managed to forge, in the forties, between their own and the working classes, already in considerable decay, became definitely undone. It was indeed the collapse of that temporary alliance which forced them all, to a greater or lesser degree, increasingly to rely on "police measures" and "riot control" to ensure "stability." That so many among the younger, university-educated members of that middle class, at once the inheritors and critics of the world their elders made, increasingly identified with the need for change and a redefinition of terms only further deepened the crisis.

Cuba radically accelerated the process of rejection of the neocolonial arrangements that, over the course of that same period, had become the status quo. It revivified as it redefined the terms and content of the anticolonial movement in the hemisphere. By so doing, it gave new dimension and vitality to the cultural articulation of the area. One of its notable achievements was, precisely, the inauguration of what amounted to something akin to a cultural renaissance. During the period between 1898 and 1959, the poet Nicolás Guillén recalls, "the American way of life became (especially for the middle and upper bourgeoisie) a 'Cuban' way of life." The Revolution, the poet continues, made it possible to "cleanse and strengthen our spirit, as we recognized ourselves in the midst of a victorious jubilation."[4] The Uruguayan novelist and poet Mario Benedetti was even more all-inclusive and pointedly eloquent:

> The Cuban Revolution [he declared] forever put an end to some of the balances that appeared to be stable, with the routine resignation of certain sectors on the left. It similarly did away with the most accepted schema created or publicized by the empire, destined for the neocolonial slum. Fundamentally, the Cuban Revolution showed our peoples that the picture of Latin American man proposed by the empire was a caricature, a deformation that only served its plunderous intentions. With the Cuban Revolution[as a result] there began . . . a new way, experimental and imaginative, of moving ahead with an anti-imperialist politics.[5]

Aesthetic conventions were, of course, not unaffected:

> Curiously, Latin American literature (in particular, the narrative, but also, though to a lesser degree, poetry and theater) also broke the old molds, with the old rhetoric, with the old routine, and began enthusiastically to experiment.[6]

Edward Brathwaite argues that its impact on the English-Creole islands, of which Grenada is one, was no less significant:

> Not since the revolution in Haiti in 1792, had a West Indian territory gained world significance *and* local integrity through the courage of opposing, and defeating, the jagaurnauts [*sic*] of Western mercantilism. . . . the success of the revolution was based upon a reliance on native resources in a way that illuminated and expanded them from West Indian island to Caribbean matrix and from this to a resonant contribution to the aspirations and ideas of the entire family of nations. Cuba, then, . . . recalled us from isolation to Caribbean responsibility, and though at first our various establishments tried to prohibit our contact, they could not effectively censor our listening and understanding . . . by the middle sixties, Cuba had become an ideal for most of the progressive thinkers in the Caribbean: why look abroad when the pride and practice of revolutionary change was *indeed* at home?[7]

One immediate consequence was the discovery and reappropriation of the work of the West Indian writers and poets who, in the forties and early fifties, had found it necessary to emigrate to the major metropolitan centers of Europe or the United States. The list includes practically every West Indian writer of note over 45. The lack of a sustaining infrastructure at home left them very little choice at the time. They had to leave, George Lamming recalls,

> if they were going to function as writers since books, in that particular co-lonial conception of literature, were not—meaning, too, are not supposed to be—written by natives. Those among the natives who read also believed that; for all the books they had read, their whole introduction to something called culture, all of it, in the form of words, came from the outside: Dickens, Jane Austen, Kipling and that sacred gang.[8]

Relying primarily on the overseas service of the BBC and English publishing houses, these writers had virtually to smuggle their work back into the region. The airwaves over which they so effectively transmitted their "Caribbean Voices" became the equivalent of the heroic little magazines edited by Frank Collymore and A. J. Seymour. The orality of the medium made it all the more accessible to a largely unschooled population. It, therefore, contributed, in its way, to the self-conscious articulation of an indigenous audience for West Indian literature. The pressures consequent upon the emergence of that audience would not finally be felt until the late sixties. It was then, too, that the pioneering re-examination of the region's historiography undertaken by the early Eric Williams, Elsa Goveia, C. L. R. James, and, later, Walter Rodney would achieve popularity. The passionately humane intransigence of the Martinican Frantz Fanon gave a palpable urgency and immediacy to the need to "turn over a new leaf . . . work out new concepts, and try to set afoot a new man."[9]

The (at first gradual) influence of their critically reassessive assumptions upon an initially reluctant University of the West Indies provided important new points of departure for an entirely new generation of writers, teachers, students, and scholars. The various manifestations of the Black Power movement extended at the same time that they partially reflected that influence. Recognition of the imperative for an inversion of perspective and the centrality of the primarily black underclass in the historical evolution of a peculiarly Caribbean ethos became the common emphasis of a multivalent restiveness with the old regime.

The Cuban Revolution, acting as both culmination and catalyst, confirmed and intensified this long-brewing discontent. By increasingly extending their compass to include the non-Hispanophone countries of the archipelago, moreover, institutions like Casa de Las Americas, encouraged the re-emergence and consolidation of a genuinely Pan-

Caribbean outlook. N. D. Williams, Angus Richmond, Harry Narain, Shake Keane, and John Agard are among the names its annual prize introduced to the Hispanophone islands and a wider international audience. Guyana's inauguration, in 1972 of Carifesta, too, is a tribute to the growing currency of that outlook, the earlier (1962) demise of the West Indian Federation notwithstanding. It would also contribute to a greater cross-fertilization in the popular and creative arts. The revival of the PNP's moderate socialism, Michael Manley's identification with the masses of unemployed and appropriation of Rastafarian symbology— all part of the sympathetic appreciation of the change in conditions since his father's time—were similarly indicative and symptomatic. His "Third World" vision and open friendship with Fidel Castro were of a piece with that appreciation.

This was the sociopolitical landscape and cultural climate in which the Grenadian revolution was fertilized and nourished. Maurice Bishop himself testified as to its importance: " . . . we must acknowledge the most important fact about our relations with Cuba," he announced on the first anniversary of The People's Revolutionary Government. "The greatest debt of gratitude owed to the Cubans is that if there had been no Cuban Revolution in 1959 there could have been no Grenadian Revolution in 1979."[10] He was clearly referring to the compelling power of its example and the forces it accelerated or set in motion.

The Grenadian Revolution was, nonetheless, a direct response to specifically local realities. The facts of the Gairy years, since conveniently placed in the background, are the subsoil in which it steadily germinated.

Eric Gairy emerged in the aftermath of the black middle-class protest against Crown Colony government and the emergence of a working-class movement that covered the period between the end of World War I and the mid-twentieth century. It was the pioneering liberal T. A. Marryshow's "cooperationist" Grenada Labor Party and the city-centered trade unions, inspired by the subsequent example of Tubal Uriah Butler, that were the immediate precedents for Gairy's organization of the rural peasantry in the early fifties. Having thus contributed to the erosion of planter power and the patrician, pigmentocratic leadership of the middle class, Gairy went on, in the period 1952–1979, to reach an accommodation with his erstwhile adversaries, to establish his own political dominance and, in the process, to transform Grenada into his personal fiefdom. Patronage, the exacting of sexual favors in exchange for jobs, malfeasance, public corruption, the harassment of incompliant officials, and domestic repression became increasingly common. The rigid centralization of the administrative bureaucracy and neglect of the public sector became equally typical features of his regime. The infrastructure of roads, medical and other supportive services were allowed to deteriorate as the *patrón* enriched himself. In an effort to gain Gairy support in the face of a progressively more disenchanted populace, the economy came more and more under the control of the foreign and domestic capitalists with whom he allied himself. Unions outside the official circle, despite Gairy's increasingly hollow populist rhetoric, were muzzled or disabled. Unemployment by 1978 stood, officially, at 49 percent. Those fortunate enough to find work, however modest, fell victim to the rapid decline in real wages as the cost of living rose with the profits of the local elite and the multinationals.

The personalization of state power brought with it a frantic, opportunistic anticommunism and Gairy's unambiguous identification with the right. Accepting military aid and training in counter-insurgency techniques from Chile, he became, early on, a defender of Augusto Pinochet's and other dictatorial regimes.

The cultural situation was equally disheartening. A conscientiously antieducational policy did nothing to lower the illiteracy index. Teachers, in general, were regarded with suspicion as a threat to Gairy's rule. His refusal to pay Grenada's share of the cost to the regional university system denied Grenadians access to the system. This cut them off from an important locus of creative activity and intellectual renewal. It significantly contributed to the island's growing isolation from even its sister islands in the Anglophone Antilles. Censorship of ideas, most particularly those which the overwhelming majority of the area's writers were espousing, became the order of the day. Newspapers were either in the pay of the government or subject to its whims. Magazines and literary journals, where they existed, were, for all intents and purposes, practically underground affairs. Publishing houses of any consequence were nonexistent. The traditional link to Trinidad, which made Gairy noticeably uneasy, became all the more important. The example of its emerging national theater, its established and budding novelists and poets, critics like Gordon Rohlehr, the comparatively vigorous tenor of its literary and cultural life, to the degree they managed to filter through at all, became Grenada's primary connection to the creative ferment then sweeping through the Caribbean. Grenada was increasingly unable to shake its image as a cultural backwater. The ambiance was decidedly uncongenial to the encouragement of local talent. For Gairy, intellectuals were, *tout court*, the enemy. Writers and poets, aspiring men and women of letters, were, like the working classes, given very few choices: complacency, disillusionment, emigration, or silence. Unavoidably, they passed into the opposition.

When Grenada eventually became independent, in 1974, it did so under a dictatorship that rivaled Papa Doc's in Haiti. It even had, in the thugs of the Mongoose Gang, its own equivalent of the dreaded Tonton Macoute. Like Duvalier, Gairy also enveloped himself in an aura of quasi-divine mysticism. His notorious obsession with UFOs made his country, as well, the laughing stock of the international diplomatic community.

The New Jewel Movement, which only a year earlier had brought together the most important elements of the intellectual, middle-, and working-class opposition, offered a genuine alternative and represented the only available hope for a ventilation of the atmosphere. The revolution it brought to power on March 13, 1979, was greeted, reasonably enough, with an enthusiastic popular support.

Its first priorities were, of course, political and economic: consolidation of the Revolution, the strengthening of its popular base, and the task of reorientation and reconstruction of the country's economic infrastructure. Among its several accomplishments were the creation of an agro/industrial sector, reduction and stabilization of food prices as well as other essential commodities, and a dramatic decrease, to 13 percent by 1983, in the unemployment rate. Subsistence food production doubled by the end of 1982. Dependence on foreign food imports was, similarly, reduced to 12 percent. The creation of four new agricultural training schools, it was hoped, would help reduce that figure still further. There was an increase in the delivery—number and quality—of social services available. Free medical care and day care centers were established throughout the country. The principle of equal pay for equal work, regardless of race, gender, or class background, along with two months' paid maternity leave for female workers, became law. Public participation in the development of the national budget helped insure a democratic receptivity to popular demands. The mass organizations of the People's Power movement provided a vehicle for the increasingly active participation of women, youth, and workers in the political process. Michelle Gibbs, an Afro-American poet who bore witness to some of these changes, captured the energy and optimistic spirit of the time in her poem "Pride of Bearing," to whose feminist emphasis a wider resonance is attached:

> The women walk
> bodies balancing
> each day's measure
> of history's weight.
> Belly's birth
> Toil's triumph—
> the fruits of our labour
> early and late.
> On hips
> in hands
> on heads held high,
> each one's load
> determines her stride,
> paces her future,
> becomes her pride,
> yesterday's pressure,
> the new day's guide.[11]

Tourism remained the island's single most important source of foreign exchange. It would continue to be encouraged. Its guiding assumptions, nonetheless, would have to be radically changed. The old tourism, Bishop pointed out, "was foreign owned and controlled, unrelated to the needs and development of the Caribbean people . . . it brought with it a number of distinct socio-cultural and environmental hazards such as the race question and undesirable social and economic patterns such as drug abuse and prostitution . . ."[12] It encouraged imitation of metropolitan consumerist values, an enclave-like divorce from other sectors of the local economy, and a mutually detrimental inter-island competition. The policy of the new government sought to "break the relationship between tourism, class and colour [by] . . . consciously encourag[ing] non-white visitors and particularly West Indians" and Latin Americans.[13] Insisting on linkages to the domestic economy, it anticipated "the development of our handicraft, culture and other art forms as expressions of our own reality and aspiration, and tourist consumption following that expression rather than our culture being determined by some preconceived notion of what the tourist might expect."[14] It was no more than the specific articulation of a more comprehensive vision.

Popular education was a crucial element of that vision. A massive campaign to wipe out illiteracy, the elimination of school fees, free books and uniforms to the most needy, the granting of more scholarships in the revolution's first year than the combined total of the preceding five years—these were all a part of it. The real goal, though, was an authentically radical, profound and lasting, transformation of the cultural and psychological status quo. "The institutions which left the most permanent scars," Maurice Bishop informed his audience during the inauguration of the National In-Service Teacher Education Program (NISTEP) on October 15, 1981,

> were those associated with education. For those institutions scarred the minds and assaulted the intelligence of our people and wore them down for centuries. We were taught to look to Europe [and more recently to the United States] for the answers to our problems. . . . We were taught to stare over the Atlantic Ocean . . . for our political institutions, our drama and songs, our poetry and literature, in the same direction as the boats steaming North-eastwards full with our nutmegs, bananas and cocoa . . . we were gradually realising the need for a *cultural* independence.

This realization entailed a creative new departure:

> We need to look to ourselves, our own land and people, to be the base of that body of knowledge and activity that takes place day by day in our classrooms.[15]

Grenada consequently required

> a mathematics syllabus that can exploit our natural resources, and gives us an apprenticeship in building our industries, and agro-industries; a language arts syllabus that teaches our children to love and respect their own people, their workers and farmers, to give words and meaning to their hopes and aspirations and the basis to understand, discuss and criticise the many dimensions of experience and development around them; a history syllabus that seeks to analyze the process of emancipation of our working people and the struggles of working people all over the world, . . . a science syllabus which sets out to investigate the potential in our own land and people, to establish an inventive, creative technology, whether it be bio-gas, beetle traps, new fishing techniques, the possibilities of hydroelectric power from our rivers or the development of new strains and flavours of our jams and nectars.[16]

From its earlier marginality, Grenada had thus suddenly catapulted itself into the forefront of the cultural movement that had helped to prepare its ground. It naturally became a magnet of attraction to the Caribbean intelligentsia. Its effect on the Anglophone islands was, understandably, especially dramatic. Grenada, choosing its own way, was now at the height of history. It could no longer be ignored. Writers, poets, and intellectuals of every calling converged on St. George's as the U.S., the Jamaican prime minister and leader of the conservative Jamaica Labour Party Edward Seaga, and the prime ministers of Barbados, Trinidad, and Dominica, themselves facing increasingly restless populations, looked on with undisguised anxiety. The Trinidad-born novelist Merle Hodge immediately put herself at the service of Grenada's revolution. George Lamming, Edward Brathwaite, Robin Dobru, Jan Carew, and Clive Y. Thomas, among the better known whose names come immediately to mind, also actively identified themselves with events in Grenada. Their solidarity effectively contributed to the erosion of Grenada's cultural isolation. It also significantly contributed, despite the press of more urgent difficulties, to the revitalization and enlivening of the local literary scene. At least one Grenadian author was added to the list of Casa literary prize winners mentioned earlier. A quick glance at the available bibliography confirms, too, the considerable degree to which Grenada's currency as a subject of serious scholarly interest, though hardly equal to that of the Greater Antilles, had risen in value, at home and abroad, after March 1979.

The integration of the socioeconomic with the cultural goals of the revolution acquired still greater prominence. The first Conference of Intellectual Workers for Regional Sovereignty of the Caribbean Peoples, held in St. George's in November 1982, which Lamming et al. helped to organize, brought together some of the area's most prominent authors, artists, sociologists, economists, and historians. Underscoring the island's growing stature as a protagonist in the articulation of "a comprehensive definition of culture" and in the debate on the role of the intellectual in contributing to that articulation, it, in addition, established a line of continuity with the policy on culture intimated by Bishop's earlier quoted remarks.

> A false concept of culture [he averred] has made a serious division between the masses in the Caribbean population and the work of those individuals and groups we refer to as intellectual workers of the region. This division has not only deprived the majority of our people of a true consciousness of their struggle, it has also retarded the development of the intellectual workers themselves.[17]

Conscientiously reaching out to them, the Grenadian Revolution was at the same time issuing a fraternal challenge to the region's intellectuals. They willingly picked up the gauntlet. A second conference, pursuing the same theme, met a year later, once again in St. George's. It struggled to articulate ways to confirm, promote, encourage, and uphold the cultural vision of the revolution and to forge more enduring links between intellectuals and the ordinary people without whom their work had little meaning and would not flourish. It was a time of fertile ferment. It was a time, too, of contradictory omens. Michael Manley's electoral defeat in Jamaica radically shifted the configuration of forces in the area. The continuing escalation of the U.S. campaign of propaganda and destabilization gave more dramatic urgency to those meetings: the end of the revolution would, after all, make the removal of "the great barriers which an external mass culture has created between them [the intellectuals] and their people"[18] all the more difficult.

The murder of Maurice Bishop and the end of the Grenadian Revolution has, as a matter of fact, widened that breech. It has abruptly plunged the country back into the depressing morass of its former predicament. Indeed, the temporary—and only apparent—assumption of power by Governor General Scoon, the local representative of Her Britannic Majesty and a former Gairy associate, virtually trumpeted the fact. That Gairy himself should return to claim his former estate was both consistent with it and predictable enough. Unemployment once again rose to pre-1979 levels. At the same time, not quite a month after the invasion, the *New York Times Sunday Magazine* and Travel Section, respectively, announced an improved climate for investment, cheap labor, and travel to Grenada. The Reagan administration, meanwhile, completed the construction of the airport at Point Salines it so bitterly—and inaccurately—denounced as a military base, while itself regarding it as a potential staging area for counterrevolutionary incursions into Central America. The chauvinism of a white supremacist imagery, already evident in media projections of the invasion, was once again in vogue; the buoyant hopes of a people who, assuming the initiative, were emerging to self-reliance and contributed with their example to the growing self-possession of the Caribbean as a whole, were yet again shattered and assaulted.

The struggle against that imagery and the society for which it stands as metaphor, stunned and disconcerted, nonetheless goes on. The declarative, cathartic starkness of the young Grenadian Peggy Anthrobus's verse, for all its lack of burnished sheen, hazy religious idealism, and occasional confusions, perhaps even precisely because of them, eloquently synthesizes both of these dimensions. Speaking, with great poignancy, out of the piercing rawness of her pain, she concludes the epic historical sweep of her poem "Grenada—October 1983: A Work in Progress" with the following lines:

> Somehow, out of these ashes
> We Caribbean people
> will find truths and strengths
> to forge our own ideology,
> born of our experience and survival
> To rebuild our shattered unity,
> our dignity,
> our faith,
> our dreams.

Seventeen years earlier Edward Brathwaite, the distinguished historian and poet from Barbados, was inspired by that very conviction to conclude his now classic "New World Trilogy" of bitter, tragedy-filled journeys, *The Arrivants,* with a nearly identical sentiment. "Jou'vert" ("Opening Day"), the poem brings to a close the long historical crossing from *Rights of Passage* and *Masks* to, tellingly, *Islands,* resolutely acknowledging the encouraging existence of:

> . . . men now
> hearing
> waiting
> watching
> in the Lent-
> en morning
> hurts for-
> gotten, hearts
> no longer bound
>
> to black and bitter
> ashes in the ground
>
> now waking
> making
> making
> with their
>
> rhythms some-
> thing torn
>
> and new.[19]

The Grenadian Revolution was at once the issue of such people, meant to represent and serve them. It was the message of Brathwaite's trilogy that, in addition to being ultimately transitory, each of our defeats was also not without some element of enduring victory.

THE YEARS SINCE 1983 have, for all that, not been especially kind to Grenada. If the Caribbean generally suffered a major political setback in the wake of the October invasion, Grenada's losses proved no less severe. American pledges of support for a "new insular democracy" proved to be hollow. "In the flush of victory," Trinidadian George Huggins notes, "the USA promised to make the new Grenada a model of democracy and development with American support. This clearly has not happened. Few of the investments promised or credits hinted at ever materialized. Politics in Grenada," he goes on, "has hardly motivated the population since and continues to seem a distant affair, not entirely or intimately related to the day-to-day life of the people, and not requiring them to become involved in [the] analysis of options and in decision-making."[20] Thrust back into its pre-1979 isolation and marginality, the island's literary and cultural effervescence has, similarly, lost much of its previous vigor and passionately animated vitality.

The governments of Herbert A. Blaize's New National Party centrist coalition (1984–1989), Nicholas Brathwaite's National Democratic Congress (1990–1995), and Keith Mitchell (1995–2003), which replaced the Interim Advisory Council that administered the island until the withdrawal of American troops, and which have since seen these two parties succeed each other in power, have certainly not been able effectively to revitalize the texture and gloomy particulars of this generally dispiriting panorama. Nature itself appears lately to have conspired still further to deepen the murky overcast and stasis of this disheartening landscape and climate. Sweeping through the island in September 2004, Hurricane Ivan left a toll of 39 dead and thousands homeless in its wake; a year later, Hurricane Emily would wreak a further devastation.

One is all the more struck by the cruel irony of the fact that, now more than two decades after the Grenadian Revolution's abrupt and tragic end, as Huggins put in 1993, "A renewed sense seems to have emerged of the vulnerability of a region of small insular countries, leading to more concerted cooperation [and that t]his [cooperation] was manifested in the decision of Caribbean governments to [re]assert their right to relate to and trade with Cuba, as a member of the broader Caribbean community [as well as of the fact that] Dame Eugenia Charles,

Dominica's Prime Minister, who was at Reagan's side during the invasion, and formerly a strong opponent of Cuba, has [since] revised her own policies towards Cuba."[21]

Notes

1. *New York Times,* October 28, 1983.

2. *New York Times,* October 29, 1983.

3. Aimé Césaire, *Letter to Maurice Thorez* (Paris: Presence Africaine, 1957), 12.

4. Nicolás Guillén, *Prosa de Prisal, 1929–1972* (La Habana: Editorial Arte y literatura), 1975), vol. 3, 375–76.

5. Mario Benedetti, *El escritor latinoamericano y la revolucíon posible* (Buenos Aires: Editorial Nueva Imagen/Editorial Alfa Argentina, 1977), 94.

6. Ibid., 95.

7. Edward Brathwaite, "The Love Axe/1: (Developing a Caribbean Aesthetic 1962–1974)," *Bim* 16, no. 61 (June 1977): 54.

8. George Lamming, *The Pleasures of Exile* (London: Michael Joseph, 1960), 27.

9. Frantz Fanon, *The Wretched of the Earth* (New York: Grove Press, 1963), 316.

10. Maurice Bishop, *Selected Speeches, 1979–1981* (La Habana: Casa de Las America, 1982), 109.

11. Included in *Grenada: The Peaceful Revolution* (Washington, D.C.: Epica Task Force, 1982), 97.

12. Bishop, *Selected Speeches,* 71.

13. Ibid., 72.

14. Ibid.

15. Ibid., 238–39.

16. Ibid., 239.

17. From text of a letter of invitation to the second Conference of Intellectual Workers for Regional Sovereignty of the Caribbean Peoples.

18. Ibid.

19. Edward Brathwaite, *The Arrivants: New World Trilogy* (New York: Oxford University Press, 1978), 269–70.

20. George Huggins, "Grenada 10 Years Later: The Impact of the Grenada Revolution on the Caribbean," typescript of unpublished manuscript, 19.

21. Ibid., 20.

El Señor Presidente

DOMINICAN PRESIDENT Joaquín Balaguer has, surely, never been in any serious danger of being mistaken for a man of even moderately liberal ideology or opinions. Octogenarian dean of the most pusillanimously colonial and racially pretentious wing of the Dominican Right, Balaguer has devoted more than half a century to the rationalization and defense of its most jejune orthodoxies and clichés.

His recent book *La isla al revés: Haiti y el destino dominicano* (The Island Turned on Its Head: Haiti and Dominican Destiny, Santo Domingo: Editora Corripio, 1989) is a self-contradictory pastiche of the would-be aristocracy's most shopworn and flatulent bromides. It is also a clear, if offensive delineation of the racist ideology that permeates a significant portion of Dominican society. For all its pretense to scientific objectivity and broad-mindedness, Balaguer's thesis has the delusive partiality of a planter's fallacious syllogism. The Dominican Republic, he ahistorically postulates, has always been a "white and Christian" country. This country has now, alas, fallen victim to a "progressive ethnic decadence" (p. 45) and gradual disappearance of the nation's somatic characteristics that threaten the imminent loss of "its Spanish physiognomy" (p. 43).

The trouble, Balaguer tellingly suggests, originates and is symbolically embodied in the final triumph of the 1791 uprising of slaves in Haiti and the Black Republic's "imperialist" occupation (1822–1844) of the eastern half of Hispaniola. He dismisses out of hand as plain treachery a considerable body of annexationist and abolitionist Dominican sentiment, which he regards as radically suspect or out of place in a Spanish colony in which he contends slavery was "more benign" (p. 197) and "racism has never existed" (pp. 188, 198).

Save for a "miniscule" (p. 23), "obviously" marginal unrepresentative portion of the population, he argues, the black presence in the Dominican Republic constitutes a foreign intrusion, something alien to the authentic national spirit of the place: in a word, something actually or effectively "Haitian." Genuine patriotism requires "our" unrelenting resistance to this exotic, pagan, and primitive, foreign penetration and its inevitable train of ominous effects.

Haiti, admittedly, no longer poses any political or military threat to the sovereignty or territorial integrity of the Dominican Republic. But, Balaguer insists, "Haitian imperialism is now an even greater threat to our country than before for biological reasons" (p. 35). Principal among these are the regressive genetic impact and cultural influence that are a consequence of miscegenation and "the vegetative increase of the African race" (p. 35).

Race, predictably enough, gradually emerges as synonymous with nationality. The least de-nationalized section of the country, we are told, the one that best conserves "the spirit of nobility that survives in Santo Domingo like an inheritance from the colonial golden age," is Baní, an isolated rural community of "whites." "The least miscegenated zone in the country . . . where the [white] race has the best sense of its capacities . . . a firmer notion of its culture . . . and its dignity" (pp. 61–62), Baní is Balaguer's wistfully nostalgic, emblematically ideal polity. His notion of the Republic's proper destiny can, in effect, be reduced "to mak[ing] the entire Dominican population a community like Baní" (p. 62).

Balaguer's methodological triad of race, demography, and eugenics— the cornerstone of his argument—betrays a distinctively anachronistic, nineteenth-century slaveholder's anxiety: the all-consuming fear of an "Africanization" of "our nation" whose Social-Darwinist and patrician temper is only too apparent. "If the government continues to ignore the problem of race," Balaguer writes, "the white race will eventually be absorbed by the African" (p. 97). The twentieth-century personifications of that dread possibility—and the manifest villains of the book—are Haitian immigrants and "guest workers."

Balaguer, evidently, sees no contradiction in the fact that successive Dominican governments—and most notably his own—both directly profited from and significantly encouraged that immigration. The state regularly recruits Haitian workers for the plantations of the State Sugar Council, offering exploitative terms and living conditions which ensure the migrants' isolation and relative powerlessness and preclude their ability to exercise anything like the nefarious omnipotence attributed to them by El Señor Presidente.

Balaguer holds Haitian immigration responsible for everything from the deterioration of his *homo dominicanus'* sense of loyalty to traditional Christian family values, the native working class's increasing lack of nationalist solidarity and the middle class's meager strength, to the discouraging state of the country's overall health, its economic instability, and the general failure of current development strategies.

What a less jaundiced observer of the frontier zones might have recognized as an ordinary example of reciprocal adaptation and cultural exchange, Balaguer invariably regards as evidence of the corrupting subtlety and malevolent ingenuity of "Haitians" intent on sabotaging the locals' sense of moral rectitude and patriotic purpose. Cross-cultural exchange becomes, under the circumstances, virtually synonymous with sedition.

Consistent with his dim view of blacks in general and "Haitians" in particular, the president invokes a phobic vocabulary of elemental sexuality, primeval excess, social pathology, and enervating disease. Negroes are all "instinct-governed" (p. 36) ferally and incestuously promiscuous, "vegetally fertile" (p. 36) while, consonant with their ancestral inheritance, "Haitians" are "heathens" (p. 40), "generators of indolence" (p. 52), "of primitive mentality" (p. 37), and a "contagion" (p. 49). To the extent they may be said to possess any culture at all, it is a derivative veneer, the result of mimetic assimilation. Those few Haitians whose intellectual stature Balaguer favorably singles out as exceptional are finally redeemed, with condescending paternalism, as oblique tributes to the civilizing force of their European educations.

Except for the enthusiasm with which he draws on the *noirisme* of Jean Price-Mars, Lorimer Denis, Jean Dorsainvil, and François Duvalier to enhance his own dubious credibility, Balaguer appears to be wholly ignorant of the work of even a single Haitian intellectual from among the multitude of those active during the last 50 years. Certainly he does not make reference to any. This allows him conveniently to elide their nearly unanimous critique of his chosen sources and what, with a keen sense of political irony, René Depestre bitingly calls their "Adventures of Négritude."

Balaguer's remedies to inhibit any further spread of the Haitian "blight" include a Malthusian free-marketeering, broadening of the rural base, and centrality of Catholic instruction, bringing the borderlands under tighter government control, promoting the "spontaneous immigration" (p. 143) of white capitalists from abroad and entrusting the future to "a vast eugenic plan" (p. 136) directed by those already of "raza selecta" (p. 148). "To make a people free," he maintains, "is less important than to regenerate it" (p. 99). Balaguer's undisguised apologia for Trujillo's October 1937 massacre of more than 17,000 Haitians—as a measure leveled at "the very causes . . . of our ethnic regression" (pp. 76, 97)—leaves no doubt that he is not beyond contemplating a policy of deliberate genocide.

It comes, then, as something of a surprise when, against the force of its own pernicious logic, *La isla el revés* concludes by proposing a conciliatory confederation of the Dominican and Haitian states to ensure the independence of each and, after a century and a half, put an end to their tension-fraught relations. Haiti's comparative vulnerability, it appears, and no doubt the Duvalieristes' political consanguinity, now make such a compact particularly attractive. Balaguer's tacit supposition is that, under such an arrangement, the Dominican nation he envisions would emerge as first among "equals." The offer, in any case, rings hollow and is entirely suspect. Certainly, Haitians and the ethnically mixed population of ordinary Dominicans have every reason to view so unexpected a gift of unity with at least as much skepticism (which the Greek who here comes bearing it necessarily inspires) as Balaguer's protestations that he is not a racist.

La isla el revés adds yet another volume to the already monumental library of raciologist tracts which includes texts by such notables as Ernest Renan (1823–1892), the Spaniard Marcelino Menéndez y Pelayo (1856–1912), the Argentines Domingo Faustino Sarmiento (1811–1888), Carlos Octavio Bunge (1975–1919) and José Ingenieros (1877–1925), the Bolivian Alcides Arguedas (1879–1946), and the Peruvian Francisco García Calderón (1883–1953). The impertinent presumption and terrified consciousness Balaguer shares with these supposed paragons of humanism is a barometer of the intensity of their mutual distrust of an authentic democracy's egalitarian impulse and of the racially heterogeneous masses of their own peoples. Their dreams are, in truth, the stuff of nightmares.

"The Pirate Ambush of Remorse"

BETWEEN 1929 and the mid-fifties the Caribbean saw a succession of historic, transitional, sociopolitical, and cultural realignments. Eclipsed by the vigorously imperial presence of the United States after 1898, European hegemony in the region was decisively, if not absolutely, superseded by a neocolonial Pax Americana. Seigniorial economies controlled by conservative local agricultural oligarchies, whose superannuated techniques and outmoded systems of production put them at a comparative disadvantage, were effectively captured, secured, reorganized, and reoriented by dollar diplomats, "modernizing" capitalists, and industrialists from abroad. The political monopoly of the old plantocracies was also successfully undone by a temporary, uneasy alliance between an increasingly restive indigenous (predominately black and mulatto) working class and the emergent (predominately "brown" and "white" *mestizo*) Creole middle classes. By the end of the period, these latter had to all intents and purposes transformed themselves into the new patricians of the Antillean domestic scene. By the late sixties, with their coalitions conclusively dissolved, they would themselves be confronted with the pointed resentment and menacing disenchantment of their erstwhile allies and, among the most prescient and alert, the disquieting recognition of their own looming historical contingency.

The racial conceit of a pigmentocratic social hierarchy sanctioned by colonial tradition, still stubbornly though less confidently in place, came under increasingly sustained scrutiny and attack as more provocatively syncretic and self-affirming notions of Caribbean reality, cultural identity, and nationhood acclaimed the positive ethnographic centrality of the contemned African ancestor and emerged to gradual rhetorical and ideological dominance. "The Antillean," poet Luis Palés Matos (Puerto Rico, 1989–1953) insisted, in defiance of more conventional Hispanophile cultural assumptions, "is a Spaniard with the manners of a mulatto and the soul of a black."[1] "Jamaica," poet Nicolás Guillén (Cuba, 1902–1989) celebrated, "says she's happy being black / and Cuba now knows she's mulatto."[2] C. L. R. James (Trinidad, 1901–1990) likewise applauded the late eighteenth- and early nineteenth-century "transformation of [Haitian] slaves, trembling in hundreds before a single white man, into a people able to organize themselves and defeat the most powerful European nations of their day"[3] Regarding the Black Jacobins' epic struggle as a pan-African parable for his own time and place, James went on to make the case for West Indian political and cultural self-reliance. Once routinely regulated by the canons of colonialist discourse, an exuberantly innovative, anticolonial mood of fertile tumult swept through the archipelago.

More than any other writer from the "French" West Indies, Aimé Césaire (Martinique, 1913) epitomizes the subversive intellectual sweep and passionately anticolonial political temper of that epoch, its signal achievements, and the sharpening edge of frustration and disillusionment to which its shortcomings would later give rise. His signature *Cahier d'un retour au pays natal* (1939) conferred dramatic currency to the neologism *négritude*. A surrealist tour de force, it gave that movement's antiassimilationist effort to break "the yoke-bag / that separates me from myself" its most catalytic, stylistically sumptuous, and inclusive lyrical monument. Césaire's poetry of the immediate postwar years—*Les armes miraculeuses* (1946), *Soleil cou coupé* (1948), and *Corps perdu* (1950)—confirmed the insubordinate *marronage* of the poet's lapidary heresies. Césaire's fusion of poetry and partisanship, his novel blend of associative metaphorical synthesis, strategies of syntactic rupture and discontinuity, exacting esoteric reference, intermingling of the mythopoetic and epic, both dazzled and stirred. His prose *Discourse on Colonialism* (1950) brought identical panache to the exposé of what he regarded as the counterfeit universalism of a Western liberal humanism intent on refusing equality or any genuine autonomy to the colonized. Six years later, convinced that the European Left itself was invalidated by its no less paternalist assumptions, as well as its continuing fidelity to the tired orthodoxies of Socialist Realism, Césaire resigned his long-standing membership in the French Communist Party, calling for "nothing short of a Copernican revolution, so deeply entrenched in Europe, in every party and in every sphere . . . is this habit of making our arrangements, this habit of thinking in our behalf, in fine, this habit of contesting our right to initiative which . . . is ultimately the right to a personality of one's own."[4]

The ex-Communist delegate to the French National Assembly went on to found his own Parti Progressiste Martiniqais. Less sanguine about his island ever being granted a truly viable independence—as, in truth, it has not—he argued instead for a program of qualified autonomy as its continuously reelected mayor of Fort-de-France. By the end of the sixties, Césaire was securely in place as the most influential member of the island's new political establishment, as well as its most illustrious exemplar of a new breed of insurgent Third World intellectual and the undisputed dean of Antillean poets and black dramatists then writing in French.

The eruptive rhetorical force of his revolutionary literary agenda remained almost wholly intact. Plays like *The Tragedy of King Christophe* (1963), *A Season in the Congo* (1966), and *A Tempest* (1968) were, nonetheless, distantly reminiscent of *Corps perdu*'s insinuating ambition to "fell the trees of paradise" in their shift to a more critical emphasis on some of the more illusive pitfalls of *négritude* and national consciousness. The plays' stress on the painful ironies and impasses confronting historic revolutionaries also lent a material immediacy and, in Césaire's adaptation of Shakespeare for a black theater, an intertextual complexity to his more lyrically abstract envisionment of The Rebel in *Et les chiens se traisaient* (1946). Their less buoyantly hopeful, if unrepentantly heroic stress is, arguably, emblematic of the elusively paradoxical figure that, as harbinger of a revolutionary vanguard, as confirmed literary icon, and as fully practiced colonial statesman, Césaire himself had become.

It was to the evolving progression of this interval of emergence, definitive literary consecration, and, between *Corps perdu, Ferrements* (1960), and especially *Noria* (1976), the first glimmers of skepticism and ideological crisis, that Clayton Eshleman and Annette Smith's 1983 compilation of *The Collected Poetry* primarily turned our attention. Its scrupulously edited and conscientiously translated pages are dominated by the calculated *demesure* and orgiastic self-surrender of a herald of "the furious We," by the verbal sortilege that "shall command the islands to be," by "the blackness of this unforgetting scream / squirt against the whiteness of the wall," and by the communally primal search for transcendent "fresh oasis of fraternity." This new volume of

Lyric and Dramatic Poetry splendidly completes Eshleman and Smith's sustained enterprise of translation, the intimidating task of making the corpus of Césaire's verse available to an English-speaking public.

More compact and selective, the new volume offers the reader a succinct overview of Césaire's *ars poética* and, in particular, the importance of an imaginative unconscious, tragic myth, and symbol to it. The surrealist conviction and hortatory optimism of Césaire's Promethean phase, represented here by the first complete English translations of the important essay "Poetry and Knowledge" (1944) and *And the Dogs Are Silent,* are set in revealing contrast to the somber concision and starkly, uncharacteristically elegiac mood of the early eighties' *i, laminaria.*

In the first of these works, Césaire lays siege to the prosaic, rationalist, utilitarian citadel of science. Summarizing his own "barbarous" poetic faith, he proposes "that all true poetry, without ever abandoning its humanity, at the moment of greatest mystery ceases to be strictly human so as to begin to be truly cosmic." "Only myth," he insists, "satisfies mankind completely." Indeed, in the extended dramatic poem *And the Dogs Are Silent,* history itself assumes mythical proportions. Its Africa is allegorical, composite, totemic, and ecumenical. Its portrayal of The Rebel protagonist who murders the colonial master and whose own regenerative "death was not cantankerous but sweet," is more heroic and allusive than historically specific or geographically localized. At the heart of its characteristic dialectic of destruction and renewal is Césaire's lyrical determination simultaneously to achieve a liberating Fanonesque catharsis, regain the ancient harmony of man and nature, and, as A. James Arnold emphasizes in his introduction, "restore to the logos its sacred function."

Still, it is "the rites of shipwreck," "the pirate ambush of remorse" and "energy of ashes" at the core of *i, laminaria* that constitute this latest collection's most conspicuously arresting revelation. A mood of melancholy, a "lucidity . . . of despair and collapse," which in the two decades immediately after 1950 had rarely and only tentatively encroached on the cosmic ambition and expansive tone of Césaire's verse, pervades this crepuscular book.

The gloomy fruit of Césaire's years of embattlement as communist *griot* and official head of government of a neocolonial island, *i, laminaria* reveals the poet at his most individual and intimate. The turbulent, utopian intemperance of youth also gives way to the resigned sense of mortality of a reflective old man keen to set his house in order and settle his accounts.

Identification with the potency of telluric forces remains essential to the poet's defining imagery. But the once commanding volcano, apparently spent and exhausted, has shrunk to a smoldering mountain of smoke. The hurricane, the embracing wind, the overshadowing, immutable tree yield to the cunning tenacity of the mollusk, the suppleness of alga, and the meditative, vegetal germination of a mangrove swamp in which, we are told, "it is quite possible to survive limp / by anchoring oneself into commensal mud" on the insular landscape.

Even Césaire's faith in the clairvoyant and restorative power of poetic speech has been badly shaken. The *négritude* poet's earlier grandiloquence is now "only the boom of distant cannons in the sky," his incantatory magic wand of words altered to a lexical debris, "out of sense. out of it. out of tune," a "saliva reswallowed by the surf." The orphic insurgent now deems himself "this avatar of an absurdly botched version of paradise." History and the debilitating assaults of a discouraging present have exacted their unmerciful, enervating toll. *Négritude*'s divining suprarealism no longer offers its consoling, idealist benediction. The emotional landscape is strewn with the sobering relics of loss, wreckage, and failure. The past itself seems almost a foreign country: "thus / all nostalgia / rolls / into the abyss."

Césaire, for all that, is not entirely engulfed by this atmosphere of dejection. Tributes to Léon Damas, Frantz Fanon, Miguel Angel Asturias, Wifredo Lam and, in particular, a poem devoted to his "second adventivity" attest to an abiding belief in the revolutionary significance of the man of culture. Like the anonymous mollusk and enduringly patient mangrove he invokes, the poet clings, in spite of himself, to an unwavering faith in the future: "to deliver the world to the assassins of dawn is [still] out of the question." Thus, the collection concludes, "a new kindness is ceaselessly growing on the horizon."

The language of these poems, though unusually transparent and accessible, is richly layered and sensuously textured. Sensitive to the rhythms and conceptual reverberations of a stylistically demanding poet, the editors demonstrate an apposite verve and inventiveness in translations that effectively capture both the letter and distinctive spirit of Césaire's verse. Brief notes to his poems' unfamiliar, more obscure, or exotically Antillean references supplement their text, and give a still greater general accessibility to what is, all in all, an illuminating and welcome addition to the swelling body of Césaire's work now available in English.

Notes

1. Arcadio Díaz Quiñones, "La poesía negra de Palés Matos," *Sin nombre*, vol. 1:1 (September 1970).

2. *Man-Making Words: Selected Poems of Nicolás Guillén,* trans. and ed. Roberto Márquez and David Arthur MacMurray (Amherst: University of Massachusetts Press, 1972).

3. C. L. R. James, *The Black Jacobins: Toussaint L'Ouverture and the San Domingo Revolution* (New York: Vintage, 1989), ix.

4. Aimé Césaire, *Letter to Maurice Thorez* (Paris: Présence Africaine, 1957), 12.

Index